REGENCY EDITOR

Clan badge used by Scott as a bookplate

REGENCY EDITOR

LIFE OF JOHN SCOTT

PATRICK O'LEARY

ABERDEEN UNIVERSITY PRESS

First published 1983
Aberdeen University Press
A member of the Pergamon Group
© Patrick O'Leary 1983

The publishers gratefully acknowledge the financial assistance of the Scottish Arts Council in the publication of this book.

British Library Cataloguing in Publication Data

O'Leary, Patrick
    Regency editor: life of John Scott (1784–1821)
    1. Scott, John   2. Journalists—Great Britain
    —Biography
    I. Title
    070'.92'4   PN5123.S/

    ISBN 0-08-028456-6

PRINTED IN GREAT BRITAIN
THE UNIVERSITY PRESS
ABERDEEN

Contents

	LIST OF PLATES AND ILLUSTRATIONS	vi
	ACKNOWLEDGEMENTS	vii
Chapter 1	Aberdeen to Glasgow by way of Windsor	1
Chapter 2	Whitehall and Fleet Street	13
Chapter 3	Country Editor defies the Lash	30
Chapter 4	The Champion of Reform	47
Chapter 5	Paris Revisited and a Row with Byron	65
Chapter 6	Tragedy Dogs the Continental Traveller	86
Chapter 7	The London Magazine: Introducing Table Talk and Elia	109
Chapter 8	Cockneys *versus* Blackwoodsmen	132
Chapter 9	Mystery at Chalk Farm	155
	CHRONOLOGICAL OUTLINE	172
	BIBLIOGRAPHY	173
	INDEX	181

Plates
(between pp 102 and 103)

1. Catherine Scott by John Phillip
2. Alexander Scott (artist unknown)
3. Helen Kidson Scott (left) and a sister in 1815 by John Boaden
4. Caroline Colnaghi before her marriage to Scott (artist unknown)
5. John Scott at 19. Miniature by Joseph Pastorini
6. John Scott at 30 by John Boaden
7. John Scott at 34. Pencil sketch by Seymour Kirkup (*Source* Scottish National Portrait Gallery)
8. Scott's second son, John Anthony Scott at 45. Drawn by John Horrak (*Source* Scottish National Portrait Gallery)
9. Frederick, Duke of York and Albany by David Wilkie (*Source* National Portrait Gallery, London)

Illustrations

1. Schoolboy John writes home to his sister Margaret from Clewer (*Source* National Library of Scotland)   6
2. Title page of Scott's first travel book   60

Clan badge used by Scott as a bookplate   *Frontispiece*

Acknowledgements

One good reason for embarking on a biography is that you encounter so many friendly and hospitable people who share your enthusiasm for the subject. In writing this book I have had the most generous encouragement from Dr Donald A Low, author of two lively Regency studies, *Thieves' Kitchen* and *That Sunny Dome*. I owe a similar debt to Dr Willard Bissell Pope, the scholarly editor of *The Diary of Benjamin Robert Haydon*, published by Harvard University Press; extracts from the *Diary* and from letters of John and Caroline Scott to Haydon are reprinted by permission of the manuscript owners, the Houghton Library at Harvard University, and of Dr Pope and his publishers.

Five Scott family portraits appear with the very kind consent of descendants of John's sisters—Mrs J R Whittaker, Mrs V P W Lowe, who overcame problems in having the portrait by John Boaden copied, and Dr J S F Watson who, with his wife, welcomed me to their home and also allowed me to use unpublished letters in their possession.

The Seymour Kirkup drawing of John Scott, and the John Horrak sketch of John Anthony Scott appear by generous permission of the Trustees of the Scottish National Portrait Gallery. Caroline Colnaghi's portrait formerly belonged to the late Miss G Tassinari who gave me a copy of the Scott bookplate and allowed me to examine manuscript notes on family history; I have been unsuccessful in efforts to trace the present owner of the painting. The original of the John Scott letter from Clewer belongs to the National Library of Scotland, and I am grateful to the Trustees of the Library for permission to quote from unpublished manuscripts in their collection, notably those in the papers of William Blackwood and Sons, and of Dr John Brown.

Permission to reproduce the David Wilkie portrait of the Duke of York has been granted by the Trustees of the National Portrait Gallery, London.

Letters from John Scott and Benjamin Robert Haydon to William Wordsworth are reproduced by permission of the Trustees of Dove Cottage; Longman Group Limited permitted the use of material from their archives; John Murray Ltd agreed to publication of a letter from Scott to the company; the Town Clerk of Aberdeen sanctioned use of extracts from the city's Burgess Register and Grammar School Visitation Books; extracts from Crown-copyright records in the Public Record Office (WO46/151 and WO4/986) appear by permission of the Controllers of Her Majesty's Stationery Office; the copy of Thomas Medwin's *Journal of the Conversations of Lord Byron* annotated by Haydon is in the Byron Collection at Newstead Abbey, Nottingham Museums; for permission to quote from two letters to Samuel Whitbread I am grateful to S C Whitbread Esq; copyright in the letters of John Taylor is owned by members of the Brooke-Taylor family, and the executors of R W P Cockerton; extracts from the Inventory and Deed of Settlement of Alexander Scott appear with the consent of the Keeper of the Records of Scotland; manuscripts of some individual letters quoted in this biography belong to Liverpool City's Hornby Library, the W Hugh Peal Collection in the University of Kentucky Libraries, the Humanities Research Center at the University of Texas at Austin, the William L Clements Library, Ann Arbor, Michigan, the New York Public Library Astor, Lenox and Tilden Foundations, Maine Historical Society, and Berkshire County Library. The P G Patmore papers are held by Princeton University Library.

Copyright in material quoted from Aberdeen parish records belongs to the Kirk Session of St Nicholas Church; the Vicar of St Martin-in-the-Fields, the Reverend Austen Williams, granted permission to quote from its parish register.

My grateful acknowledgements for permission to quote from the following works: *The Letters of William and Dorothy Wordsworth: The Middle Years* Part II edited by Ernest de Selincourt revised by Mary Moorman and Alan G Hill (Oxford University Press); *The Letters of Charles Armitage Brown* edited by Jack Stillinger (Harvard University Press); *Memoirs and Correspondence of Coventry Patmore* by Basil Champneys (George Bell and Sons); *Henry Crabb Robinson on Books and Their Writers* edited by E J Morley (J M Dent & Sons); *The Letters of William Hazlitt* edited by Herschel Moreland Sikes assisted by Willard Hallam Bonner and Gerald Lahey (Macmillan); *Collected Letters of Samuel Taylor Coleridge* edited by Earl Leslie Griggs (Oxford University Press); *The Letters of Charles and Mary Anne Lamb* edited by Edwin W Marrs (Cornell University Press); *The Letters of Charles Lamb* edited by E V Lucas (Dent, and Methuen); *The Letters of Sir Walter Scott* edited by H J C Grierson (Constable), and *The Letters of Thomas Moore* edited by Wilfred S Dowden (Oxford University Press).

Among people who have been particularly helpful in providing information were: the Reverend Professor David Cairns; Mr Claude A Prance, who has written about John Scott and *The London Magazine*; the Town

Acknowledgements

Clerk of Stamford, Mr D A O'Leary, and his archives staff; staff of the Keats Memorial Library, Hampstead; East Midland Allied Press and their History Editor, Mr David Newton; Dr James C Corson, Honorary Librarian of Abbotsford, who kindly sent me a transcript of part of a letter of Sir Walter Scott known only from a bookseller's catalogue; Mrs W O Manning; staff of P & D Colnaghi; Mrs Mary R Wedd, editor of *The Charles Lamb Bulletin*, and the former editor, Mr Basil Savage; Mr James Norrie, Curator of Provost Skene's House, Aberdeen; the Courts Administrator of the Central Criminal Court (Old Bailey); staff of the Regimental Headquarters of the Gordon Highlanders; members of Barnes History Society; and staff of the Royal Archives at Windsor Castle. Others who have been, as American spokesmen say, specially supportive in this way are: Mrs Winifred F Courtney, author of *Young Charles Lamb*; and Professors Stephen M Parrish, Stuart M Tave, and Edwin W Marrs. Mrs Maxwell-Scott gave me permission to quote from unpublished letters in the Abbotsford Collection.

Cambridge University Library, the Bodleian Library (Oxford), Birkbeck College (University of London), and the Pusey Library at Harvard University allowed me to study unpublished dissertations.

Apart from bodies already mentioned, my research has been assisted greatly by the courteous, efficient service provided by Aberdeen University Library, the London Library, the British Library at Bloomsbury and Colindale, the Guildhall Library in London, Westminster Public Library, the National Register of Archives, Haringey Libraries, University of Reading Library, Derbyshire, Berkshire, Bedfordshire, Lincolnshire and Wiltshire Record Offices, Somerset House, Aberdeen Public Library, Stamford Library, St Bride's Institute, the Greater London Record Office, Edinburgh Central Public Library, Edinburgh University Library, and Highgate Literary and Scientific Institution.

Other bodies and individuals who were good enough to answer my enquiries included: the English Faculty Library, Oxford; Coutts & Co; the Royal Automobile Club; the Historical Societies at Dedham and Norwood, Massachusetts; the Royal Commission on Historical Monuments; the Reverend Denis Shaw, Rector of Clewer Parish Church; Aberdeen Sheriff Clerk's Office; University Libraries at Wisconsin, Yale, Guelph (Ontario), Iowa, John Rylands (Manchester), Leeds, and Durham; Burghley House Preservation Trust; Salisbury Diocesan Record Office; the Huntington Library; Wigan Record Office; the Institute of Bankers in Scotland; *Hobbies* magazine, Chicago; the Royal Bank of Scotland; Camden Central Library, the Institute of United States Studies, University of London; the National Gallery of Scotland; Mr F H Marchbank; the National Trust for Scotland; the National Register of

Archives (Scotland); Vera Watson, author of the *Life of Mary Russell Mitford*; the *Morning Advertiser*; the Worshipful Company of Upholders; the United Reformed Church History Society; Lambeth, and Chelsea Libraries; the Museum of London; and David Wainwright, author of *Broadwood by Appointment*.

If anyone has been overlooked I hope they will attribute the sin of omission to inefficiency rather than discourtesy, and accept my genuine apologies. Any other blunders in this work are also mine alone.

Two notes on editing. For the sake of clarity and to avoid the use of (*sic*), when transcribing John Scott's own letters and published writings I have silently corrected slips of the pen and the press, and occasionally modernised his spelling. I have not tampered with the sense. The familiar form of names such as Horace Smith and Fanny Kelly has been used.

Chapter One

ABERDEEN TO GLASGOW
BY WAY OF WINDSOR

On May 24 in 1784 the grey columns of the back page of *The Aberdeen Journal* were punctuated by this announcement:

> ALEXANDER SCOTT
> Upholsterer from London
>
> Begs leave to inform the nobility, gentry, and the public in general, that he has taken the first floor in Mr. Farquharson's house, end of the Broadgate, which he intends to open as a shop next Thursday, when he proposes to sell all sorts of upholstery goods, in the present taste, and on the most reasonable terms. . . .
>
> A. Scott has been employed in the first shops in London for these nine years past, and particularly for the last five years was foreman to an eminent master in that place; flatters himself he is capable of executing every part of the upholstery business in the most elegant manner; and had the pleasure of furnishing a house in this place last year, to the satisfaction of his employer.

The style reflected the man; his bold signature 'Alex^r Scott' can still be seen in the Burgess Book of Aberdeen. His portrait shows a plump face with a pugnacious look. Not yet thirty, he was active, quick-tempered and generous. Alexander spent the rest of his life building up and diversifying his business in the city, with frequent trips to London and other manufacturing centres to buy stock.

Scott took to Aberdeen the English girl he had married in 1782, Catherine Young, five years his junior. She was well educated, with strong religious principles. In the years ahead she bore eleven children and brought up ten of them, while supervising the business when her husband was away.

Their first child was John, born on Sunday 24 October 1784. During his career he showed much of the irascibility of his father, tempered by literary tastes inherited from his mother. According to the register of the parish of

Aberdeen, John was baptised by the Reverend George Abercrombie, in the presence of Adam Watt, baker, and William Dewar, who was stamp master.

The Broadgate, where the Scotts lived, now Broad Street, was described as the most spacious, airy and sanitary in the city. Their house had been rebuilt a few years before, and William Farquharson had his saddlery shop on the ground floor. In 1786 his tenants moved; business was expanding and with it the family, for their first daughter, Margaret, was born that summer.

Trade in Aberdeen was controlled by societies descended from ancient craft guilds, their privileges reinforced by royal charters and local agreements. Upholsterers did not have an organisation of their own, but were classed with tailors.

So the Burgess Book recorded:

> At Aberdeen thirtyfirst day of the October seventeen hundred and eightysix In presence of Magistrates & Council.
> The said day Alxr Scott Taylor in Aberdeen was admitted & received a freeman Burgess of said Borough of his own Craft only, with all the liberties and privileges competent to the said Craft by virtue of the Decree of Indenture, past betwixt the Brethren of Guild and Craftsmen of the said Burgess of Abd^n, dated 7th of July 1587, for payment to the Dean of Guild of a composition of fiftyone pounds eighteen shillings Scots, and of five shillings Scots to the Provost in a white purse, as use is, At which time the said Alex^r Scott swore the usual Burgess oath for payment of whose Taxation John Winton Taylor Burgess in Aberdeen became Cautioner and the said Alxr Scott obliged himself to relieve the Cautioner of the Premises.

Fortunately for the new burgess, the Scots pound was worth only one-twelfth the English one at that time. The premises he took over were in the Back of the Narrow Wynd, a short road at the south end of Broad Street. Alexander Scott's place of business there and in Broad Street have been swept away by redevelopment, as have others to which he moved later.

The Aberdeen Journal provided a running commentary on the business. In April 1785 readers learned Alexander Scott 'has just returned from London, where he has purchased a great variety of the most fashionable paper-hangings for his rooms, moreens of all colours . . . a neat assortment of ladies dressing glasses. . . . A. Scott has made it his particular study to select the above articles from the first shops in London. . . . All sorts of Cabinet work done in the best manner'.

His affairs prospered, and two years later, after one of his expeditions to the capital, he claimed that since 'most of the above goods were purchased on the spot for ready money, he can therefore afford to sell them on most moderate terms'. The cabinet-making side developed, and by 1788 he was telling customers that, in addition to chairs, sofas, tables, sideboards, and chests of drawers, he had for sale 'an exceedingly fine Piano Forte, by

Johannes Broadwood, London'. A 1790 advertisement concluded: 'Funerals performed in the most decent and frugal manner.'

Competition was keen. George Bartlett had an old established business, and by 1791 there were others in the field, including John Strachan & Co, advertised as upholsterers from London.

Meanwhile, more daughters were born, Nancy in 1787, Catherine two years later, and Jane in 1791. John Scott had begun his education under his mother's eye. As he recalled late in life, 'we held our horn-book in our hands. A was then an Apple; B was a Book; C was a Cat; D was a Duck.'

Lessons were the key to being able to read fairy-tales. 'What enchanting details lurked under the variegated cover of Mother Goose', John wrote, 'Our literary horizon in those days was peopled with dragons, was lit up with chariots of fire, and beautified with magical rainbows.'

Even the feel and look of what he termed the literature of the nursery lingered in his memory: 'When our primers and story books were enclosed in firm, compact, gilt covers, assurance seemed given externally, that there were golden stories within.'

At eight John began studies of a sterner kind. He went to Aberdeen Grammar school, where lessons were confined mostly to Latin grammar and literature to prepare boys for university.

Young Scott took this heavy fare without flinching, for in his first year he was one of ten boys in the lowest class to win a prize. These annual presentations, or visitations as they were called, were solemn affairs. On this occasion in 1793, on John's ninth birthday, Provost John Abercrombie, preceded by a scarlet-coated halberdier, walked in procession with several bailies, other city dignitaries, and local clergymen to the premises in Schoolhill.

John's prize was a copy of George Buchanan's Latin metrical versions of the Psalms, stamped with the city's arms. He was not among the successful contestants the following year, but returned to the winning lists in 1795, receiving a Greek Testament in the third class.

Boys were limited to three weeks vacation in summer and ten days at Christmas, but they spent only five hours a day at their desks, and had frequent half and full days off, including one to visit the races.

There was much else to occupy a lad growing up in Aberdeen at the end of the eighteenth century. In spite of its remoteness—the coach journey to Edinburgh took nearly a day and a half, even when the road was not blocked by snow—the city was a royal burgh with an important role in the political and commercial history of Scotland.

The population of more than 20,000 were split between Old Aberdeen with its cathedral up by the river Don, and the other city where the Scotts and their business friends lived close to the Dee and the harbour.

Fishing and whaling fleets were based on the port, while cargo vessels sailed to the Baltic, the Low Countries, and to London, Edinburgh, Hull and other centres, sometimes chased by French privateers. It was said a prudent man made his will before embarking.

Alexander Scott encountered opposition from yet another upholsterer from London, but continued to increase his range of goods and services, selling 'four-post and tent bedsteads, stained in the English manner', and offering pianos and harpsichords for hire. Aberdeen was a musical city, with a concert hall and a theatre. It also had bookshops, among them one opened by Alexander Brown on the corner of Broadgate and Queen Street. Mr Brown later became Provost of the city, and was a close friend of Alexander Scott.

Early in 1795 he married the eldest daughter of James Chalmers, printer and proprietor of *The Aberdeen Journal*. It seems likely John was influenced in his literary ambitions by his father's friends.

After some argument in the business community, a police board was established in Aberdeen responsible among other duties for paving, lighting and cleaning streets. At the same time magistrates were alarmed by talk of political reform.

This stemmed partly from the revolution in France, but sprang as well from dissatisfaction with the narrowness of the franchise in Aberdeenshire; in 1786 Mr George Skene received only sixty-two votes, but was elected MP with a majority of ten. It was not surprising John Scott became an advocate of Parliamentary reform. Craft freemen like his father resented the town council being drawn from the merchant guild, which excluded craftsmen but included a number of local landowners.

In the 1790s the future Lord Byron lived in Aberdeen with his mother, who was of noble birth but brought to the edge of poverty by a spendthrift husband. John Scott's eldest sister recalled seeing Mrs Byron and her son pass by. Late in life Margaret wrote: 'Lord Byron. What regretful thoughts cling around his Memory—I remember him. He was a boy about nine and I a girl about the same age. . . . He was walking with his mother, a very stout good-looking Lady down Broad Street in Aberdeen. His cap thrown back and shewing pretty, heavy curls of dark chestnut hair, and as I looked I thought "You are a bonny Laddie".'

Byron attended the Grammar school for four years, and more than twenty years on, when he and John met in Venice, they exchanged reminiscences of Aberdeen. But it is unlikely they enjoyed any friendship as boys, since Scott was three years older than the heir to a peerage, and Mrs Byron would never have let her son mix with an upholsterer's family.

It is even less likely that either was aware of the visit to the city in 1796 of a man they came to admire deeply, Walter Scott. He was not then a baronet or novelist, but a young advocate in love. The heiress he had travelled from Edinburgh to see, Williamina Belsches of Fettercairn, rejected him.

One link between the three men was the unhappy recollection they carried through life of the puritanical Sundays of their boyhood. John Scott's comment was: 'I had the advantage of a strict Presbyterian education, and remember well how a boyish wish to take a walk on a fine Sunday evening was checked with a—*We* certainly should know better. I might sigh but could not doubt.'

His parents belonged to the Secession church, which broke away from the Presbyterian establishment in the 1730s. The Seceders themselves split over the introduction of a religious clause into certain burgess oaths. Anti-Burghers refused to take such oaths, while the Burghers accepted them. Scott's family belonged to this second sect.

In spite of his strictness over observing the Sabbath, Alexander Scott must have been an indulgent father. In 1796 he took John with him on one of his excursions to London, and on to Clewer, then a separate village from Windsor, where both parents had relatives. Mr Scott's sister Ann was the second wife of John Davis, a clockmaker who was locksmith to George III at Windsor Castle. According to family traditions, the father of Catherine Scott, whose maiden name was Young, superintended the gardens at Windsor. On 22 May 1796 John wrote home to Margaret:

> Dear Sister
> I received your very kind letter yesterday. We intend to set off for Aberdeen on Wednesday. I have been at Clewer more than a week. I have spent my time very happily. Mr George Davis has been so kind as to make me a present of a bow and arrows. I have been at a Review of the Prince of Wales Regiment of Dragoons where I saw all the Royal family. Upon Sunday last I saw the King coming out of the Chapel at Windsor. I also saw the Stadtholder. I have been at the Montem which is a collection made by the Boys at Eton college to support the best Scholar at Kings college Cambridge at which time the Boys are all very well drest the Salt bearers run about with a bag of Salt, asking money from every body they see it is said that they got 700 pounds. I hope you are going on very well at the singing I suppose you will all be excellent Singers and all the different parts of Music sung in our church by the time I come home, give my kind love to all there. I hope my Mother & Sisters are well. I long very much to be home Papa [and *I*] are both well. I hope the Pigeon is alive I thought you would have told me so in your letter. Excuse bad writing I see you are improving very fast. I hope Nancy is doing the same. I have nothing more to say but remain
>
> your affectionate Brother

George Davis was probably John Davis's grown-up son, since he succeeded him as royal locksmith in 1798. The Stadtholder was the Dutch ruler who fled to England when ousted by French revolutionary forces.

Dear Sister   Ab'n May 21 1796

I received your very kind letter yesterday. We intend to set off for Aberdeen on Wednesday. I have been at Clewar more than a week I have spent my time very happily there. Mr George Davis has been so kind as to make me a present of a bow & arrows.

I have been at a Review of the Prince of Wales Regiment of Drag'ns I saw all the Royal family. Upon Sunday last I saw the King coming out of the Chapel at Windsor I also saw the Stadtholder I have been at the Montem which is a collection made by the Boys of Eton college to support the best Scholar at Kings college Cambridge at which time the Boys are all very well drest the Salt bearers run about with a bag of Salt asking money from every body they see it is said that they got 700 pounds. I hope you are going on very well at the singing I suppose you will all be excellent Singers and all the different parts of Music sung in our church by the time I come home, give my kind love to all there. I hope my Mother & Sisters are well I long very much to be home Papa are both well. I hope the Pigeon is alive I thought you would have told me so in your letter excuse bad writing I see you are in a very great I hope Nancy is doing the same. I have nothing more to say but remain

                                    your affectionate Brother
                                            John Scott

1 Schoolboy John writes home to his sister Margaret from Clewer

John, at eleven, already showed an instinct for observation and descriptive writing. The review he saw was held on Ashford Heath, near Staines, and according to *The Times*:

> The Prince gave the word of command in the most General-like manner . . . the grand charge was one of the finest manoeuvres we have seen. . . . All the branches of the Royal Family were present, the Queen and the Princess Royal in a postchaise, the Princess of Wales in her coach.

Unknown to the world the Prince and his Princess were already estranged, a scandal roundly condemned by Scott when he became a journalist and the Prince became Regent. But he always wrote with respect of the man known as the good old king, George III.

The letter from John would have been read eagerly by Margaret, who had visited Windsor with her mother and sister Nancy a year or two before. Margaret recorded her recollections of that visit: 'We were taken to the Terrace where the King and R. Family walked on fine evenings. The Queen nodded to my sister and the King said "Davis, Davis, are these your Grandchildren" . . . how disappointed my poor sister was. After the Cortege had passed she said "And that's the Queen is it, she is no better dressed than Mamma, I thought she would have been all over silver and Gold!" We had new bonnets bought from the Queen's Milliner, Mrs Snow.'

John Davis, who died in 1801, was the third generation of locksmiths of the same name to serve Windsor Castle. John Scott's own ancestry was more obscure, which encouraged later speculation that his parents made a runaway marriage. John himself referred with affection to a kind but unidentified grandmother, who was skilled at making milk punch.

As a man John used a heraldic lion's head for a seal on his letters, and his bookmark was the same with the addition of the motto *Tace aut Face* (Keep Silence or Act). The device and motto belonged to the Roxburghshire Scott of Ancrum family, and was also used by the Scotts of Dunninald, who shared a common ancestry with them. This taste for heraldry did not imply John claimed aristocratic descent, merely that he belonged to the clan whose badge he used.

Since Alexander Scott favoured sea travel, he and John probably returned home on board the *Mary & Anne*, which, *The Aberdeen Journal* noted, arrived from London on 31 May loaded with boxes. The newspaper carried Alexander's announcement that he had 'a neat assortment of upholstery goods, such as painted papers for rooms, elegant furniture, cottons for Beds, printed in London. . . . The above goods being picked by himself on the spot.'

John went back to his studies, and again received a prize, on 26 October 1796 at the end of his final term at school. Five days later he presented himself at Marischal College in Broad Street to compete for a scholarship to the university there. Out of twenty-six successful applicants he came seventh, being awarded the James Cargill bursary worth £6 10s. annually. Work started the day after the competition, and John spent the next three years studying Greek, history and natural philosophy.

The curriculum laid down that in their third year the boys, in addition to natural philosophy, would be instructed in the principles of criticism and the Belles Lettres, if time allowed. It was perhaps this flirtation with literature which led to John's departure from the college with the fourth year of his course still to go. Nearly twenty years later he wrote: 'I shall never forget the sad, disheartened sense which struck, as it were, heavily down on my then growing and searching spirit, when one, who had my boyhood in his power, uttered with a savage earnestness, a coarse and contemptuous exclamation against some expression that I chanced to utter that showed a turn of mind towards the pursuit of those gallant and graceful visions which the path of study was then first giving me a glimpse of.' The powerful one was presumably his father, who may have felt he needed a helping hand rather than a budding Belles Lettrist in the family.

Three more girls, Marion, Helen and Eliza, had been born between 1792 and 1795, and Alexander and his wife must have despaired of having another son when Hannah Kidston, their eighth successive daughter, arrived on 10 October 1797. Trading conditions were worrying as well, for in the same year the Provost of Aberdeen took the chair at a meeting of merchants, manufacturers and other leading citizens to tell them, because of unusual demands for specie, the two Aberdeen banks had agreed only paper money, not gold, would be paid out. Alexander Scott and several of his friends, including Alexander Brown, were at the crowded meeting. Rumours spread quickly that banks had stopped payment, and French warships had been sighted, heralding an invasion.

In the following year one more upholsterer opened in the city, and Alexander Scott appealed against his taxes. On 16 August 1798 the Provost and bailies heard his plea his rates and window tax should be reduced because he had ten children, 'and also as having a shop in his dwelling place, the windows whereof have always been charged with the window duties of his house'. His appeal was allowed although, unless an addition to the family went unrecorded, he had only nine children at the time. By the summer of 1799 the business was in Huxter Row, another small street which has disappeared.

For a time John seems to have been a dutiful son, the routine enlivened by his first visit to the city's Theatre Royal to see 'The Celebrated Drama, *The Castle Spectre,* with all the scenery, decorations and dresses as presented in London'. Playgoing later became part of his professional life.

In December 1800 the family suffered their first bereavement when a boy who had been christened Alexander died after only a year of life. Six months later Alexander Dick was born, taking his name from his godfather, and Catherine Scott's child-bearing was at an end. But by that time the family had suffered a loss of a different kind.

After a quarrel with his father John left home in the middle of winter and went to Edinburgh. The cause is not recorded, but it seems likely his role in the business lay at the root of it. On 24 November, 1800 Alexander Scott inserted an announcement in *The Aberdeen Journal* which showed little of his usual ebullience: 'A. Scott flatters himself that on trial his goods will at least afford equal satisfaction with any others.' Soon after his son's desertion he advertised: 'Wanted, a sober person as Porter, to carry out small parcels, and also an apprentice is wanted, in the upholstery line.' These were not duties to appeal to a youth who had acquired a love of reading at Grammar school and Marischal college.

John did not cut himself off from his parents' money, or from their influential connections. In Edinburgh he lodged at a public house but dined with a Mr Scott, probably a brother of Alexander's who worked in a bank, and then went on to Glasgow where he stayed with the Reverend William Kidston, minister of East Campbell Street Secession Church and godfather of the Scotts' youngest daughter.

From Glasgow John wrote to his father on 28 January 1801 a remarkably mature letter for a sixteen-year-old:

> My dear Father,
>   Although by my past conduct I have I am afraid incurred your displeasure, yet I should esteem myself very far wanting in my duty should I omit writing you, whether I have done right or wrong would be a needless discussion I shall only observe that had I not thought by some of your expressions that my absence would give as much pleasure to you as my presence perhaps I should not have so hastily adopted my present line of conduct. I arrived at Glasgow on Monday night, I would have been there on Saturday but I was not well. I had kept my bed for two days before but found myself easier on taking a vomit. I went all but 13 miles on foot going on the top of the coach for that length. On Tuesday Mr Kidston went with me to some of his friends, all seemed very anxious to serve me, but have not yet heard anything in particular, but there is the probability of another vacancy in the Bank . . . if there be Mr Wardlaw promises to exert himself to procure it. I was obliged to get another guinea note from Mr Scott. I had got it before you sent me the 10/– I bought new shoes at Edinr. pair new stockings, these as I was at Mr Scott's table and appeared with his company I could not do without. Mr Scott desired me also to get another pair of breeches my old ones were all holes and I could not appear with decency at his house with them. . . .
>
> I hope my mother is getting better. I am very sorry to hear by your letter to Mr Kidston she was then still weakly. I would wish very much to hear soon

an account of her health. I would desire my kindest compliments to be presented to my Sisters and believe me

Your ever affectionate Son,
John Scott

The Mr Wardlaw of the letter may have been William Wardlaw, merchant and bailie, whose son Ralph was a Secession minister. A note from Mr Kidston accompanied John's letter. The minister told them: 'Johnny shall have his great coat without delay. . . . I shall count it a happiness to do for him any service in my power.'

Another Secession minister visiting the Kidston household who also knew the Scotts, Dr John Jamieson, put in a sharper comment: 'It gave me no little surprise when I reached the house of our friend to find there your son John and to be informed that he had passed thro' Perth without visiting Scoon. For this I have not failed to reprove him.'

He did not say why this offended him. Dr Jamieson was an enthusiastic antiquary, whose work won the respect of Walter Scott, and he may have thought no Scotsman should miss historic Scone.

John was taken on at the bank. Glasgow was expanding as a manufacturing and commercial centre, and a branch of the Royal Bank, whose headquarters were in Edinburgh, had opened in the High Street. It was managed by two merchants, David Dale and Robert Scott Moncrieff. It was presumably the latter, a dour-faced man to judge from the Raeburn portrait of him, who was the Mr Scott of John's letter to his mother on 21 March:

> I am still in the Bank, and will remain in all probability as we both as yet seem mutually pleased. The very great variety keeps the mind from wearying, which might otherwise happen in such a hurry and bustle . . . we sometimes go from eight to nine in the morning but not often, we are always there before 10, continue till near four return before 5 and come out after six, when business requires it we go again after Tea but this does not always happen. . . .
>
> What I have seen of the transactions as yet do not seem near so difficult as I expected and my superiors in the Office seem very ready to show me any thing I want. Mr Scott however has not yet spoken certainly of my continuance, but it is the opinion of all my friends here that he will never speak on the subject as he is that sort of a man but I will just be doing.

John was lodging at Mr Kidston's home, an arrangement which did not suit the minister's sister. On April 9 he informed his mother: 'From what Miss Kidston has repeatedly said I conjecture that it would be fully as well for me if I could immediately get an agreeable room, to take it.'

Catherine was evidently torn between anxiety for the welfare of her son and fear of irritating him, for he wrote tenderly:

> So far from thinking your advices tedious they are to me the most valuable gifts you can present. I should wish to observe them & if I swerve from the path of right my conduct will surely appear inexcusable after having had the advantage of such a Mother.

In the middle of April Alexander Scott paid a brief visit to Glasgow before going on to London, and invited the staff of the bank to supper. Mr Scott seems to have left his daughter Catherine in Edinburgh and then taken her with him to London, for on 23 April John wrote to his mother:

> He did not bring Kate to Glasgow, which rather disappointed her Glasgow acquaintances & me with the rest. . . . My father did not appear very stout when here, I hope however the voyage will have a good effect. He speaks in doubt whether or not he will leave Kate in London if he does the family will be more widely scattered than ever it was before.

His evenings began to grow tedious and he asked her to send him books, indicating a catholic taste which covered William Godwin's novels, Milton, and even craggier fare:

> I would like Guthries *Grammar,* Aberdeen Magazines, Nicholson *Philosophy,* Kennets *Roman Antiquities,* Dupatys *Travels, History of Belles Lettres, Universal Traveller,* Cronstad on *Mineralogy,* Watts *Improvement of the Mind, St Leon,* Robertson's *History of Scotland, Telemachus,* Addison's *Evidences,* Thompson's *Seasons,* Milton, Fuller—Also any other book I may have forgot and which you may think I would like. The Encyclopedia would I suppose be too large for carriage neither would you like it out of your house. I would thank you also to send me my manuscripts and all my papers as they will not take up much bulk.

John had rented a room at 4s. a week, but soon abandoned fending for himself, for he informed his mother he had decided to share lodgings with a fellow bank clerk.

> I find disadvantage in housekeeping by being by myself as my meat has now twice spoiled the butchers refusing to sell a small enough quantity. . . . I suppose you have not heard from my father, the mildness of the season has almost rendered his safety from storms certain, and I trust he has been equally lucky with regard to the enemy.

John was now firmly on the staff of the Royal Bank, for he told his mother to write to the office in future. While he was in Glasgow, another future journalist named John Gibson Lockhart was a young boy at the city's High school. Their paths were to cross dramatically later.

It was after he went to live in Glasgow that John caught his first sight of the Highlands. He and a friend spent a long weekend walking to Loch Lomond where, he recorded: 'The highland scenery burst upon us, for the first time of our lives, just as the sun was setting, with enough left of the light to give the glow of enchantment to the sudden spectacle . . . the road to Ben Lomond turns soon after it touches the Loch. In the adjacent forest of stunted pine firs, we met, not a party of Sunday wastlers, but a pair of tender lovers; the darkest shade of the "gloamin" prevented the gratification of our curiosity as to who the unguarded lady might be. We supposed she was a Glasgow belle.'

John Scott seemed to have settled to a career as a bank clerk. But he was to secede from Scotland as he had already seceded from Aberdeen.

Chapter 2

WHITEHALL AND FLEET STREET

From Glasgow John moved to London, where he entered the War Office as a temporary assistant clerk in July 1803. The work of the department was expanding rapidly, for in May Britain renewed the war with France after the brief peace which followed the Treaty of Amiens.

Although the post was a humble one with a salary of £81.18s. a year, it must have required influence to obtain Government employment. James Henry Leigh Hunt, who became a War Office clerk about the same time, obtained his appointment through the Prime Minister, Henry Addington (later Viscount Sidmouth). When another applicant wrote to the department, an official replied: 'I am directed by the Secretary at War to acknowledge the receipt of your letter of the 2nd instant and to inform you that having several young men well recommended to him already on his list for any vacancy which may occur in his office he cannot hold out any expectation of being able to serve a person however deserving who is totally unknown to him.'

Scott's immediate superior was Thomas Dods, principal clerk, whose father William lived in Scotland and knew the Aberdeen upholsterer. William Dods had himself been a principal clerk before retiring. But John probably owed his appointment to recommendations from some of Alexander Scott's aristocratic customers. These included the Earl of Kintore, and the young Earl of Aberdeen.

Mr Charles Philip Yorke was Secretary at War, but there was also a Secretary of State for War and the Colonies, Lord Hobart, who was in the Cabinet. Mr Yorke and his successors (the post changed hands frequently at that time) shared administrative duties with the Commander-in-Chief, the Duke of York. The War Office was in Whitehall, overlooking Horse Guards Parade.

There, with two other assistants Alexander Mackay and John Peevor, Scott helped Mr Dods in his duties, officially described as: 'The care of forming the Estimates and Establishments of the Army and of preparing the Authorities for the issue of Field Allowances, Off Reckonings and the Pay of Officers of the Staff & Garrisons.'

Britain was seized by near panic when Napoleon became the ruler of France and threatened to sweep across the Channel. Militia men were called to arms and William Pitt returned from the back benches to form a war ministry. It meant extra work and a supplement to his pay for John Scott. He wrote home to his second eldest sister, Nancy, from the office on 12 April 1804:

> I have been longer of writing to you than I intended, but of late I have been fully as much employed out of the office as in it, having procured Extra Work which must be done out of the Official Hours of Business—and is paid for by itself independent of my Salary.—It's terrible hard work tho'—and 'to a Gentleman of my gallantry' rather unpleasant to have every minute taken up in poring over Calculations. . . . .
>
> Knowing this, you will at one glance perceive the extreme difficulty I must experience in gratifying your wish (N.B. I consider Margaret and you as one Correspondent) of couching the finale to my Essay in harmonious Numbers. . . . As I see however You are determined to have Rhyme if You cant get Reason
>
> > I must even saddle Pegasus
> > And ride up Parnassus
> > To please the fair Lasses
> > Of Gay Aberdeen.

He then launched into five pages of doggerel for his sisters, tilting at their Presbyterian upbringing, and their father's position as a tradesman, while reminding his readers he had left university before taking his degree in its hall; some of the more felicitous lines ran:

> And here Divines I make apology
> For rashly meddling with Theology
> Yet I've some right to show my Knowledge
> As I've been bred at Marischal College
> And tho' I ne'er was at the Hall
> Yet with many Preachers great & small
> I've so often had communication
> That I've imbibed some Information
> I hope You'll keep your wrath from rising
> Tho' I encroach on Sermonizing
> For well I know that every Trader
> Runs down a Man that's not been bred
> And Prentic'd to that same profession
> So its the same in the Secession.

Postage was expensive for the Georgians, especially on long letters going hundreds of miles, but the mail of Members of both Houses of Parliament and some Government officials went free, and they could frank the correspondence of friends and acquaintances, by signing the outer cover.

Franking was an uncertain business, as John found when he tried to get his rhyming essay sent off by Francis Moore, Deputy Secretary and First Clerk at the War Office. His letter carried a series of postscripts:

> April 14th. After concluding in a very great hurry to get this sent off on Saturday, I find I am too late for a Frank. . . .
> Apl 16th. After going with my ill-fated Pacquet to get it Franked I hear that Mr Moore did not Frank Saturday's Letters, that of course they must be done today, that of course Monday's Letters cannot be done. . . .
> April 17th. Misfortune upon Misfortune, how often have I seen the brightest horizon suddenly partially darkened by the appearance of a solitary cloud, soon however to be totally overcast by those which follow in gloomy succession, so I, disappointed Saturday, am doubly disappointed on Monday & fated to be trebly disappointed on Tuesday. Mr Dods on coming in this morning locked the door, which we always do when in a hurry to prevent Intruders, having heard of some papers which we had to get ready being wanted in Parliament that very evening. I was therefore kept without the possibility of release driving my Pen till my fingers ached from 20 minutes past 10 o'clock till $\frac{1}{2}$ past 5.

Scott's description of himself as a gentleman of gallantry was more than teasing, for reminiscing some years later he wrote: 'On my first entrance into London, I happened to meet, at an evening party, a Roman Catholic lady and her daughter; the latter being pretty, was eagerly asked to a ball intended for the next Friday, which was a Saint's Festival. . . . Alas, the look sent to the mother for permission, was answered with an emphatic..."We, my dear, should know better"... What, thought I, are these persons, and Papists too, who know better on religious points, than my parents!'

In spite of his duties, John went home that summer on holiday, perhaps because his health was poor. He left with his family a miniature portrait of himself, dated 30 March 1804, showing a wide-eyed, curly-haired young man wearing a fashionable high stock. It was painted by Joseph Pastorini, who became a Royal Academy exhibitor.

Aberdeen and his family quickly restored the clerk's spirits. An account of their life early in the century was given by an unknown writer in *The Aberdeen Herald* in 1870:

> Mr Scott employed a number of hands and had the principal trade in his line in the town and country. His correct taste, and the substantial quality of the articles sent out from his workshops were appreciated by the late Premier, the Earl of Aberdeen, who entrusted him with the furnishing and decoration of Haddo House. . . .

> Mr Scott was a man of quick and fiery temper, but of noble and generous disposition, easily roused and easily pacified. He was an influential member of the Burgher Secession body, and made a present to the congregation of a costly and beautiful mahogany pulpit when their first church was built in St. Nicholas Lane.

This was in 1802, and the lane was then known as Correction Wynd. The writer continued:

> Mrs Scott was a highly-accomplished woman, gentle and lady-like in manners, with a firm and equable temper. . . . Mrs Scott may be said to have personally directed the education of her family of two sons and eight daughters, and to her they owe the turn for literature and intellectual pursuits, in which they all shared more or less. She had them raised at an early hour in the morning to study along with her the best English and foreign authors, and taught them to distinguish what was excellent in matter and style from the merely superficial and flimsy. Her choice of books was unrestricted, for although a conscientious Seceder she allowed her children free scope among novels, romances, the drama, and all the light and heavy literature of the day.

He added there was always a welcome at the Scotts' evening parties for 'the probationers of the Secession Church who journeyed through the country on horseback, with their travelling kit and a few crack sermons stowed in their saddle bags, to make their gifts manifest to the church, and as candidates for vacant charges . . . but to some raw and unpolished youths it was a severe ordeal to have to encounter so many sharp-witted females of high and cultivated intellect, quick to perceive, and ready to quiz any absurd sentimental extravagance of language in their pulpit discourse, as well as to repress stilted and stuck-up fools, who thought the assumption of a solemn pomposity essential to the dignity of the ministerial character; and many a time Mrs Scott has had to come to the aid of these self-important personages, whose pretensions were seen through, and unmercifully ridiculed by her frank outspoken daughters'.

It says something for the resilience of the young preachers that at least two married sisters of John. Margaret became the wife of the Reverend Lawrance Glass, minister at the chapel which received Alexander Scott's pulpit. The Reverend Robert Balmer, a prominent theologian of the Secession Church, married Jane Scott.

Scott returned to London with pleasant recollections of fishing, and of good company. Writing to sister Margaret from the War Office on 27 August 1804 he told her: 'It took a long time to wean my affections from that love of ease and sauntering which my mode of living while with you was so calculated to inspire . . . my thoughts will sometimes run, nay often run, on Miss Blank & Misses Severall, & Mrs You know who—Ladies whom you introduced me to at Aberdeen, I can assure you that

Miss *Blank* has made a wonderful *Blank* in my heart, which were she not at such a distance might be transmogrified into a Prize, that Misses *Severall* have made several indelible impressions—& that *Mrs You know who* has occasioned *You know what.*'

He assured her his holiday recollections had interfered with his official duties of sending letters to the Commander-in-Chief: 'Writing to a correspondent of mine, His Rl Highness The Duke of York, on the best method of opposing the Enemy with advantage, I told His R. Hs. that His R. Hs. must allow them a good deal of Play, but at the same time keep the Rod very tight, that by so doing he would soon weary them & kill them.' A few years later Scott was to speak less playfully of the Duke, second son of George III.

He continued his extra duties, and in two years at the War Office supplemented his income by £78.10s. He had taken lodgings in what was then the country to the west of London. Scott's letters do not identify the exact location, but the description seems to fit the home at that time of Jean Marie Delattre and his family in St John's Villas, North End, Fulham.

On 28 February 1805 he wrote to his mother, describing his life and the prospects of a permanent post in Whitehall:

> Your assurance of Remembrance, *particular* Remembrance, on the little festivals of the family give me the warmest pleasure—next to being with you they afford the most satisfaction. I am happy to inform you that I am in perfect good health. I am very comfortably situated and the country now gets pleasant. My Landlord is a very eminent Engraver, he is an old Frenchman, his wife and two Daughters constitute their family, they are every thing I want, attentive and quiet, and my accommodations are excellent, my room looks into the Garden which is large and affords abundance of choice vegetables, the road across the fields is in good weather extremely pleasant, the distance about 3 miles from Hyde Park Corner. I certainly think I have to thank this walk for the perfect restoration of my health.
>
> We have been extremely busy since I wrote you more so than ever since I went into the Office, this you may recollect is our Estimate time—they were altered so often and changed etc. by Mr Pitt that for 3 weeks we had not a moment's spare time. Mr Dods has got an additional £100 a year for his exertions on this occasion. I mean to push the Secretary at War through Mr Dods for a change for the better in my situation when I have been there 2 years which will be in July.

On 10 June Scott was able to tell his mother that Mr Moore had sent for him and said that because he had worked well he had been placed on the establishment: 'I have £90 per annum the 1st year, £100 the second, £110 the 3rd and 4th to rise progressively £10 every two years after that besides casual promotion.'

He went on to ask after his young brother and to acknowledge the gift of some salmon packed on ice in what was then a new method of conserving fish sent by sea. 'I am sorry to hear of poor Alexander's illness. . . . What is the reason that Nancy never writes me—is she so busy courting that she cannot find time—The Salmon was excellent.'

A letter to his father a few weeks later was devoted to business and political gossip. First he mentioned Mr Scott's piano supplier, John Broadwood, with a wry word for his son and partner, James:

> Mr Broadwood has I find acknowledged the receipt of the Money you sent him by me, I suppose the reason of his long silence was his going out of Town the day after he received it, & Mr J.B. seems now too intent on pleasure to take much concern with business. He is almost constantly in the country.

John showed astuteness in assessing the war situation, and the impeachment of Viscount Melville. This member of the Cabinet and First Lord of the Admiralty was of particular interest to Scotsmen because he controlled Government patronage in their country. Walter Scott described Lord Melville as the great giver of good things. He was finally acquitted of any crime except carelessness in superintending the financial activities of a subordinate, but resigned.

John wrote to his father: 'Margaret told me you wished me to insist more on Politics in my Letters, particularly on Lord Melville's business—that is now a stale topic—"*Every dog must have his day*"—and the public clamour which so furiously railed at him, is now entirely absorbed by the combined Fleets, and prospect of Invasion. With regard to Lord Melville's crime, there seems to be but one opinion, that he is guilty, but his good nature, affability, and great abilities, have in the Metropolis raised him many friends.'

Although Scott shared the reforming zeal of the Whig and Radical opposition, he was scornful of their lukewarm attitude to the struggle with Napoleon, and went on:

> It certainly too must be remarked that upon no one occasion when any National subject was agitated, did the Leaders of the opposition exert themselves so strenuously, as on this comparatively trifling affair. And surely if patriotism was their motive, it ought to break out as furiously when suggesting measures to curb the ambition of Buonaparte, as when endeavouring to crush a man who whatever may have been his faults, was at that moment endeavouring by every means in his power to raise the British Navy from that state of weakness into which it had fallen through an administration composed of imbecility, cunning, and more than pharisaical hypocrisy.

It is to be hoped John sealed this letter, with its libellous comments on former ministers, firmly before leaving it at the office for franking.

Writing two months before the Battle of Trafalgar, John told his father: 'It is undoubtedly a serious consideration that at this moment, when invasion is so much dreaded, a hostile fleet of above 60 Sail, may very probably be enabled to assemble, and that within no great distance from our shores. . . . Everyone here *acts* as if he expected to hear of a French Army landing in England tomorrow, yet no one appears to believe it when you come to ask him—for my own part I should think the Ruler of the French too much taken up with preparations for those scenes which appear likely to be performed on the Continent, to attempt an enterprise in which he must undoubtedly lose an immense number of men, and which must so engage his Forces as to render him very vulnerable to his hostile neighbours. I have just this moment got intelligence of Lord Nelson's having arrived at Portsmouth. . . . It is dreaded that he means to give up his Command on account of bad health.'

He added a note on his own health: 'I have not been so well lately as hitherto, but I am now getting better again, though I am very thin.'

Work was taking its toll, for the War Office at this time was a hard taskmaster. *The Monthly Mirror* told readers: 'The Admiralty, Treasury, Secretary of States, Council Offices, Post Office, War Office, and many other departments, have no holiday but the Sabbath.'

By 1807, when an official inquiry was held into the military departments, the situation had eased only slightly. The Commissioners conducting it reported the ordinary hours at the War Office were 11 o'clock to 4, and added: 'There are no established holidays. It is, however, usual to dispense with the attendance of most of the Gentlemen on Christmas Day and Good Friday; and of late years the indulgence of being absent on Saturdays, during the Recess of Parliament, has been frequently granted to a proportion of the officers.'

The results were revealed nearly twenty years later when Viscount Palmerston told the Commons no set of men worked harder than his clerks, and in a few years twenty-six of them, all in the prime of life, had died of pulmonary and other complaints arising from sedentary habits.

The Georgians' reaction to ill-health was to take vigorous counter-measures which sound worse than the disease. John Scott was not immune to such over-kill, for he wrote to his mother:

> I am excessively nervous, consequently bracing weather and exercise are the two best remedies. I have got lately quite well, tho' very thin. I in general walk from 15 to 20 miles a day and sometimes more, and find the most beneficial results from the exertion. My lodgings are 4 miles from the Office, and I repeatedly walk to town before 7 o'clock, work in the War Office till 8, get back to breakfast by 9, set off again at 10, and reach the Office by 11, this with returning to dinner is pretty well, but often when I wish to make any calls, I set off again for town after dinner and reach home again to sleep.

Not surprisingly, he added: 'I have however generally lately breakfasted in town.'

John continued to send rhymes to his sisters, including some lines *On the Rain-bow*, which began:

> Hail beauteous Arch! that, in the darkling sky,

His verses were beginning to show the influence of the fledgling Romantic movement, as well as thoughts of romance. It is natural to suspect he had come into contact with Leigh Hunt, then a clerk of John's own age working in a temporary department of the War Office concerned with settling old accounts, but whose mind was occupied with poetry and dramatic criticism.

It may also have been in 1805 that Scott first met William Hazlitt, to whom he became a loyal friend. Charles Lamb records in a letter that Hazlitt saw 'a Mr Scott' at the house of Joseph Hume. Lamb thought at first this was Nelson's secretary, John Scott, who died with the Admiral on board *Victory*, but was told by Mrs Hume it was not the same man. Hume was a Government clerk in the victualling office at Somerset House in the Strand. Many years later Hazlitt wrote of talking with Joseph Hume about their mutual friends, Leigh Hunt and John Scott.

A Birthday Ode was dispatched to Aberdeen by John to celebrate his coming of age on 24 October, the series of quatrains opening:

> The beauteous landscape adorning
> How sparkling and bright is the Sun,
> With lustre he honors the morning,
> That hails me of age—twenty one.

Stanza 9 probably contained some genuine self-revelation:

> Then Mama's pretty Jacky so petted
> Delighting in mischievous fun,
> (Change worthy of being gazetted)
> Shall grow thoughtful when turned twenty one.

He intended to complete twenty-one verses, but invention ran out after fourteen, a foretaste of the ambitious failures which marked his life. Writing to his mother a few days later, 'Jacky' told her he spent the evening of his birthday at the house of a friend. But his thoughts turned to Aberdeen, where the family celebrated over supper, and Alexander Dick was saddened by his brother's absence.

John's letter was serious in tone: 'Everything at the War Office goes on as well as can be expected, that is to say as well as 21 *ought to* expect. But not so well as 16 foolishly *will* expect. I have however now given up looking for windfalls.'

He told her the family with whom he lived were attentive, but not intrusive: 'I sometimes think that it will never do for my temper to form a constant connection with any human being. I mean such a connection as requires you constantly to be together, and unites the happiness of one with the happiness of the other.'

This was clearly the letter of a young man about to fall in love. The girl was Caroline Antoinette Colnaghi, two years his junior. A portrait painted apparently about this time depicts her as a ringletted brunette with a roman nose, humorous mouth, and the eyes of a Mona Lisa, impressions reinforced by the later comments of Leigh Hunt and artist Benjamin Robert Haydon on her attractions.

John did not entirely let his heart rule his hard head. He admitted his beloved was a little vain, over-sensitive, and given to coquetry, which must have made her irresistible. Caroline herself said she once tormented a Frenchman engaged to teach her the language so cruelly he gave up appearing for dinner to avoid meeting her.

Her mother was English, but her father, Paul Colnaghi, was the son of a Milanese lawyer. Paul worked in Paris before settling in London in the 1780s, and taking British citizenship. He was a printseller, a term which covered most forms of picture-dealing. His shop was at 23 Cockspur Street, at the east end of Pall Mall, not far from John's office. One of the firm's most profitable speculations was a portrait print of Nelson published the day news of Trafalgar reached London. Two sons, Dominic and Martin, worked in the business, and Caroline had a young sister.

John Scott faced heavy odds in his courtship. He was young, his income was just £100 a year, there was a rival for Caroline's hand, and the news John wished to marry a beautiful stranger with a foreign name must have alarmed his family.

Alexander Scott paid one of his regular visits to London in the spring of 1806, and probably reacted angrily to the latest example of his son's impetuosity. But John set about his campaign with his usual tenacity, and ability to argue a case.

He revealed his strategy to his mother on 12 May in a long letter in which he used the word 'friends' in its old Scottish sense of relatives:

> From my father you will have learned what passed during his residence in London, also his sentiments on the Affair.

He emphasised he was determined to pursue his courtship, but acknowledged his present salary was inadequate and said he was not seeking to rush into marriage:

> I know my own disposition and I know it is not at all calculated to be happy under those deprivations which a straightened income requires (I mean in a married state)—I not only would be miserable myself, but would most certainly render my Partner so by my discontent, if I had not means sufficient to live in the manner I have accustomed myself to look to in prospect. . . .

> When I requested the approbation of Caroline's parents to my addresses, which I saw the necessity of doing, sooner perhaps than I originally intended, from not only observing that they expected, but also being conscious that they had a right to expect, some explanation of my behaviour, the immediate answer was "What would your friends think of this"—I replied that I had no reason to suppose my friends could have any objection to a Connection so essential to my happiness, and so indisputable in point of respectability—but that I expected my Father in town in a couple of months, when I should take an opportunity of speaking to him. . . .
>
> When that time came, and when week after week passed without any settlement or even conversation on the subject, I could evidently see their manner alter, and that so much as to convince me that should he depart in this way, I must give up my hopes, at least so far as depended on them.

In the end it seems a reluctant Alexander Scott gave his approval provided the young couple waited for a year. John told his mother:

> The period mentioned, viz. twelvemonth, I intend . . . to be lengthened if necessary, to be shortened if convenient—Many things make me sure not only that a set time was indispensable but also that the same ought not to exceed a year—one of which is, that to my certain knowledge, a Gentleman in a very extensive Line, and living at present in superior style, an old acquaintance of the family & on terms of particular intimacy, had expressed his wish to Mr C. to pay his addresses to his Daughter.

Alexander must have taken two or more of his daughters to London with him, for John wrote to his mother: 'With regard to Caroline herself I must refer you to my Sisters—as I suppose what I say might be received with caution.' But he did take up the delicate topics that would interest Catherine Scott most, the character and religious sentiments of her prospective daughter-in-law:

> She is, as I daresay you have already heard, a Protestant, and altho' certainly not brought up with those strict notions of Religion, inculcated by you, and in my opinion consistent with its truth, possesses as much respect & regard to its dictates as is to be found out of the pale of a few particular Sects—
>
> However preferable this nicety may be when to be found yet I should be sorry indeed for the great mass of mankind were I of opinion that Virtue, & goodness were not to be met with separated from it—She has got an amiable sweetness of temper, as much Sense as is necessary, or is usually to be found, and a superabundant store of sensibility . . . the knowledge that she contains in her Breast the germ of misery under certain casualties of Life must render me tremblingly careful, with the affection I bear for her, and knowing the responsibility I incur, of my future conduct towards her.

He agreed she had some faults which he hoped would diminish with time—'a small portion of Vanity—rather more of giddy coquetry—and a tinge of affectation'. No doubt feeling Catherine would be more sympathetic to his plans than her husband, John urged his mother to visit London in the summer.

Facing a year's engagement, or more accurately twelve months' probation in which to prove he could support a wife, Scott considered making money by writing, encouraged by an unnamed friend who sounds like Leigh Hunt. The poems sent to his sisters, and hints he gave them about writing a play alarmed his mother, who understood her son's failings better than he did himself. He tried to reassure her in a rambling letter written a week after that about his love problems.

Referring to the poems, he commented: 'It was first suggested to my mind by the hint of a friend of mine, that the hours devoted to relaxation in this manner, might perhaps at some future time, be turned to an additional use were I to turn my attention to any mode of writing, likely to catch public notice. . . . The plan of making an attempt for the stage I pitched on, as being easier in attainment (I mean in getting it brought forward) than any other, as being unattended with expense in the event of a failure, and as affording more ample remuneration in the case of success, than almost any other channel of writing whatever.' He did not consider writing would interfere with his career, since 'close attention for five hours a day, will procure for me every possible rise in the War Office'.

No more was heard of play-writing, but the War Office, with its salary increases of £10 at two-year intervals, had lost the loyalty of the young man in love with Caroline Colnaghi. The following spring Scott's career underwent another abrupt change.

Among family papers preserved in the National Library of Scotland are newspaper cuttings belonging to John Scott with a note by his brother, Alexander Dick, saying 'they are contributions of his own to *The Statesman* after he became Editor'. One bears the inscription 'May 10th 1807 the day I commenced the Paper'. *The Statesman* was an evening newspaper whose principal owner was Daniel Lovell, a radical and former linen draper. It cost sixpence and was published from 87 Fleet Street.

During the first few weeks of his editorship Scott wrote vigorous leading articles in a style which became his hallmark as a political commentator. A Whig Government headed by Lord Grenville had fallen in March, and been replaced by a Tory administration with the Duke of Portland as Prime Minister. Special targets for attack were two able and rising ministers, George Canning who had drawn the fire of reformers by his satirical verses in a publication called *The Anti-Jacobin* some years earlier, and Viscount Castlereagh, believed to have condoned savage measures while Chief Secretary in troubled Ireland.

A rumour Lord Melville was to rejoin the Government brought the comment: 'The Restoration of Lord Melville to a seat in the Cabinet, an event announced in a Ministerial print of Tuesday last, shows that the *effrontery* of his Majesty's advisers falls nowhere short of their misconduct.' Scott also decried the refusal to grant emancipation to Catholics, who were barred from sitting in the House of Commons, and from holding various offices. When the Government introduced an Irish Insurrection Bill he wrote two powerful articles opposing it.

John printed a piece entitled 'Burlington House Card Party', that being the residence of the Prince of Wales. He sneered at the efforts of a man who was to be a life-long opponent, writer and Government MP John Wilson Croker, and crossed swords with the Tory *Morning Post*. He had a scornful remark for wordly bishops and ambitious parsons 'of all bickerings, God preserve us from the religious ones'.

Scott reserved praise chiefly for Sir Francis Burdett, a radical reformer elected MP for Westminster in April, although he chided him for being rash. Even at twenty-two, Scott tempered his enthusiasm for change with discretion, fearing a violent approach would raise the spectre of revolution and delay progress. These leading articles were forthright but showed maturity and balance.

They were hardly the outpourings of a novice, and it seems obvious John had already served an apprenticeship in journalism. Possibly he did so while still at the War Office, writing in his spare time after doing his five hours a day. In this he would have been following Leigh Hunt, who combined official duties with contributions on the drama to a series of publications. Leigh Hunt admitted in his *Autobiography*: 'I made a bad clerk, wasting my time and that of others in perpetual jesting, going too late to the office.'

In 1805 Leigh Hunt joined his brother John, a printer and publisher, in launching a Sunday paper called *The News*. The following year they were concerned in founding *The Statesman*, which was perhaps why Scott became its editor in 1807. Their most famous venture, *The Examiner*, a political and literary weekly which appeared on 3 January 1808, was owned jointly by the brothers.

Newspaper historians state John Scott edited *The News*: if he did it was probably either just before or while he was writing for *The Statesman*, and he certainly contributed one article and possibly more to it some years later. *The News* repeated many short items that appeared in *The Statesman*, and called it a respectable evening print. The term editor was used loosely in Georgian London; editors came and went on some journals much as football club managers do today.

Leigh Hunt hinted in his later writings that Scott was indebted to him in some undefined way. It was one of his foibles to exaggerate his influence on every young man of talent he met, from John Keats to Lord Byron, but in this case the Hunt brothers may have opened the door to Fleet Street for editor Scott. John Hunt was respected as a man of business and advocate of liberal principles by everyone, except the ministers who prosecuted him for his opinions.

Byron's friend John Cam Hobhouse, later Lord Broughton, stated both Leigh Hunt and James Perry, proprietor of *The Morning Chronicle*, played a part in introducing Scott to journalism. Perry was an Aberdonian who attended Marischal College. Nearly thirty years John's senior, he went to London, and took control of the *Chronicle*, which became the recognised organ of Whig politics. It could have been Perry Scott had in mind when, late in life, he spoke of advice he received from an elderly Scotsman in his early career.

The early nineteenth century was an exciting time for journalists. Dozens of new papers and periodicals sprang up each year, although most vanished swiftly. *The Times* had not yet achieved the eminence it was to assume under proprietor John Walter II and editor Thomas Barnes, but *The Morning Post* made Daniel Stuart a wealthy man. When he sold the paper in 1803 it became an uncritical supporter of the Prince of Wales and of Tory Ministers, and an object of contempt to John Scott. Stuart turned his attention to an evening paper, *The Courier*.

Journalists of the day included names now famous in literature, among them Charles Lamb, writing humorous paragraphs and political squibs. Samuel Taylor Coleridge wrote for the newspapers owned by Stuart, who also had the help at first of another intellectual, James Mackintosh, his brother-in-law. Mackintosh studied at Aberdeen before becoming a lawyer, and was to prove an influential friend of Scott.

He first caught public attention by supporting the principles of the French Revolution against the thundering of Edmund Burke. But later he denounced the excesses of the Terror in Paris, and accepted a knighthood from a Tory Government to go to Bombay as a judge. This was regarded as desertion by his old comrades in reform.

Modern readers glancing through newspapers of the Napoleonic era find it hard to recognise the quality of the authors and the importance of the events they discussed. Articles were normally unsigned or closed with a pseudonym. Papers were small, four pages for wholesheets and eight or sixteen for halfsheet publications. Few headlines exceeded one column, and were often just labels. Short items, including satirical or scandalous pieces, might have no headings at all. Most daily papers carried advertisements on the front page.

Reputable papers were increasing in power, and had become bolder in resistance to Government attempts to curb their independence than those of earlier decades. But corruption, by direct bribery or indirect patronage, was common. People paid to air their views in letters to the editor, and occasionally to suppress paragraphs which reflected on their reputation or business. Much space was given to war news, Parliamentary reports, and legal proceedings.

An evening paper, such as John Scott's *Statesman,* copied whole columns of material from morning papers.

The newspaper had been going more than a year when he became editor. Some of the delicate manoeuvring involved in operating it was revealed in a memorandum sent by Lovell to Samuel Whitbread, an opposition MP. In it he stated the original purpose of *The Statesman* had been to oppose William Pitt, but when the war leader died and was replaced by a Whig Government, it came out in support of that administration in February 1806. Its policy was explained to the Earl of Moira, a minister of whom Lovell said:

> Lord Moira was then told it had been the practice of Mr Pitt's administration to order a circulation of newspapers and that *The Sun* had distributed upwards of One Thousand at the expense of Government in addition to the Advertisements for the Public Offices—Lord Moira said he would consult his colleagues . . . a few days afterwards his Lordship ordered a circulation of four or five Hundred Papers daily & the Advertisements for the Public Offices.

However, according to Lovell, when bills totalling £1800 were presented only £550 was paid. The matter was unresolved when the Whig ministry fell, and as this happened a few weeks before Scott became editor, he did not benefit from their patronage. However, the paper must have been profitable, for Lovell claimed to have paid Wilmer M Willett, who succeeded John in the editorial chair, nearly £600 a year. No doubt this was a considerable exaggeration, but Scott's switch from Whitehall to Fleet Street served the purpose of raising his income.

For on 30 September 1807, according to the register of St Marylebone Parish Church, John Scott, bachelor, and Caroline Colnaghi, spinster, were married by the curate, Benjamin Lawrence. Witnesses were the bride's mother, Elizabeth Colnaghi, and brother Dominic. The modest-looking church in Marylebone High Street, scene of Lord Byron's christening nearly twenty years before, has since been demolished.

It was to the grander St Martin-in-the-Fields the couple went the following year for the baptism of their own son. Paul Alexander was born on 6 May 1808. The arrival of a seven-months child could have raised some eyebrows, and may account for the ceremony being delayed until 21 July. However John and Caroline made no attempt to conceal his exact age in later life, and when a second son was born in 1816 he too was premature.

No letters from John have survived from this period. On 4 July he published an attack on the man he once described jovially as his correspondent, the Duke of York.

Britain was about to send troops to the Peninsula to support the Spanish insurgents against the occupying French forces. A report circulated the Duke, as Commander-in-Chief, wished to take charge of the expedition. He had commanded British forces in the unsuccessful campaigns in the Low Countries in the 1790s, and *The Statesman* declared nothing but misfortune and disgrace would follow from his appointment: 'Now, when Spain is just coming to her senses, and looking to talent, and to rank, for men able to guide her through the present crisis of her fate, what, in the name of goodness, has the Duke of York, of all men in the world, to do in such a Country, at such a time.'

Two weeks later Scott drew on his own recollections of the War Office to write: 'It is, we are ready to allow, natural enough that his Royal Highness should feel mortified at being fixed to the Horse Guards, like a Private in the old Lumber Troop, or a fat Beef-Eater, to count the chime of the quarters as they sound from the clock, while Generals less favoured by birth, but more by fortune, are proclaiming the renown of their Country in peals of British thunder.'

The royal Commander had a special reason for wishing to leave the country. His duties involved recommendations for Army commissions, and for promoting officers already serving. It was common practice for appointments to be bought and sold, but the public were scandalised when it was alleged the Duke was influenced in his decisions by the beautiful Mrs Mary Ann Clarke, who had been his mistress while Scott was at the War Office.

The Government decided to act over the attacks. On 14 December 1808 John wrote to his mother: '*The Statesman* is, I am sorry to say, prosecuted for a libel on the Duke of York, inserted in that paper in the month of July last. Contrary to the express terms of our agreement, the Proprietors were all eager to make me the scape-goat, if by so doing they could have saved themselves. Most fortunately, and at the same time most unaccountably, the manuscript copy of the article in question could not be found, although the copy is generally preserved with great care. They very unwarrantably made affidavits that I was the author, although such an Oath could only be made at hap-hazard. These affidavits, however, being no proofs, are returned to them as useless; and consequently they must go to prison without the pleasure of my company.'

Daniel Lovell did not go to gaol over the Duke, although he did for subsequent offences. The prosecution was dropped because the case of Mrs Clarke was taken up in Parliament by Colonel Gwyllym Lloyd Wardle, and the Duke finally resigned. But the affair apparently ended Scott's editorship of *The Statesman*, and he turned to a new undertaking.

This was a weekly newspaper called *The Censor,* of which he seems to have been both editor and proprietor. It was from his office at 1 Catherine

Street, off the Strand, that John wrote home in December. No copies of it are held at the British Library, but judging from this letter it followed his usual anti-Tory line. Apologising for not answering Mrs Scott's letters before, he said:

> Your anxiety relative to my safety, in consequence of the ticklish topics on which the Censor, in virtue of his office, must necessarily touch, is I hope groundless. I have heard nothing of any prosecutions against me. . . . It cannot be denied that my situation is one of some danger; but if I did not make up my mind to run a risk, it would be idle to continue *The Censor*. A young work must be noticed, or it must die; and I think that everyone who undertakes what I have undertaken, should face the hazards incidental to his profession, more especially at the present moment, when there is an evident combination against all free discussion whatsoever, on the part of the men in power.

His family and friends were playing a part in the venture: 'I feel much indebted to you all for your very active exertions in my behalf. Aberdeen and the surrounding country do wonders for the Censor. . . . I shall have some volumes of the work to dispose of at Christmas, printed on unstamped paper, half bound, with Index, Title page, etc. and sold I believe about 8s. or 10s. per volume.'

The reference to unstamped paper was a reminder normal sales of newspapers were taxed at the rate of $3\frac{1}{2}$d. a copy. Publishers had to get the blank paper stamped at Somerset House before publication. Payment was in cash, although a discount of 20 per cent was allowed on large quantities. A separate duty of 3s., later raised to 3s.6d, was charged on each advertisement.

John's letter explained the burden of taxation, especially as the vendors who distributed the papers were often slow in paying:

> I hope I shall be able to make the Censor answer. The great difficulty is to manage to get stamps—this requires prompt payment; and the newsmen receive one, two and three months' credit—1,000 stamps cost £14; and a less number cannot be purchased without losing the discount which is a very material consideration. The above number will not make out the fortnight; and sometimes the intervention of several holidays one after another renders it necessary to purchase in advance.

From Scott's purchase of stamps it seems *The Censor* had a circulation not much above 500 a week. Whatever its selling price, probably ninepence at most, expenses would leave little profit. He later referred to the year 1809 as a time of embarrassments and difficulties.

He got into debt, and quarrelled with Caroline's parents. Mr Colnaghi was approaching sixty, and had his own business problems. In spite of the war he visited Paris to renew contacts there, and on his return journey had to escape through Holland disguised as a sailor. His Continental links brought him into contact with important officials, leading later to patronage by the Prince of Wales. Some articles by his son-in-law must have caused him uneasiness.

Although Alexander Scott sided with Paul Colnaghi in the family row, he helped the young couple, for in his will drawn up in 1810 he referred to cash advanced to John. This money, which otherwise would have been left to him on his father's death, appears to have totalled £400.

It was not enough to keep the creditors quiet. By the time Margaret Scott married the Reverend Lawrance Glass in Aberdeen on 17 October 1809 her brother had put nearly ninety miles between himself and his debts, and started afresh as a country editor.

Chapter 3

COUNTRY EDITOR DEFIES THE LASH

The chosen retreat was Stamford, in the southwest corner of Lincolnshire. This charming place of stone houses and fine churches, over-looking the River Welland has changed less in the intervening years than any other associated with John Scott. In his day it was a market town of between 5000 and 6000 inhabitants, and a staging post on the Great North Road to York and Scotland.

Scott was the editor of a new weekly, *Drakard's Stamford News*, produced at 14 High Street. The house still stands, although the printing works behind it was demolished.

He intended to spend a year in Stamford, and stayed for three; but they were not wasted years, or uneventful. Freed from the burden of running the business side of a newspaper, and backed by a proprietor who gave him his head, John refined his skills, and weathered his first direct clash with authority. In his writings, even at their most pugnacious, you sense this was a happy time.

The *News* was owned by John Drakard, an outspoken radical with a string of shops in the villages of Uppingham, Bourn, Corby and Crowland, as well as his Stamford premises. They sold all sorts of articles, from patent medicine to pianos. But the chief interest of Johnny Drakard, as he was known, was waging war on local Tories.

In this he had the support of Octavius Graham Gilchrist, town councillor and owner of a High Street grocery business. He took a hand in the new journal, for Gilchrist had published a book of poems, dabbled in scholarly criticism, and in spite of his liberal views was friendly with William Gifford, editor of *The Quarterly Review*, recently established in London as the Tory answer to the Whiggish *Edinburgh Review*. Gilchrist's literary activities could be as controversial as his politics, John Scott discovered.

The first issue of *Drakard's Stamford News and General Advertiser*, to give its full title, appeared on Friday 6 October 1809. It announced its circulation covered the counties of Lincoln, Rutland, Northampton, Huntingdon, Leicester, Nottingham, 'and the parts adjacent'. The front page carried advertisements for a range of goods and services, books, auctions, a register office for servants, liquor, a state lottery with £20,000 prize, *Old Moore's Almanack*, and the offer of a £20 reward for apprehension of a tollgate keeper who eloped with another man's wife.

Inside Scott stated in a leading article the *News* would be conducted on principles of independence, impartiality and moderation. Although anti-Napoleon and pro-British Constitution, its policy was to be equally indifferent to Whigs and Tories. This did not save the Government, just reshuffled and now headed by Spencer Perceval as Prime Minister, from unfavourable comment.

The outgoing cabinet was described as 'perhaps as imbecile in its designs, and as blundering in the execution of them, as any which has ever disgraced our national councils', while of the newcomers it was said 'the meanness and grovelling spirit of the persons who compose this burlesque on administration are glaringly evident'. Such onslaughts were reinforced by protests over the influence of the family who owned much of Stamford and the surrounding countryside, and dominated the council, as well as nominating two MPs. This was the House of Burghley, whose mansion has stood on the outskirts of the town since the first Elizabeth created the first Lord Burghley. When Scott edited the *News* the family was represented by a boy, the Marquis of Exeter, and his affairs were in the hands of trustees.

This issue contained an attack on a long-established rival, *The Lincoln Rutland and Stamford Mercury*, describing it as subservient to those in power. Its sober columns were filled with advertisements, and like most contemporary country newspapers it refrained from expressing views which might upset any large body of customers. The Mercury was owned by Richard Newcomb, a former Chief Magistrate of Stamford, who was helped in the business by his son of the same name. Young Richard was of an age with Scott and had served part of his journalistic apprenticeship on a London evening paper, *The Globe*, whose offices in the Strand were not far from those where the Aberdonian had battled with *The Censor* and its problems.

Johnny Drakard was particularly annoyed because when he announced the start of his own paper by placing an advertisement in the *Mercury*, the Newcombs launched another weekly called *The Stamford and Boston Gazette*. This carried news squeezed out of the older paper, and served as a medium through which the younger Newcomb could reply to the attacks of Scott and Drakard.

In national affairs Scott campaigned for reform of the electoral system, abolition of slavery, Catholic emancipation and fair play for other dissenters, a softening of the criminal laws, and education for poor children. His sharpest rebukes were for pettifogging lawyers, servile clergymen, and corrupt politicians and courtiers; he found room for judicious observations on the upheaval in Latin America as Spain's colonies rebelled, and on the looming war between Britain and America, as well as mounting a spirited defence of press freedom.

When the Newcombs accused him of stealing an advertisement delivered by mistake to the *News* instead of the *Mercury,* he declared: 'The Editor of Mr Drakard's Paper . . . superintends the original discussion and the arrangement of the political intelligence in the *Stamford News*—but he is much too dull to be entrusted with such important matters as Advertisements and Ship News.'

Flattery was discouraged: 'The Editor hopes . . . *Dr Dominus* will excuse the few liberties that have been taken with his letter. In omitting the complimentary passages, the Editor is not actuated by a real or affected disregard of the approbation of his readers,—but by a conviction that the praise of correspondents comes in a very questionable shape, and is justly looked upon as a suspicious *character,* by the public. The Editor of the *Stamford News,* therefore, thus gives notice, that he does not expect his friends, who favour him with communications, that they should preface them in the usual manner, with,—"Sir,—I beg permission, through the medium of your *valuable* and *widely circulated* paper, to state, etc, etc, etc". . . many people have got an idea that the Conductors of Newspapers have an unaccountable habit of writing letters to *themselves.*'

There were worse trials for the editor. Early in its career the *News* reported: 'The London Mail was, on Wednesday night, robbed at Barnet. The bag containing the letters and papers having been stolen, we have been deprived of the London news for Tuesday and Wednesday.'

Scott's main energies went into his weekly essay on current affairs. Acknowledging a letter signed Mr Sheepshanks saying that 'gentlemen editors *understand* everything', the editor replied they were at any rate expected to treat of everything.

In a tribute to Leigh Hunt, Scott continued: 'A brother journalist, whose services have not been confined to politics, but who has done much to promote literature, as well as the liberties of his country, sighed very pathetically over the

> Distaste, delays, dislikings to begin,
> Gnawing of pen, and kneading of the chin,

that are experienced by the writer, who is expected to tell of the time with the regularity of an eight-day clock.'

On 17 November 1809 the *News* made its first mention of the brutal flogging of soldiers. Under the heading 'Matrimony a punishable offence', it carried a letter about a man receiving 100 lashes for marrying against the orders of his commanding officer.

Space was found for social and literary life, such as Lord Byron coming of age and taking his seat in the Lords. There was a curious reference to Walter Scott, still known as a poet rather than novelist: 'Among the literary manufacturers of the day, the celebrated author of *Marmion* stands supreme. . . . It has been whispered the firm of John Ballantyne & Co has the honour to include Mr Scott. If so, it must be allowed that he is no *sleeping* partner.' Walter's involvement in trade as a partner in the firm of printers who produced his work was not widely known until many years later.

Sickness attacked John's own family and the Aberdeen household. Scott wrote to his mother on 19 January 1810 after a letter from his sister Margaret had made him fearful that Alexander Dick, not yet ten, was dying. He expressed the hope 'that the disorder which had before carried our dear Brother to the very entrance, as it were, of the grave, might again be overcome through the means of your unceasing efforts & attentions . . . the mental misery which an infant may suffer is perhaps never duly appreciated but by those whose feelings at that time of life have been permanently impressed on their recollection by peculiar circumstances. When surrounding a death-bed one would buy back a former act of unkindness against the sufferer at an immense price.—You will readily trace these observations to my relation as Father to him who is now looking up in my face.'

John went on to express concern that Mrs Scott's own health had suffered through the strain of looking after her young son, and remarked: 'Caroline is not stout, but on the whole better since she has been in Stamford.' He added his salary had been raised from three to four guineas a week. Alexander Dick finally recovered.

In the same month Scott wrote a very different letter, an open one headed: 'From The Editor of the Stamford News to Samuel Coddington Esq, Mayor of Stamford.' This was evidently prompted by Drakard, Gilchrist, and another supporter of reform, Thomas Blore, and arose from a parliamentary by-election held before Scott arrived in Stamford. This was won by Charles Chaplin, nominee of the Burghley interest, against an independent candidate, Joshua Jepson Oddy, by 306 votes to 142. Accusations followed that the trustees of the young Marquis of Exeter, Lord St Helens, Lord Henniker, the Reverend William Burslem, and Mr Evan Foulkes, MP, had exerted improper influence through the family agent, John Pepper. Other allegations were that voters for Mr Oddy were disqualified on the technical ground they had not paid the poor rate as householders, that some farmers on land owned by the Marquis had their tenancies terminated for voting the wrong way, and that Mr Oddy's wife and children were turned away from the George Inn. This coaching house at the southern end of the town was the headquarters of the Tories. Thomas Blore added to the list of misdeeds some complaints of maladministration of the town's charities.

In his open letter Scott said:

> The Corporation, of which you are the head, has just now resolved to take the opinion of Sir Vicary Gibbs, on the propriety of prosecuting the authors of certain Resolutions passed and published on the first day of April last— that is to say, more than nine months ago. These . . . originated in the late contested election, and were passed at a meeting of gentlemen attached to the interests of Mr Oddy, the popular candidate. . . . Surely, sir, the Corporation of Stamford was not compelled to bear about its shame, like a frail female, for nine tedious months before it could be delivered of it. . . .
>
> Why you *now* talk of prosecuting is, that John Pepper has now given his orders to that effect. In conformity to this, it is said that Mr Foulkes lately left his attorney's desk in Southampton-street, for the purpose of instigating this said prosecution; and that, on his arrival at Burghley, Pepper was dispatched with the imperative mandate, in consequence of which the meeting of your Corporation took place, when it was resolved to apply to the Attorney-General.

No more was heard of the application to Sir Vicary after this broadside. On 16 February 1810 the *News* renewed the attack on the Burghley trustees, declaring the real interests of the Marquis were being sacrificed. Scott's previous remarks must have gone home, for the last paragraph read: 'One word in conclusion to a certain great man; for great he is. We have heard from various quarters that he has honoured us, by proclaiming that "if he was *made a fool* of in Drakard's Paper, he would make good use of his horsewhip". . . . As to his horsewhip, should it ever call at our door, we trust that we shall pay our respects to it in a very becoming manner.'

At the end of March, nearly six months after the paper was launched, sales reached 1175 copies a week. Scott declared that while political reform was their policy, 'We follow no Reformer further than we think him right; and reserve to ourselves a perfect freedom to form an opinion on his conduct, and to declare that opinion. We are as determined enemies to tumult as to oppression.'

Scott elaborated his views on reform in a pamphlet published by Drakard. In it he pleaded for moderation, to win over those who occupied what today would be called the middle ground in politics.

His principal proposal was that every man who paid taxes should have a vote in parliamentary elections. Scott was far-sighted enough to realise that reform, when it came, would not destroy the influence of the landed gentry, and in fact the House of Burghley continued to dominate Stamford until mid-century. He could see no remedy for this but time.

In July the Government struck at the radical William Cobbett, who was tried for writing about military flogging in his weekly *Political Register*. He was commenting on English militiamen who mutinied being lashed by German mercenaries at Ely. Convicted of criminal libel and sentenced to two years gaol and fined £1000, Cobbett apparently tried to reach a compromise with his prosecutors. Ministers frequently offered to overlook offences if journalists and newspaper owners agreed to modify criticism in future. But negotiations failed, and Cobbett went to Newgate prison.

Writing on *The Law of Libel* on August 3 John Scott made a daring assault on the Lord Chief Justice, Lord Ellenborough. Referring to sentences passed on Cobbett, and on John Gale Jones and Peter Finnerty, who had been convicted of libelling Lord Castlereagh, he wrote:

> It is rather a delicate matter to meddle with the opinions of judges, but we hope that what is well meant will be well taken . . . the article for which Mr Cobbett was convicted, and sentenced to a severe punishment, was undoubtedly written in very unguarded, and, we will add, improper language. . . .
>
> In the action brought by Lord Castlereagh against Mr Jones and Mr Finnerty, for libelling his character, it was wished by one of the defendants, to bring witnesses to the *truth* of the matters alleged by them against his lordship. But this Lord Ellenborough would not hear of. If the writings were calumnious, said the Chief Justice, its *truth* would not acquit the writer. . . . It is highly important, particularly to us newspaper writers, that we should have clear instructions from our legal authorities as to what is and what is not libellous; for we write with an awful responsibility hanging over our heads.

Scott reminded the Lord Chief Justice of a libel action he had tried two years earlier. This case was brought by Sir James Carr, who wrote travel books, including one on Ireland which earned him the nickname Jaunting Carr. Edward du Bois, barrister and journalist, ridiculed the author in a small volume called *My Pocket Book*, and its publishers were defendants in the action. Lord Ellenborough dismissed the prosecution with scorn. Scott's article went on:

> If we may legally hold up to the detestation of all good men, an unprincipled author, who inculcates base maxims, why may we not direct general execration to the profligate public servant, who uses his authority to serve the most guilty of purposes . . . *Lord Ellenborough* may speak only of bad authors and contemptible books, but the *law* says nothing particular about these. There is not one argument used by the present Chief Justice in the case of Carr *versus* the booksellers, but will apply much more forcibly to the case of a wicked minister, than to that of a trumpery author. It remains for Lord Ellenborough to explain why the latter may be written down, by means of ridicule or censure, as the case may deserve, while the former must be held inviolable. We cannot accept this distinction between authors and statesmen on his Lordship's *ipse dixit*.

On 24 August 1810 Scott published an article which was to have repercussions on the law of the land, as well as influencing the course of his life for two years. Headed *One Thousand Lashes*! it picked up the theme which put Cobbett in gaol, and was a searing attack on punishments inflicted on soldiers, deploring a case in which Private William Clifford was sentenced after repeatedly striking and kicking his superior officer. In fact he received 750 lashes, presumably being then too weak to receive the last quarter of his punishment. The article ridiculed Sir Vicary Gibbs for his comments at Cobbett's trial in which he contrasted the treatment of British soldiers with that of French troops who could be imprisoned in chains or executed for indiscipline.

Scott wrote:

> The Attorney-General said what was very true; These aggressors have certainly not been dealt with as Buonaparte would have treated his refractory troops; nor indeed as refractory troops would be treated in any civilized country whatever, save and except only this country. Here alone, in this land of liberty, in this age of refinement—by a people who, with their usual consistency, have been in the habit of reproaching their neighbours with the cruelty of their punishments,—is still inflicted a species of *torture*, at least as exquisite as any that was ever devised by the infernal ingenuity of the Inquisition.—No,—as the Attorney-General justly says, *Buonaparte* does *not* treat his refractory troops in this manner: there is not a man in his ranks whose back is seared with the lacerating cat o'nine tails; *his* soldiers have never yet been drawn up to view one of their comrades stripped naked,—his limbs tied with ropes to a triangular machine,—his back torn to the bone by the merciless cutting whipcord applied by persons who relieve each other at short intervals that they may bring the full unexhausted strength of a man to the work of scourging. Buonaparte's soldiers never have yet with tingling ears listened to the piercing screams of a human creature so tortured; they have never seen the blood oozing from his rent flesh; they have never beheld a surgeon, with dubious look, pressing the agonized victim's pulse, and calmly calculating, to an odd blow, how far suffering may be extended, until in its extremity it encroach upon life.—In short Buonaparte's soldiers cannot form any notion of that most heart-rending of all exhibitions on this side hell,—an English Military Flogging. . . .
>
> Buonaparte is no favourite of ours, God wot,—but if we come to balance accounts with him on this particular head, let see how matters will stand. . . . He imprisons his refractory troops,—occasionally in chains,—and in aggravated cases he puts them to death. But any of these severities is preferable to tying a human creature up like a dog, and cutting his flesh to pieces with whipcord.

Scott sent a letter home on October 7 in which he referred to the money troubles of the previous year and his quarrel with Paul Colnaghi and his wife, putting part of the blame on the threat of prosecution which faced him following the attack on the Duke of York in *The Statesman*. He wrote:

My Dear Mother,
         Your last letter with its kind enclosures, I duly received; and in Paul's name return to you and his grandfather thanks for your remembrance of him. You will have been informed by Margaret, that with his Mother, he had left me on a visit to London. They are not yet returned, but I heard from Caroline on Friday, when they were both very well. Caroline had been pressed to visit her friends for some time; and as there existed a probability, which I before hinted to you, of my leaving Stamford, in November next, I thought she might as well go first, to save her the trouble attending such a removal. I have, however, lately, through Mr Drakard's kindness, been enabled to offer those who have demands against me terms which I think they probably will accept. I go to London the latter end of this week, to endeavour to arrange matters.... I have, since we have been here, remitted upwards of £30 to London—but it is foolish and useless to remit to one, while at the mercy of another.

The *News*, as perhaps you may have observed, continues to thrive: and in some late weeks, has cleared a handsome profit. It is, as you say, absolutely necessary that my exertions should not slacken; and it is equally true, what you also observe, that an abatement of them may have been discoverable in a former instance. You add 'perhaps uneasiness of mind was the cause'; Whether this be probable or not, will best appear by considering my situation at the time, and judging whether it would admit of that composure of mind which must be attained before we can speculate on subjects that however generally important, are after all but of secondary importance to individuals compared with their own immediate concerns. If Mr Cobbett on contemplating an event, which many would exult in, and which I am sure *I should,* regard as a very honourable testimony to the efficacy of my exertions, felt himself completely unnerved,—it is just possible that the same effect might be produced by embarrassments gradually yet certainly accumulating—perpetual alarms—and perpetual difficulties.

Referring to his quarrel with Mr and Mrs Colnaghi, John said:

You are not at all acquainted with the merits of the difference between Mr C. and myself. As to Mrs C. I have never treated her but with, in my opinion, *scrupulous respect,* altho' I am aware she thinks otherwise. Neither my father nor yourself have ever condescended to wait for my story: but have on the representation of others invariably attacked me with severe blame—blame certainly in part merited, but in other respects so manifestly unjust that it has worked on what is irritable in my temper, rather than on those qualities which my wife tells me I possess as a small set off against the bad.

Caroline's visit to London could have arisen because she was pregnant, for according to Colnaghi family records a daughter was born in 1810. Since there was no mention of her in this October letter the birth presumably came later. The girl was named after her mother.

An editorial in *Drakard's Stamford News* in November declared:

> We have at present an Attorney-General who feels it to be his duty to suffer scarcely a day to elapse without instituting a prosecution against some or other political writer ... the *liberty of the press*—in other words, the right to discuss the character of public measures, is not only recognized by the British Constitution, but is even interwoven with it. ... Sir Vicary Gibbs, in the short space of eighteen months has filed *three* criminal informations against *The Examiner*.

Scott stated two of these political libel actions against Leigh Hunt and his brother John had failed, but their legal costs in each amounted to £100, and the third was still outstanding. In this way a newspaper could be ruined even if innocent. By using the *ex officio* procedure of filing criminal information through solicitors employed by Government departments, ministers could circumvent the preliminary investigation of charges by a grand jury.

Drakard himself soon felt the weight of the Government's hand. On 14 December Scott's leading article began:

> *Criminal Information against the Stamford News*
>
> The Proprietor of the Stamford News has received the usual notice on such occasions, that a *prosecution* has been commenced against him by *Sir Vicary Gibbs*, the Attorney-General, for publishing an article, which appeared in the paper of Friday the 24th of *August* last, entitled "ONE THOUSAND LASHES!"—Circumstances had previously come to his knowledge that induced him to expect such an event.

Scott went on to say Leigh Hunt's *Examiner* had copied the greater part of the article, and suggested this was why the Government decided to prosecute. Drakard wanted the case against him heard by a jury. He would not adopt the easy option of allowing judgment to go by default, as many publishers prosecuted for criminal libel did, in the hope of receiving a light sentence.

Scott added: 'It is proper that these observations should not be regarded as merely expressing the ideas of the Editor, who, although the author of the article denounced as libellous, is not included in the prosecution: they are the calm, decided, and conscientious sentiments of the Proprietor.'

He offered to declare himself the author to shield Drakard, but the owner declined. It is doubtful whether the Government would have wavered in prosecuting him, for such libel actions were undertaken chiefly to damage opposition newspapers. Editors were easily replaced, but it was harder to find the resources to publish a paper, as Scott discovered with *The Censor*.

He closed by saying the Hunt brothers would be prosecuted in London for reprinting the attack on flogging, while Drakard would appear at Lincoln. Drakard had told Scott: 'If *Sir Vicary* think to disturb my quiet, he will find himself very much mistaken.'

While waiting for the trials John Scott continued to comment on current affairs. King George III was an old, sick man, and was thought to suffer fits of insanity, although modern doctors have diagnosed a different cause for his behaviour.

The Prince of Wales became Prince Regent, and the aristocratic Whigs who had been his friends in rebellious youth expected his support. They were upset when the Tories, led by Perceval, remained in office.

The *Stamford News* reported almost every wall west of London's Temple Bar had chalked upon it in large letters 'The Prince and no Perceval', but Scott's leading article was fairly mild in tone when it expressed the wish the Regent had dismissed the ministers. He came out more strongly on a topic to which he often returned, the Irish question. On 8 February he wrote:

> We are truly sorry to learn that the spirit of disaffection in Ireland is displaying itself in a very alarming manner. It is impossible that so much discontent should exist without a cause; but we are sorry to say that few in this country know or care what the Irish suffer. They are oppressed and injured in a manner almost beyond belief, and insult is added to their wrongs. We speak thus strongly from a knowledge of *facts*—facts which it will one day be our duty to lay before our readers. . . . The Irish are goaded into rebellion by injustice, and are then repressed by cruelty.

Very likely Scott's knowledge of Ireland came from Peter Finnerty, the journalist sent to Lincoln castle after being convicted of libelling Lord Castlereagh over his actions in Ireland. Judges had devised an extra punishment for newspaper men, sending them to serve sentences in gaols far from their homes, and means of earning a living.

John was called away from his duties to confer with solicitors about the coming libel actions. On 1 March the *News,* for the first time, carried a banner headline right across its front page:

LIBERTY OF THE PRESS VINDICATED
> Court of King's Bench
> Fri Feb 22
> The King against John and Leigh Hunt, on the prosecution ex-officio of the Attorney-General, *Sir Vicary Gibbs*, Knt, for publishing an article on the subject of Military Flogging, which originally appeared in THE STAMFORD NEWS

Verdict
> NOT GUILTY

The account of the trial showed the Hunts had been defended in a clever speech by Henry Brougham. This barrister and politician went on to become Lord Chancellor briefly in a long and brilliant but erratic career. Even Lord Ellenborough who presided at the London trial described it as a speech of great ability, eloquence, and manliness, before telling the jury he had no hesitation in pronouncing the article an inflammatory libel. But the acquittal owed as much to the composition of the jury as to the quality of the arguments.

In a note on the trial Scott explained that in *ex officio* prosecutions the Attorney-General usually exercised the right to have special juries drawn from lists provided by the Crown Office. 'To judge by late lists which we have seen, it would seem that the chief recommendation, guiding the Crown Office in their original selection is that the parties should either by themselves or their relatives, *hold situation under Government!*' he said. 'The gentlemen who composed the jury which brought in the late verdict on the Court of King's Bench, so completely contrary to the opinion of Lord Ellenborough, were almost entirely selected from what is termed the *common jury*—two of them alone being special jury men.'

When Drakard stood trial at Lincoln on 13 March there were six special and six common jurors. At the end of the trial they retired for a few minutes and then brought in a verdict of guilty. There were other differences in the two trials which contributed to the inconsistency of an article being declared libellous in Lincoln but not in London. Although Brougham was again counsel for the defence, the prosecution was not handled by the Attorney-General but by a barrister named Clarke. He made skilful use of *The Examiner* omitting parts of the article in *Drakard's Stamford News*, although Leigh Hunt said this was not done because the passages were considered dangerous, but to shorten the piece.

Scott's account of the trial spread through three issues of his newspaper. He was fulsome in praising the defence speech: 'Mr Brougham's address to the jury is allowed by all who heard it, to be as splendid a specimen of oratory, as of acute convincing reasoning; and its effect on the auditors was electric.—An instantaneous burst of approbation broke out on its conclusion, which was properly condemned by the Judge as an indecorous expression of sentiment in a court of justice, but for which much allowance will be made by those who consider it as the involuntary homage of the affections to transcendant talent exerted in an interesting cause.' Evidently Scott himself, who was short and dark, took a leading part in the applause, for he recorded that the judge, Baron Wood, 'repeatedly threatened to commit an obnoxious individual with a *black head*'.

There were however counter-demonstrations from Tories present:

> We shall not hastily forget the mob of gentry and clergy, assembled in a box near the Judge.... They could scarcely sit still, or keep silence, during the

proceedings, so great was their anxiety for a verdict of guilty—they evinced the most tumultuous manifestation of gladness. One reverend dignitary we could not but particularly notice;—his countenance is at all times calculated to reflect radiance on his cloth,—but on this occasion it was animated with a more than usual suffusion—his cheeks swelled beyond their normal amplitude—his eyes twinkled from the bottom of those deep caverns of fat, in which they were immersed—his capacious chest rose and fell, with the breathings of rapture.

The main burden of the prosecution case was that the article was designed to incite mutiny, and the comparison it drew between treatment of British and French troops meant support for Napoleon. This was specially resented by Scott who opposed the French dictator in his writings. However he drew comfort from the knowledge the campaign against military flogging was producing results: 'In the Mutiny Bill for the present year, the punishment of *imprisonment* (as we gather from the Parliamentary Report in the London papers) is substituted in many cases, in lieu of the lash.' Identifying himself with the expected fate of Johnny Drakard, the editor spoke emotionally of what would happen 'while we are immured in our dungeon,—cut off from domestic and social comforts'.

But the only hardship Scott himself suffered was shelving his plans to return to London with Caroline and their young children, for he could not desert a newspaper he had led into conflict with the law. It was surely no coincidence the issue of 29 March carried this advertisement: 'Wanted, a neat house, fit for a small family, in Stamford or Stamford Baron. If with a garden it will be preferred. Apply at the News-office, Stamford.'

While Scott had fallen under the spell of Brougham, the politician was equally impressed with the editor. He referred to him as a writer of great power, and his newspaper as distinguished for constant adherence to the cause of civil and religious liberty, and praised Drakard for refusing to name Scott as author of the article. Brougham was himself a prolific writer, contributing to *The Edinburgh Review* and masterminding Whig campaigns in the press. Looking back late in life on the attempts to silence the *News* and *The Examiner,* Brougham wrote: 'These trials were not without their influence upon the great question to which they related. The speeches delivered, the discussion of the merits of the case in the public papers, the conversation to which in the course of the session, they gave rise in Parliament brought, for the first time, the subject before the country, and also turned the attention of military men to it much more than it had heretofore been.' He believed the vindictive way the cases were pursued played a part in bringing state prosecutions for libel into discredit, and finally to their disuse. But although military discipline was steadily relaxed flogging in the Army was not totally abolished until 1882.

Some time elapsed between conviction and sentence in criminal libel cases, and it was May when Scott accompanied Drakard to London to attend the Court of King's Bench. Mr Justice Grose pronounced sentence on Drakard: 'That the defendant do pay a fine of £200 to the King, be imprisoned in the Castle of Lincoln for 18 months, and at the expiry of that period, do enter into recognizances to keep the peace for three years, himself in £400, and two sureties in £200 each, and be afterwards imprisoned until such fine be paid and sureties found.'

Announcing the decision Scott served notice on the Government his newspaper would not be cowed. He commented on a case in which a Liverpool militiaman had received fifty lashes for passing round a song protesting about rations of bad bread. John cited this as an example of flogging inflicted for trivial as well as serious breaches of discipline.

A subscription was opened to meet Drakard's fine and legal fees. Contributions from many parts of the country reached over £500 before the end of the year. Lord Folkestone raised his case in the House of Commons, presenting a petition complaining at the severity of his sentence. This repeated arguments Scott used in commenting on the trial, and he pointed out with pride that, although ministers ignored it, since the petition was ordered to lie on the table it would be entered in the Journals of the House, and 'thus form part of the history of the land'.

He continued to range widely in his leading articles, and on 20 September 1811 wrote: 'It being the duty of a journalist to *shoot flying*, or, in other words, to notice events as they rise, the subjects which most properly present themselves for discussion at this time, are the aspect of our connection with America, and the recent appointment of the Prince Regent's friend to a lucrative sinecure. . . . With respect to America, the question whether she has given us reason to be angry with her, is of much less import than the interrogatory we ought to put to ourselves, whether, in the present circumstances of Britain and the world, it would be advisable in us to go to war with her, because she happens at present to be ill-tempered.'

Britain and America were in dispute over the freedom of the seas. British merchantmen were excluded from ports dominated by Napoleon, and in retaliation the Navy stopped and searched neutral ships trading with those ports. Scott suggested it would be wrong for the two countries to spill blood in such a dispute when the fate of Europe was being decided in the great struggle on the Continent:

> The period is too sublime, its dangers are too great, its hopes too splendid, for two countries of common origin, language, and dispositions, each distinguished by zeal in behalf of liberty, and each possessing it in a peculiar degree, to expend their energies in a mutual quarrel on a point of punctilio, or even of interest, unless it were of the most essential description. . . .
>
> The Americans, we say, are hasty, unjust, and insulting; they carry themselves with a haughtiness of demeanour derogatory to our dignity, and

indulge an aptitude to anger which seems to court a quarrel. . . . We should recollect that disposition is hereditary, and that, as to this country she owes her birth, so most probably from this country she derives the habits and feelings of her people.

Having disposed of peace and war across the Atlantic, Scott turned to the post of Paymaster of Widows Pensions being given to the Regent's secretary, Colonel John McMahon, pointing out this was a sinecure whose abolition had been recommended by a parliamentary committee.

The *Stamford News* and the Newcomb publications in that town and Boston continued their running battle, and the year 1812 began with Scott writing two long attacks on the opposition. He complained the younger Newcomb, using a pseudonym, had insinuated 'the Southern Scott' was guilty of scurrility and was a traitor, Jacobin, and blackguard. John hinted he would welcome an open charge against his honour which could be met by a challenge.

Reports of duels were common in the paper. Duelling was illegal, but judges treated leniently most combatants brought before them, while society not only condoned these senseless conflicts, but ostracised men who refused to settle a trifling quarrel by exchanging pistol shots at a few paces. Even the philosophic Coleridge once wrote seriously to Lamb that he might have to challenge a mutual friend, Basil Montagu, over a reported slight. The poet, Thomas Moore, went on the field against Francis Jeffrey, editor of *The Edinburgh Review*, who questioned the propriety of some of his verses. The affair ended in farce when the seconds failed to load the pistols. This almost led to another meeting after Byron poked fun at the leadless encounter, but the peer and Moore became friends instead of duellists.

It is curious that Byron himself, for all his peccadilloes and self-proclaimed eagerness to avenge slights, seems never to have fired a shot in anger, although he once took the field against an opponent who failed to appear. He was careful to let the world know he was an excellent shot; and he put his affairs of honour in the hands of sensible seconds who could be relied upon to avoid a battle if possible. He himself boasted of the times he performed a similar service for friends.

Scott continued sniping at the Newcombs, hard-hitting editorial notes being varied by insipid attempts at satire. Some items were probably inspired less by indignation than by shortage of material to fill his columns, for John apologised frequently during the year for deficiencies in the paper caused by absence on undisclosed business. Octavius Gilchrist added to the controversy when he looked after the *News* in the absence of the editor.

But Scott still contributed trenchant articles. On 6 February 1812 he took a tilt at the banking system, and the great increase in paper money during the war. His comments might have been applied to the fringe banking collapse of the 1970s:

> In the *Arabian Nights' Entertainments* (a work which we quote to show our deep reading) there are many events recorded, which aptly illustrate the present system of British Finance, in its several results. Our Banks seem proto-typed by the magnificent palaces, that suddenly shoot up out of nothing, and into which the people enter, and fill their pockets with riches; shortly after which, they totally vanish from before the eyes of the deluded multitude, and by their disappearance convert the treasures, they had circulated, into their original rags, that had been made to assume the appearance of money, only by the power of enchantment.

On 3 April the editor fired a warning shot across the Government's bows, singling out the Prime Minister and his brother Lord Arden, over rising discontent in the country at hardships imposed by a poor harvest, disruption of trade by the war, and the expense of paying for it:

> The people are called upon to pay taxes which wax heavier in proportion as the means of paying them grow more scant—their profits are surcharged as the trade diminishes—but they are told that the hard measures are necessary in order to meet the emergencies of the period—they are told by those who draw their incomes of from five to thirty thousand a year from the national coffers, that these are times in which every good subject will submit to deprivations—will be contented, even with bread and water, rather than not uphold his country's honour.

Two weeks later the front page carried a series of reports: 'Riots at Manchester, Violence at Bristol, Riots at Leeds, Cornish Riots, Fatal Riots at Carlisle.' Whatever his sympathies with workmen driven to desperation, Scott condemned the violence, and declared riots must be put down forcibly before complaints could be met.

His ability to stick to his guns and not be swept along by events was tested when Mr Perceval was assassinated by a deranged gunman in the lobby of the House of Commons in May 1812. While deploring the event he resisted attempts to turn the dead Prime Minister into a martyr. He attacked the granting of pensions to Perceval's widow and children, and condemned opposition MPs who reviled the minister in life, but praised him when he was dead:

> We, therefore, as opponents to the political system so stubbornly persevered in by Mr Perceval, thus declare, that we deem the grant of public money, made to his family since his decease, *unmerited*, and therefore improper: and, further, we think that the distressed part of our population have a better claim on the money so granted, than those to whom it has been given. Mr Perceval, not very long ago, told the petitioning manufacturers, that he knew their distresses to be great, but as they were brought about by the dispensations of Providence, there was no recourse but in patience, for the public coffers were too deeply drained to supply the wants of misfortune. These manufacturers, who were thus dismissed to their famished families,

have now seen upwards of *one hundred thousand pounds* voted to alleviate the misfortune, originating in the dispensation of Providence, of the family of the man who made them the above reply . . . our solicitude for political consistency and integrity, has impelled us to dissent from the propriety of a tribute being paid to the merit of Mr Perceval as a public servant, by those who have pertinaciously and warmly denied that he possessed any.

Scott's task of keeping the *News* going for its imprisoned proprietor was drawing to a close, and when on 24 September he wrote more than two columns on 'The Newspaper Press and the Principles and Conduct of the Stamford News', he did so with the air of a man summing up.

But he was not quite finished with Stamford and its affairs. During his absences from the town, Octavius Gilchrist had borrowed the signature 'Ed.' for some of his own contributions to the *Stamford News*, which led to a rumour Scott had gone back to his native country and been succeeded by his friend. Young Richard Newcomb published in the *Boston Gazette* an attack on the supposed new editor which Gilchrist considered so serious as to warrant a challenge. Scott intervened, telling the elder Newcomb he was the conductor of the *Stamford News,* and responsible for all articles in it.

However, the duel went ahead, the belligerents exchanging one shot each on Sydenham Common. The seconds, Edward du Bois and William C Ayton, then intervened, and Gilchrist and Newcomb returned to Stamford. They published contradictory accounts of the duel, and according to a pamphlet published by Newcomb, he was assaulted in the street by Gilchrist and his brother, Horatio. Scott then went to the Mayor and said he feared there would be another duel, and Newcomb was ordered to keep the peace towards Gilchrist. However, three months later there was a further meeting between the two men, both emerging unscathed again.

The death of Perceval was followed by a period of political uncertainty which ended in the new Prime Minister, the Earl of Liverpool, calling a general election. John Scott reported:

> The usual civil war of electioneering is already commenced, and Noble Lords and Honourable Gentlemen are running about from one end of the kingdom to the other with great promises in their mouths, like ants carrying their eggs when the nest is broken open.

He was in ironic mood, for he told readers:

> Not a breath of news is stirring of any interest. We honestly confess we have not received any private letters addressed by ourselves to ourselves, containing intelligence from headquarters; accompanied by those grave conclusions of certainty drawn from the premises of doubt, with which our numerous contemporaries so interestingly abound . . . nor shall we stop the press for a second edition which informs the public that we have nothing to add to the first.

When polling took place for the two parliamentary seats in Stamford, the Burghley interest triumphed again, Lord Henniker and Mr Evan Foulkes being returned. Opposition was provided by a local landowner, Colonel Gerard N. Noel, who professed Reformist views. Among those recorded as voting for him was John Scott, Gentleman, of the Parish of St John. The church of this small parish, on the west side of the constituency, was a few paces from Drakard's premises.

Johnny Drakard was released from Lincoln Castle, having served his sentence and paid his fine. In true Regency fashion the occasion was celebrated with a dinner (tickets with wine 12s.6d.) at the White Hart Inn, Boston, on 24 November. After the loyal toasts, Drakard's health was drunk, followed by 'Mr Scott, and thanks to him for the able conduct of the Stamford News'. Scott's reply was the first time, and probably the last, he spoke in public. Perhaps this was why, in the long report in the *News*, most space was devoted to his own eloquence.

It was a rousing oration, especially when he referred to Drakard as 'one of the worthiest,—and I will add, and challenge contradiction,—one of the firmest and most independent men breathing—who is now liberated from a long and severe imprisonment, which he has borne with exemplary courage, and even with cheerfulness... feeling how much I am personally concerned in the peculiar circumstances that led to his punishment—I am indeed most sensibly affected—I am agitated by emotions which I will not attempt to express, but for which if you will consult your own hearts, you will very readily give me credit.'

The company dispersed at eleven, but not before Scott had proposed a toast to the man who presided over the evening, Challis Sheath, partner in a Boston bank. He must have done so with special fervour, for the bank had agreed to lend him £500 for his next step as an editor.

Chapter 4

THE CHAMPION OF REFORM

In January 1813 Scott was back in Fleet Street as editor and owner of *Drakard's Paper,* described as the London edition of the *Stamford News.* Some of his articles continued to appear in the other paper, and Drakard apparently had a financial interest in the new publication, but the ties were slackening between the two men who had defied the Government and the law of libel. Scott's paper did not carry the local advertisements of the country edition giving him room for general topics in addition to political essays in his eight folio pages; Drakard himself pursued a more radical line, reprinting many of Cobbett's *Political Register* articles.

After setting out his policy on Reform; Scott told readers: 'The Literature, the Morals, and the Manners of the day, will occupy regularly a portion of our attention: in short, it will be our aim to render our publication a sort of *moving Panorama.*' The offices of the new weekly were 177 Fleet Street, it was published at the weekend and cost $9\frac{1}{2}$d., threepence more than the *Stamford News.*

Format followed that of *The Examiner* closely, and at the end of the month Leigh Hunt acknowledged this form of flattery by his old War Office colleague. He quoted from its pages and commented: 'We reckon this new paper a more than common accession of strength to the cause of Reform,—not only on account of the Editor's talent and independence, but from the liberal spirit that seems to adorn them . . . though it must be confessed that the lively attention which Mr Drakard's Editor pays to the belles lettres, rather makes us tremble for some of our readers, particularly the theatrical.'

The paper's first dramatic review showed gusto. A spectacular presentation at Covent Garden, called *The Aethiop,* was dismissed with the words 'although almost every character in this Piece was a Conjuror, it was soon discovered that the Author was not'. Drury Lane fared no better: 'Only one novelty has been brought forward; but as we had not an opportunity of seeing it on the first night, and the piece had no opportunity of seeing us on a second. . . .'

The tribute from Leigh Hunt was particularly handsome, since he and his brother John had at last been trapped by Lord Ellenborough in a libel action. They were sentenced to two years imprisonment for calling the Prince Regent a libertine who had reached the age of fifty without a single claim on the gratitude of his country, or the respect of posterity. To make it more difficult for them to produce *The Examiner,* the brothers were sent to prisons on different sides of the Thames. John going to Coldbath Fields, Clerkenwell, while Leigh Hunt was detained in the new Surrey gaol in Horsemonger Lane.

Scott devoted nearly six columns to the trial in his paper on 14 February, describing it as a blow to the liberty of discussing the conduct of rulers, and saying two men of exemplary lives had been imprisoned. Less weighty remonstrances were delivered on another page:

> It has happened very unfortunately for us, that the sixth number of our Paper falls to be published on St. Valentine's Day. For the usual expense of commencing a Journal we were prepared; but certainly not for the enormous demands that have this week been made on our coffers by the twopenny postman. Why this Paper should have the preference, and be selected by every rhyming inamorato, from the Prince to the potboy, to give publicity to his *effusion,* as they are in the habit of calling them we know not; but this we know, that it is a preference we could very well have dispensed with.

In spite of the imprisonment of the Hunts, Scott continued to attack the Prince Regent, particularly over his treatment of his separated wife, Princess Caroline, and their daughter, Princess Charlotte. He dismissed accusations that in doing so he wished to weaken respect for the institution of royalty: 'To such calumnies we shall never cease to reply that if the exposure of the errors of men in high stations be dangerous, the errors themselves are still more so,—nay, that the former is our only safeguard against the pernicious effects of the latter.'

The paper was beginning to recruit talented contributors, but not all were of equal merit. A series of pieces entitled *Ancient English Literature,* written in a vein of laboured pseudo-scholarship, must have been tedious even to the Georgians who liked that sort of joke. Another occasional series signed S^x varied wildly in quality and seems to have been the work of several hands, including Scott's own.

Although the law of libel was oppressive, journalists were freer in their comments on judges than would be tolerated today. In April Scott lectured the Lord Chief Justice in these terms:

> Lord Ellenborough must be told, that the respectable part of the public are much dissatisfied with his mode of conducting himself as a Judge, and that

the dissatisfaction is not confined to any political party, and exists entirely distinct from any political feeling. There is a character of violence, and of arbitrary will predominant in his proceedings, which, while it entirely destroys his personal dignity, sadly deteriorates from that of the office he fills.

Meanwhile Leigh Hunt, who had felt the verbal lash of Lord Ellenborough, continued to edit *The Examiner* from his cell. Prisoners could make themselves comfortable if they had money and influential friends with which to impress the gaolers. He played host to a succession of visitors. These included Charles Lamb and his sister Mary, and John Scott and his wife the handsome Caroline, of whom Leigh Hunt wrote: 'Her veil, and her basket of flowers, used to come through the portal, like light.' On 26 April she joined the Hunts at dinner, and John and some other friends called in at the Horsemonger Lane prison in the evening.

Another regular visitor was artist Benjamin Robert Haydon who had an electrifying effect on people, his overwhelming personality obscuring the fact his pictures were second-rate. Hazlitt said of him, 'He sets one upon one's legs as it were better than a glass of champagne.' In May Leigh Hunt wrote to his wife: 'Haydon was here yesterday morning before I was up, calling for his breakfast, and sending those laughs of his about the place that sound like the trumpets of Jericho.' A few days later the Scotts were invited to dine at the gaol with the artist David Wilkie, who was much more successful than the ebullient Haydon and later received a knighthood.

But the jailed editor's proudest evening was when he welcomed two poetical lions. Thomas Moore already knew Leigh Hunt, and took with him Lord Byron, famous following publication of *Childe Harold's Pilgrimage* in 1812.

In his *Letters and Journals of Lord Byron* Moore described the occasion in June when they dined with Leigh Hunt: 'I had, for Lord Byron's sake, stipulated with our host beforehand, that the party should be, as much as possible, confined to ourselves; and, as far as regarded dinner, my wishes had been attended to:—there being present, besides a member or two of Mr Hunt's own family, no other stranger, that I can recollect, but Mr Mitchell, the ingenious translator of Aristophanes. Soon after dinner, however, there dropped in some of our host's literary friends, who, being utter strangers to Lord Byron and myself, rather disturbed the ease into which we were all settling. Among these, I remember, was Mr John Scott,—the writer, afterwards, of some severe attacks on Lord Byron.'

According to Haydon, who was not at the gaol on this occasion, but spoke to both Scott and Leigh Hunt afterwards, Byron snubbed his old fellow schoolboy. The painter wrote: 'Scott said several things but Byron never replied; Scott called on me as he returned home, and appeared evidently mortified at something—a day or two afterwards, I saw Hunt, he told me Byron said "Scott has got a dance about eye". Nothing further—Scott never forgave a slight—he always alluded to this matter, continually.'

These recollections should be treated with reserve. Both Moore and Haydon were writing long after the prison incident. Moore, a conscientious biographer, had to consult Thomas Mitchell to confirm Scott was present on the occasion referred to, while Haydon had quarrelled with John by the time he commented on it.

However, it would be natural for Scott to remind Byron they had both been at Aberdeen Grammar school; Byron, very conscious of his rank and his literary success, would not relish this unexpected reference to the days when he was a poor lame boy pulled along the streets by a slightly ridiculous mother. It was aristocratic practice to ignore verbal approaches from people of inferior rank. Scott was sensitive, and he did attack Byron, but not for another three years. His temperament was scarcely that of a man who would wait so long to avenge an insult.

John had special cause to think of his home city and family in the middle of 1813. Early in May his sister Margaret became a widow after four years of marriage, the Reverend Glass dying of consumption at thirty-four.

Scott suffered the usual trivial problems of editing a newspaper. On 27 June this note appeared: 'The French words, in the paragraph relative to Madame de Staël, under the head "Literature", are made sad havoc with by the compositor—similar murders of language have been committed before.'

The outspoken French authoress visited London that summer. She was a social success, particularly as she was escorted by Sir James Mackintosh, home from India after service as a judge. Sir James was a renowned conversationalist and a rising man in the Whig Party; his support for penal reform and other measures of social improvement received warm commendation from *Drakard's Paper*.

Whatever Scott's feelings about being snubbed by Byron, he devoted nearly two columns of the same issue to a favourable review of his poem *The Giaour*. It concluded by saying *Childe Harold* had raised Byron to the rank of a first-rate poet, and the latest poem would sustain and even enhance his reputation. The ability to appreciate a man's work without necessarily approving his actions was to remain a strength of Scott as a literary critic, an art he was beginning to exercise.

On 11 July Scott hailed a subject he said was in everyone's mouth and in everyone's heart, the victories of Wellington and his Spanish and Portuguese allies in Spain, especially the great battle of Vitoria, which broke French power in the Peninsula. He praised the genius of the British commander, who had just been made a field marshal and within a year would be given a dukedom. But he suggested the best hope of establishing stability in Europe was to allow Napoleon to remain ruler of France, with his powers curbed, rather than continue the war and seek restoration of the Bourbon dynasty. In the next two years Scott's views on France were to change radically, mainly because he realised the Emperor had to be crushed rather than curbed. This brought him into conflict with those who regarded Napoleon as heir of the French Revolution, and the necessary scourge of reactionary royalty poised to return to power in countries he had transformed.

A notice in the same issue that 'a few sets of this paper, from its commencement, may be procured through the newsmen, or by application at the office' indicated sales were slower than the editor would like. It was probably about this time Scott turned to Thomas Hill, a City merchant, and to a friend of Hill's, Horace Smith, for financial assistance; they became part-owners of the paper. A cryptic note from Scott addressed to Hill at Sydenham and dated 28 August 1813 said: 'I think five minutes conversation will set the matter at rest, one way or the other—I shall do myself the pleasure to come down to you tomorrow morning—by one of the earliest coaches that goes to Dartford. I shall be with you, I suppose, by 10 or 11 oc. I am engaged to dine in town.'

The last sentence would have been added with regret, for the dinner parties at Hill's country retreat were famous among literary men. One who described these parties and their host was Horace Smith, stockbroker, novelist, and prolific contributor in verse and prose to periodicals, but best known for writing with his brother James *Rejected Addresses,* a book of parodies on leading poets. He described Hill as 'a fat, florid, round little man, like a retired elderly Cupid', who was 'an inexhaustible quidnunc and gossip, delighting more especially to startle his hearers by the marvellous nature of his intelligence, not troubling his head about its veracity, for he was a great economist of truth'. Smith added: 'Pleasant and never-to-be-forgotten were the many days that I passed beneath that hospitable roof.'

Scott, a family man and busy editor, had to decline invitations to such parties. In a note to Hill about this time, couched in legal language in mock deference to barrister Edward du Bois who acted as messenger, John wrote: 'du Bois has forwarded me an order which I should have been most happy to consider a rule absolute, but for an engagement to preside at my own table tomorrow, where some *"near & dear"* friends assemble. Hoping, in consideration of the premises, to be acquitted of contempt of Court....'

At the beginning of November 1813 *Drakard's Paper* moved from Fleet Street to No 1 Catherine Street, premises occupied by master printer David Dean and some others in the trade. It was familiar ground to Scott, who had issued *The Censor* from the same address five years before. Although less than 200 yards long, Catherine Street was the headquarters of two daily newspapers, *The Morning Herald* and *The Morning Advertiser.*

It ran into the Strand, then a much narrower thoroughfare than today, where other papers were published.

The Napoleonic War was at last moving towards victory for the allies, and on 28 November Scott wrote:

> It has never yet fallen to the lot of any Journalist to publish so overflowing a sheet of gratifying facts, as that which the Editors of the Weekly Papers have it now in their power to publish. Never before in the course of seven days, has England received so much and such a variety of good news, as has come to her delighted shores since last Sunday. Our publication of today contains three *Extraordinary Gazettes,* and one *Extraordinary Supplement,* all full of Victories—Victories from North to South;—Victories proclaimed by the sound of Cannon in our streets, sometimes twice a day!—For remark we have not a line of space.

As the year ended Scott noted the Stadtholder, son of the man he had seen nearly twenty years before at Windsor, had become ruler of the Netherlands in the wake of the retreating French armies. He commented:

> It may seem that a limited monarchy is entitled to this praise, that whereas an arbitrary government may be more prompt and decisive in its measures, and a republican more free from the pernicious effects of corrupt influence, it secures on the whole a greater proportion of private happiness and public security than either of these. It may be compared to a temperate climate, which is more comfortable to the inhabitants than either of the extremes.

When 1814 came, the paper's change of address was followed by a change of name to *The Champion*. The new year saw the introduction of fresh talent. First to make his mark was Thomas Barnes, afterwards editor of *The Times*. His principal contributions to *The Champion* were a series of essays on leading authors signed *Strada*. Their appearance, after a while, was erratic, and Horace Smith described the difficulty Scott encountered in extracting copy from Barnes. He said the writer's habits were rarely temperate and never methodical. Finally Barnes himself suggested writing materials should be placed on a table by his bed, with the works of the author he was to review.

According to Smith: 'At his customary hour he retired to rest, sober or not, as the case might be, leaving orders to be called at four o'clock in the morning, when he arose with a bright, clear, and vigorous intellect, and, immediately applying himself to his task, achieved it with a completeness and rapidity that few could equal, and which none, perhaps, could have surpassed.'

Strada began on 16 January by saying of Robert Southey: 'Upon the whole, my admiration of Mr Southey far exceeds my dislike.' He was less friendly in writing about Walter Scott a month later, and positively hostile to Thomas Moore. The charge Barnes levelled against the Irish poet was the heinous one, in Regency eyes, of indelicacy in his early love poems. To modern readers it seems strange a writer who later set up house with another man's wife should raise such an issue. But at the time men might act scandalously as long as they did not talk about it, a convention Byron ignored at his peril.

Moore was dismissed as 'the idol of wanton boys and silly young women'. This attack in *The Champion* did not stop the poet becoming a friend of John Scott. Byron himself was not spared. Barnes said that for the 'disgusting character of his lordship's poetry, two reasons are assigned; his lordship is young, and, forsooth! his lordship is melancholy'.

Scott went out of his way to dissociate himself from this. He preceded it with an editorial note pointing out his own criticisms of Byron's poetry in the paper differed from that of *Strada* and promising to take up the subject again before long. Byron accepted the abuse in good part, praised the ability of the writer, and told Moore he intended to become a regular reader of *The Champion*.

Employing writers like Barnes, who was apparently paid £1 10s. an article, added to the paper's costs, as Scott told a reader who complained about space devoted to advertisements. But he added, 'We admit *only such as are connected with Literature and Art,*—and even of these limit the number.'

The introduction of advertisements led to some puffing of those who paid for them, publishers Longman and partners. In a letter to Hill Scott wrote: 'I have been busy this forenoon, drawing up an article from Messrs Longman's Book on Moreau. This I thought particularly necessary and interesting at the present moment, and as likely to benefit them as the Article on the Catalogue, which is accordingly postponed until next week.'

A review of Longman's catalogue of books for sale appeared in *The Champion* on 30 January 1814. Moreau was a French general whose life had been published in Paris. Scott wrote from the home to which he had taken his wife and young family, No 3 Maida Place, in the Edgware Road, then a rural area. He must have appreciated living somewhere named after a British victory at Maida, in Italy.

One hazard of writing about events as they unfolded was illustrated when, in the same issue that carried threequarters of a column on the Longman catalogue, Scott reviewed a Covent Garden production of *Coriolanus* and praised John Kemble, saying he was 'confessedly the greatest actor of this age, whose *best* exertions are, we doubt not, equal to anything that his art ever produced, as indeed it is impossible to conceive that they can ever be surpassed'. Three weeks later, after Edmund Kean had captured London as *Richard the Third,* the rash writer conceded Kean was the first male performer of the day, adding: 'We speak these words guardedly, and duly admiring, as well as recollecting, the great attainments of the veteran who has hitherto occupied that place, and who has been very lately the subject of our panegyric.'

So overwhelming was the new actor's success that a later issue carried the note: 'The Editor could not get into the Theatre to see Mr Kean in Hamlet, on Saturday se'nnight, the crowd was so great.' In March the paper attempted to boost circulation by publishing a biography of Kean, with a free print of his portrait. Kean was drawn by John Boaden, who exhibited at the Royal Academy. He also painted John Scott, showing a handsome, quizzical face, aquiline nose, dark eyes, full lips, and thinning hair over a high forehead.

When Napoleon abdicated and retired to Elba, the exiled Louis XVIII passed through London on his way to reclaim his kingdom, Maida Place was on the route of the procession, and *The Champion* carried a moving account of it:

> The Prince Regent had taken every means to give splendour and effect to the ceremony. The Horse Guards were ordered out on the Edgware Road, in their most showy regimentals; military of all sorts, and Volunteers were posted in the Parks; the State Coaches and servants in full livery were sent on to Stanmore, the first stage on the road to Hartwell, which has been the residence of the king in his exile. . . . Bodies of cavalry, and gentlemen on horseback, all displaying the white cockade, preceded and accompanied six Royal carriages. . . .
>
> The concourse of people by the road-side was incredibly great; they had been assembling in carriages, on horseback, and on foot from ten in the morning. The villages of Kilburn and Paddington were all decked out with white streamers, inscriptions, laurel leaves, etc. The pressure of horsemen and persons on foot, increased as the procession drew near the park-gate, so as to be alarming: all waving their hats and huzzaing.

Meanwhile another powerful writer, William Hazlitt, joined the paper. For a year he wrote regularly for *The Champion*, as well as contributing to *The Examiner*. He took over dramatic criticism from Scott—his direct approach contrasted sharply with the editor's discursive essays—but his most telling pieces were on the Fine Arts. Although Scott and Hazlitt differed on politics, particularly in their attitude to Napoleon, they respected each other's talents and John played an important part in shaping his friend's career.

Towards the end of April 1814 the art world witnessed an event expected to mark the beginning of an epoch, the exhibition of Haydon's *The Judgment of Solomon*. Scott was among many friends who made a practice of calling on the painter in his first floor studio at 41 Great Marlborough Street in London's West End. After seeing the picture at an exhibition held by the Water-Colour Society in Spring Gardens, not far from Colnaghi's shop, he dashed off this note:

> Dear Haydon,
> I congratulate You very heartily on the success of your picture—I was there yesterday with some Friends & found the whole room full of people with eyes rivetted on it. The M. Herald says Your Brother Exhibitors are not Solomons, to admit Your Solomon—or rather *I* say this—the Herald only doubts their prudence.

Haydon replied he had already sketched an idea for an even greater picture of Christ's entry into Jerusalem. But this was not completed for several years, and then it caused a rift between the friends.

In July Scott was quick to grasp the significance of an event now part of literary history, devoting three columns to the just published *Waverley*. Its authorship held no mystery for him—perhaps John had learned the secret from Longman's, who joined with Constable in issuing the novel, but he was on the defensive about this lavish use of space. He wrote:

> The first chapters of this work, though not likely to be the most popular, shew that the author has both read and thought:—this is saying enough to avert the reader's indignation, which may have been suddenly collected against us, under the idea that we were about to claim his attention to a common novel. But we have a prodigious secret to tell our friends. . . . Approach, then, every ear! while we loudly whisper, that it is reported,—and that is to say, it is surmised,—that is to say, it is understood by those who, like us, know more than their neighbours; that *Waverley* is the last offspring of the very prolific brain of Walter Scott, Esq.—Bless us, what an instantaneous rushing we have caused to the circulating libraries!

Scott assessed the strength and weakness of his namesake's switch from poetry to prose: 'It is true we cannot flatter *Waverley* so far, as to place it on equality with our best novels—such as *The Vicar of Wakefield*, *Tom Jones* and *Amelia*: but . . . if his pages never give to the enraptured soul, fresh and more refined consciousness,—he runs with much effect over all its usual susceptibilities,—he sets them all, if we may so speak, into play, and thus causes us to feel the full enjoyment of what we possess, although we must not look to him to enlarge its amount.'

When Covent Garden opened for the season in September, Scott headed his review 'Miss Foote's Performance of Amanthis'. She received high praise, but only in the final paragraph of a column devoted otherwise to condemnation of managements who encouraged prostitutes and their clients to use the theatres. 'The profligacy of the lobbies and saloon, however, has a beneficial effect on the receipts at the door, and therefore the managers do not scruple to act in a capacity, the proper appellation of which is too coarse to be publicly mentioned,' he said. 'The present theatres are built large in order that they may serve the purpose, and enable those who are concerned in them to share the profits, of the bagnios. It is evident, too, that their dramatic character is now made subordinate to their

Paphian;—the business of the stage is placed beyond the reach of both the eyes and ears of the audience, that there may be room enough to be let out as the rooms of a brothel are let.'

During the summer many English tourists had taken the first opportunity for years to visit France, and among them was Haydon, who wanted to see the pictures in the Louvre gathered during Napoleon's conquests. Scott decided to follow his example, and on 1 October he wrote to Haydon, by that time holidaying at Hastings to rest his always weak eyes: 'I have had a grievous stomach attack—which prevented my writing in the Paper. I am going to Paris, to Draw up a Sketch of the Capital for Longmans. . . . I think the trip will bring me some money, afford me some pleasure, & restore my health.'

Hazlitt played the chief role in filling the gap caused by Scott's absence. It was not until 30 October the editor told his readers of his adventure in the first of a series of articles spread over four weeks on *The State of Public Feeling and Thinking in Paris.*

Scott poked fun at Parisians attempting to switch loyalties with the return of the Bourbon king: 'One of the first hotels in Paris was named by its proprietor, *Hotel de la Guerre,* during the predominance of the good fortune of Buonaparte—but scarcely had the Eagle given place to the Lily, when a re-baptism was celebrated, and *Hotel de la Commerce,* in large letters, now confers an important sanction on the returned family and their system. The *Hotel de la Victoire,* its dream of glory o'er, has subsided into the *Hotel de la Paix.*'

His opinion of the future prospects of Louis XVIII, which was quickly proved right, was sombre: 'Whether the house of Bourbon is or is not to continue to reign over this sort of people, is the same kind of question as whether tomorrow it will be sunshine or rain.'

Hazlitt's articles in *The Champion* on the Fine Arts, had attracted the attention of Lady Mackintosh, wife of Sir James, and a friend of the editor of *The Edinburgh Review,* Francis Jeffrey. She wrote to Scott at his Maida Place address saying: 'Lady M. has written a strong recommendation of Mr Hazlitt as a clever writer to Mr Jeffrey and will communicate his answer to Mr Scott as soon as she receives his location at Paris.'

The letter was forwarded to Sir James Mackintosh, who was visiting the French capital. Lady Mackintosh was his second wife, and their relationship was not always cordial, principally because the couple and their children seemed unable to live within his £1,200 a year pension. Sir James also resented the fact his acceptance of a judicial knighthood from a Tory Government was attacked by Hazlitt and other radical writers. He wrote to his wife:

> Finding that Mr Scott had returned to England I ventured to open your letter to him supposing it might contain something of political and literary

news with which you do not indulge me. I was not disappointed—but I was rather amused at the effrontery of Mr Hazlitt either the writer or the writer's brother who abused me in *The Examiner* & who now employs you to procure him influence & income in the Ed: Rev.'

In a later letter he asked: 'Why do you not write me some part of the literary news & criticism which you so generously bestow on Mr Scott?'

Perhaps when he opened his wife's letter Sir James wondered whether she and the lively young author were exchanging rather more than literary gossip. There is no evidence Scott was ever anything but a devoted husband to Caroline. Nevertheless, Lady Mackintosh wrote him a cordial note on his return saying: 'Lady Mackintosh is happy to hear of Mr Scott's safe arrival and hopes for the pleasure of seeing him any day this week most convenient to him.'

Hazlitt became an Edinburgh Reviewer, and his connection with Jeffrey proved of value to him for the rest of his life. Readers of *The Champion* had noticed some falling off in the paper during Scott's absence, and on 27 November he inserted a note: 'The Editor's return from his visit to Paris will enable him next week to continue his weekly labours for the Champion, with his accustomed regularity.'

The following day Scott received a note which heralded a literary relationship, whose first stage was short, but which became famous six years later. It read:

> Sir,
> I beg leave to offer you the accompanying Essay (originally written for Mr Hunt's *Reflector* but not published, owing to the stopping of that work). Should it suit you to pay for occasional trifles of this sort at your common rate, I should perhaps trouble you sometimes. If not, I will send for the Ms next week, & you will have the goodness to leave it out for that purpose,
> I am, Sir, with respect
> C. Lamb

The new contributor was engaged to write regularly, and on 4 December the humorous essay signed Burton, Junior, and entitled *On the Melancholy of Taylors* was published. The following week a letter, evidently written by Lamb himself, appeared, upbraiding Burton, Junior, for an unjustified attack on an honourable trade. Lamb did not know his editor was the son of a member of the tailors' guild in Aberdeen, for writing to Wordsworth the same month he said: 'One J. Scott (I know no more) is editor of *The Champion*.' Unhappily on 12 December the essayist told Scott he could not fulfil his agreement to write regularly.

Although this is Lamb's only recorded connection with *The Champion*, he almost certainly wrote an item in the paper in January 1814. This was a letter to the editor signed 'The Learned Dog in the Drury Lane

Pantomime', about the actress, Fanny Kelly, to whom Lamb proposed marriage. The Dog protested his own trick of firing a pistol in the pantomime had been surpassed by Miss Kelly discharging a musket in the opera *Narensky,* and went on to challenge her to a duel: 'Let our place of meeting be the fields behind the Dog and Duck.'

Writing in the last *Champion* of 1814, on Christmas Day, Scott had some light-hearted exchanges with readers who sent him advice:

> *Brutus* hates long political articles, and demands that more attention shall be given to the Theatre. *Roscius* recommends, that, instead of a tedious Dramatic Review, we should publish every week a sound Agricultural Essay, which would infallibly procure us a large circulation among the farmers. *Maecenas* has an utter detestation of verse, and shrewdly suspects that one of the authors of the *Rejected Addresses* has something to do with *The Champion,*—if it were not so he would not see *such* things in rhyme, taking up the room that ought to be given to provincial news. *Paracelsus* complains that, in violation of our promise, there is more of Prose than of Poetry.

Scott realised his sometimes pawky humour could misfire:

> It was well observed to us once in the way of caution, by a grave old gentleman who is still connected with a London newspaper,—"these ironical articles are very dangerous, for most people, like myself, are inclined to take them in earnest." With certain proofs before us of the justice of this worthy person's remark. . . .

As in the twentieth century, journalists found the aftermath of war required them to pontificate on economic problems which seemed intractable. Heading his leading article on 29 January 1815 *The Finances, Agriculture, and Commerce of the Country,* Scott wrote:

> These are not subjects to be dashed off in one article of a newspaper . . . there are few among us who cannot criticise the merits of a campaign, dilate on the plan and success of an engagement, and even expatiate fluently, if not always accurately, on the stipulations of a treaty. . . . But matters of statistical economy require to be discussed with very different talents, and attended to in a very different temper, from what are usually brought to the editing and reading of a newspaper.

Discussing matters which were to be at the heart of the great Corn Law controversy in the coming years, Scott said:

> It sounds short and easy to say, the price of bread must be kept up that the farmer may pay his taxes: but suppose the price of bread, thus kept up, keeps up wages so that our goods are too high-priced for the foreign market, and cannot meet foreign competition. . . .
>
> The other side will instantly exclaim, "Oh, we must have bread cheap by all means". . . . This also is a very concise, and, to many people, very satisfactory manner of loosening the gordian knot; but it is as erroneous and

> unthinking as the other. By the latter method we would ruin those who supply, as by the former we would distress those who purchase, the commonest article of provision. The existence of the taxes, then, must be looked to as the primary cause of the present embarrassment. . . . It is the taxes that have made the gentry raise their rents:—the raised rents and the taxes were both to be borne by the farmer, and he has thrown as much of the load as he could on the buyers of his produce by raising its prices . . . farmers cannot return to the old prices, until their landlords return to the old rents, and Government to the old taxation.

On the back page of the same issue was an advertisement for the book John went to Paris to write:

> In the press and immediately will be published, in 1 vol 8vo
> A Visit to Paris in 1814
> Being a review of the Moral, Political, Intellectual and Social condition of the French capital: including descriptive Sketches of the Public Buildings, and the Museum of Art which it contains; Remarks on the Effects of these great works and the Institutions of Paris, on the National Taste and Thinking; Observations on the Manners of the various classes of its Society; on its Rulers and Public Men; on its Political opinions; on the present state of French Literature, and on the Dramatic Representations in the French Metropolis.
> by John Scott
> Editor of the Champion, a London Weekly Political and Literary Journal. Printed for Longman, Hurst, Rees, Orme, and Brown, Paternoster Row.
> Preparing for Publications by the same Author.
> A History of the Public Events of Europe, from the Commencement of the French Revolution, to the Restoration of the Bourbons.

In the introduction to his book Scott admitted France had become a hackneyed subject:

> Where is the family that has not sent out its traveller, or travellers, to the capital of France? Minute oral accounts of its wonders have been rendered at every tea-table. . . . How many letters have been dispatched, from the very spot of observation, to 'dear pappas' and 'dear mammas', and other dears, not likely to feel less interested in the communications of the writers!

Nevertheless, he believed there was room for a work which would concentrate not so much on sight-seeing, as on 'my principal and favourite design of illustrating and discussing national character and manners'.

John found plenty to disapprove of in the French. When visiting a bookseller's shop in Rouen 'the person who attended, while I was looking at a set of Rousseau's works, before words had been exchanged between us, put into my hands, with a smirk and a bow, a miserable book, full of vulgar profligacy'. As a family man, he was shocked by the looseness of conversation and behaviour in mixed society in Paris—'a woman can

A
VISIT TO PARIS
IN 1814;

BEING A REVIEW OF THE

MORAL, POLITICAL, INTELLECTUAL, AND
SOCIAL CONDITION

OF

THE FRENCH CAPITAL.

By JOHN SCOTT,

EDITOR OF THE CHAMPION, A WEEKLY POLITICAL
AND LITERARY JOURNAL.

———— " now I would pray our Monsieurs,
To think an English Courtier may be wise,
And never see the Louvre."
      King Henry VIII.

THIRD EDITION,
CORRECTED, AND WITH A NEW PREFACE
REFERRING TO LATE EVENTS.

LONDON:
PRINTED FOR LONGMAN, HURST, REES, ORME, AND BROWN,
PATERNOSTER-ROW.
1815.

2 Title page of Scott's first travel book

seldom possess a lover before marriage, and is as seldom without a variety of paramours after'.

Like all British trenchermen, he despised the Continental breakfast: 'The family, whether it be a tradesman's, or a duke's, never assemble together in the morning;—breakfast, which is so enjoyed, I might say so *amiable* a meal with us, is never in Paris partaken of in a regular way.'

His general opinion of the French was that they were boastful and shallow, they had failed to take advantage of the sweeping away of abuses by the Revolution, and merely become the dupes of Napoleon.

This was a hostile picture, but it was as difficult to speak objectively of France at that time as to be fair to the Germans in 1945. Nor was it, perhaps, an unjust report. When Hazlitt visited France ten years later, he set out with the intention of redressing the balance; in his *Notes of a Journey through France and Italy* he declared: 'The rule for travelling abroad is to take our common sense with us, and leave our prejudices behind us. . . . The first thing that an Englishman does on going abroad is to find fault with what is French, because it is not English.' Yet within a few pages Hazlitt was attacking the French with almost as much fervour as his former editor; he did not think much of the Italians either.

In fact, Scott found plenty to admire in his visit and was not blind to the shortcomings of his own countrymen. He described travelling with a young shopkeeper from England bound for Paris who spoke no French, had no passport, and carried only English money: 'Of course, he was exposed to many difficulties, which had he been alone, he would have found serious; but he treated them all with the utmost carelessness, and attributed them to the awkwardness and ignorance of the people amongst whom he had come.'

He was also impressed by the courtesy of the poorest men and women, and by seeing shopgirls read French classics when not serving customers. He noted that although there were probably more people in desperate want in France than in England at that time, an impoverished husband did not, as at home, spend his pittance on getting drunk and then go home to beat his wife and children.

He had some praise for the women, in spite of their suspect morals: 'In one particular respect, sufficient justice has not been done to Frenchwomen, or rather they have suffered under injustice. They are very cleanly in their persons and clothes:—the bath is in common use with them.'

In February 1815 *The Champion* recorded the release of Leigh Hunt and his brother from prison at the end of their two-year sentence for libelling the Prince Regent. It may have been this that encouraged Scott a few days later to write scathingly of lawyers. He complained that 'from the attorney's clerk to the Lord Chief Justice' they attached more importance to legal niceties than to common sense:

> We once saw a whole table of lawyers, with a judge at their head thrown into the most lively consternation by the entrance of one of the body without his wig:—the trial that was proceeding at the time was of a young female, accused of a capital crime: not a face in the fraternity showed any expression of interest in the girl's case,—but every face was roused even to indications of agitation when their brother entered *without his wig!* The judge stopped taking notes; the counsel ceased his examination; the accused, whose look spoke the horror of her situation, found her fate arrested in suspense, while the grave assembly to whom it was entrusted investigated with becoming seriousness the serious omission in question. This is by no means a trivial illustration of the dispositions of the profession:—the wig is to them in every thing a more important matter than the skull which it contains.

It would be interesting to know what Scott's barrister friends, Sir James Mackintosh and Henry Brougham, thought of his remarks.

Riots broke out in London in March during the passage through Parliament of the Corn Bill. The mob took to stoning the premises of anyone not on the popular side. Scott wrote: 'It might have been supposed that every company of persons, wherever met, was formed entirely of glaziers, for no one spoke but of broken windows.' He described how a great crowd had passed down Catherine Street past the offices of *The Champion* and smashed the windows of *The Morning Herald,* a pro-Government paper.

His collaborators were beginning to leave. Barnes, having embarked on a series of articles on British novelists, had become even more irregular in his contributions. On 14 February John wrote to Thomas Hill about *The Champion*:

> I enclose you a statement of paper. I have charged £1-10s. Literary—for Barnes, after I understood he could do no more for us, has offered to finish the Novelists at intervals. But the proportion for this will not be more than 10s. per week.

Barnes was contributing to Leigh Hunt's *Examiner,* and becoming increasingly involved with *The Times,* where he was appointed editor in 1817. It may have been his influence that caused Scott to attack the Tory editor of that paper, Dr John Stoddart, who later became a judge and was knighted. Perhaps Hazlitt also had a hand in this, for he was married, unhappily, to Stoddart's sister. Hazlitt ceased to contribute to *The Champion* in the spring of 1815; his political views and those of the editor differed and he found it more congenial to write in *The Examiner.*

Scott was virtually alone. Although his newspaper was widely respected, its sale was small: the lively *Examiner* with its editor now at liberty overshadowed it.

Nevertheless *The Champion* gave three columns to a review of Leigh Hunt's poem *The Descent of Liberty.* John pointed out that 'Mr Hunt sent

The Champion of Reform

this elegant poem forth from the inside of a prison's walls', gaoled for arraigning 'certain vices of a prince'.

Thomas Moore wrote to Leigh Hunt:

> I see you have been done justice to by a very interesting writer in *The Champion*.—His description of you in your prison-garden is done well and feelingly.—I was a good deal surprised, during a visit some time ago to Chatsworth, to find how very little more than the *reputation* of the Champion has reached any of the various Whig lords there assembled—they have all heard it was extremely clever, but I do not think one of them had ever met with it—which I could not help considering a little stupid in their lordships—your friend Scott is a fine fellow, and I heartily hope he may have perfect success.

In short, Regency politicians behaved towards the Press very much as those of today do: if they received favourable treatment from journalists, they regarded it as no more than their due; if they were roughly handled by the same journalists, they pretended it was beneath their dignity to acknowledge criticism. Coleridge, who was writing for *The Courier* at the time, said: 'Ministers do not *love* Newspapers in their hearts, not even those that support them. Indeed, it seems epidemic among Parliament men in general to affect to look down upon and despise Newspapers, to which they owe 999/1000 of their influence and character, and at least 3/5ths of their knowledge and phraseology.'

During May Scott had some of his sisters, including Helen, to stay with him, and at the end of the month he wrote to his mother of his dual roles as author and editor. After promising to have a specially bound copy of *A Visit to Paris* sent to her, he said:

> I am glad to hear, through Helen, that my labours have produced what does not give dissatisfaction with you—and you will be happy to learn that the work is popular here—and that the Publishers express themselves highly pleased. The subjects presenting themselves for handling, in consequence of a visit to Paris, are precisely those which I most like to take up, and which I believe I take up most successfully. . . .
>
> The Champion is a most unmovable personage: he seems to think, with some of the heavier German troops, that he does all a Champion can be expected to do, if he keeps his ground. As to advancing at all, it never enters into his imagination. From the very highest quarters I am complimented on the character of the Paper; and I have a letter before me just now, from one of the most distinguished men of talent in the country, which concludes by heartily congratulating me on the bright prospects opening upon me—whereas in truth the clouds are very thick, for the Paper does much too little for a comfortable living. . . .
>
> We should be very comfortable all of us here together, if Caroline were in but tolerable health, but she is not so:—she is very weak, and she has now a

bad cough. You will know how much these circumstances are likely to deteriorate from our satisfaction. The children (yours and mine—which are the greatest?)—are in high condition, as the horse-jockies say.'

The letter from the distinguished man of talent came from David Wilkie, Haydon's artist friend, whose work had been praised in *The Champion*, although with discrimination. Wilkie told him: 'I have very seldom met with remarks from which both in the way of encouragement & correction, I hope to derive greater advantage.'

John's youngest sister was evidently one of the visitors referred to in his letter home, for Hannah's family preserved a painting by John Boaden dated 1815 showing her and an unidentified sister.

Sir James Mackintosh joined in the praise of Scott's work, telling him: 'I hear from several quarters the highest applause of your later articles in principle as well as in talent. You are now in that vexatious position of being abused for moderation by those whose intentions at least you respect which embittered one part of my life and on some of the consequence of which I now look back with pain.'

This Whig politician, whatever his feelings about the exchange of literary gossip with his wife, also gave more tangible help to his fellow-countryman. A regular contributor to *The Edinburgh Review* he mentioned *A Visit to Paris* in an anonymous article in the spring issue. Unfortunately only one page out of thirty-two in the essay referred to the book, and the praise was not unmixed. He called Scott an eloquent and philosophic traveller, but suggested his enthusiasm for English manners and institutions led him to use 'severe and indignant invective against the vices, and even frailties, of the French nation, which sometimes more resembled the language of a moral satyrist, than that of an estimator of national character'.

However, any mention short of outright condemnation in such a publication was valuable. Sales were also helped through renewed interest in Paris caused by the return from his Elba exile of Napoleon. His second short reign, and the battle that ended it, were to have a deep effect on Scott, and led to his final rejection as a liberal patriot of the more radical position of men like Hazlitt and Byron, who revered Napoleon.

Scott wrote of him as 'again Emperor in Paris, on whose citizens he had fired as a Jacobin, whom he had cajoled as a Consul, oppressed as a Sovereign, by whom he had been banished as a criminal, and is now received with "all hail", to his returned royalty. Instead of our feelings being divided on this occasion, we have them all burning on the side of deep mortification, and of sad presage, of painful disappointment.'

He parted from old allies with regret, but without apology: 'While we write at all we must write according to our honest convictions.'

Chapter 5

PARIS REVISITED AND A ROW WITH BYRON

Scott did not forget his old colleagues in Whitehall. On 21 May 1815 *The Champion* carried the paragraph: 'It is rumoured that Lord Palmerston is about to retire from the office of Secretary at War. Mr Chas. Grant is mentioned as his lordship's successor. The War Office clerks are to be congratulated on this removal.' The congratulations proved premature, for Viscount Palmerston remained minister for many years.

In the same issue John returned to his attacks on the editor of *The Times*, who had opposed renewing the war with Napoleon. His views were dismissed as the ravings of a madman, and he was called 'that furious-headed personage'. Perry's *Morning Chronicle* also came under fire for its coverage of the Congress of Vienna, broken up by Napoleon's return.

These attacks drew an admonitory letter from Sir James Mackintosh the following day, in which he said:

> The castigation bestowed on Stoddart is most just. It is provoked by his insolence & required by the influence which he derives from the circulation of his paper.... I know the folly of Perry as much as anyone & I have little reason for personal good will towards him—but I believe him to be honest and consider his present errors only as proofs that he is too clumsy to trim his boat and cannot attack the Congress without Napoleonising. He is weak....
>
> If I am not deceived in you my frankness will appear to you the surest mark of the sincerity of my commendation & of the reality of my respect.

Hinting that he would like to enlarge on his account of *A Visit to Paris* in *The Edinburgh Review*, Sir James ended: 'I hope that I may soon find an occasion to speak more fully of a certain Traveller of whom it is more proper to speak to the Public than to himself.' But the occasion apparently never arose.

The following week Scott said of the situation on the Continent that hostilities depended solely on considerations of convenience and expediency, with the Prime Minister, Lord Liverpool, consulting leaders of the gathering allied armies on the probable success of the contest. The editor wrote: 'The Duke of Wellington, in particular, as may well be imagined, is, we hear, keen and pleased as a greyhound, bounding in the loosening slip, in the view of the game.' It seems doubtful whether the phlegmatic Duke, man of destiny though he was, quite fitted this sporting image.

The editor was feeling the defection of his talented contributors. He filled the paper with material reprinted from various sources, and on 18 June he wrote: 'We admit the justice of an *Old Subscriber*'s remonstrances. The Editor, has finally shaken off the causes of that irregularity in the appearance of the original articles which has been complained of, and of which the present number is a fresh, but, as he trusts, will be the *last* proof. In the next number of *The Champion* there will be given the usual Original Political Article, an Article on Mr Wordsworth's Poetry, and a Dramatic Review.'

Scott had met Wordsworth a few days before, a meeting which led to a close though brief friendship in which the poet showed himself a much warmer human being than the aloof egotist described in some reminiscences. They were invited to breakfast at Haydon's studio in Great Marlborough Street. Haydon described in his diary how he made a cast of Wordsworth's face, and as his victim sat in a dressing-gown with the plaster covering his eyes, 'I stepped in to Scott & told him as a curiosity to take a peep, that he might say the first sight he ever had of so great a poet was such a singular one as this'.

Wordsworth had already written to Scott to thank him for the 'pleasure and instruction' he had received from the gift of *A Visit to Paris*. He said his own experience of living in France, during the Terror more than twenty years before, confirmed John's hostile view of the French character. Released from the plaster Wordsworth entertained them over breakfast with an account of his poetical theories and his plans for a great work (never completed), *The Recluse*.

Henry Crabb Robinson, diarist and friend of Wordsworth, met Scott at the poet's lodgings in London two days later. Robinson described him as a little swarthy man, who talked fluently on French politics, and held Wordsworth in high reverence. According to a letter written later by Wordsworth, during this visit to London he called on Scott one morning at home, and there met Leigh Hunt for the first time.

Scott devoted three columns of *The Champion* to an appraisal of Wordsworth's published work. It was a clear-eyed summing up, defending him from the attacks by reviewers in the great quarterlies. It did not gloss over his defects, but Scott was unequivocal in his final assessment: 'Mr

Wordsworth is a poet of the first class. . . . He is now before the public in a variety of works,—of unequal merit certainly,—but in the collective testimony proclaiming him the greatest poetical genius of the age.' These were bold words when Byron, Walter Scott and Thomas Moore were the popular favourites.

The influence of this article may have been diminished by the war news which filled every newspaper. Dispatches from Wellington telling of the defeat of Napoleon at Waterloo reached London on June 21. Haydon was on his way home from an evening spent with Scott when he heard a Foreign Office messenger repeating the news. The painter dashed back to his friend's house, and they joined in shouting 'huzza'.

Discussing Waterloo in his paper, Scott emphasised the modesty of Wellington and the gallantry of the troops he commanded:

> No battle in the annals of the world is superior in splendour and interest to that of Waterloo. The caution and address of the British general were first put to the proof; then his desperate personal courage, which he displayed like a young enthusiast. Lastly, his eye and promptitude were shown to be unrivalled by his seizing the critical moment, described by distant and combined signs, when the army might advance with effect. . . . Great man! gallant souls!—the dispatch in which these wonderful events are detailed has not the word victory, if we remember rightly, in it.

He followed this a week later with a first-hand account of the Duke under fire during the bloody encounter at Quatre Bras two days before Waterloo. Scott's war correspondent was an old friend, Ensign Robert Logan who, with his brother, Lieutenant George Logan, was in action with the 92nd Foot, the Gordon Highlanders. Their father was a merchant in Aberdeen. Both brothers were wounded at Quatre Bras, and their brother-in-law, Lieutenant John Kynoch, adjutant of the Cameron Highlanders, was killed the same day.

In his letter, published with a sketch plan of the engagement, Robert Logan wrote:

> As it is the first battle I have been in, I shall attempt to describe it to you. . . . We marched 30 miles that night, came up with the enemy about 2 or 3 o'clock next day, viz. the 16th. We were immediately marched into the field, as there were only one British division and some Brunswickers there before we came up. The 92nd took the position in the ditch. . . . We lay in a most disagreeable situation for upwards of an hour, having an excellent view however of the fight, but exposed to a most tremendous fire, from their great guns of shot, shells, grape, etc, which we found great difficulty in keeping clear of, I say *keeping clear of*, because, what I never knew before, you can very often see the round shot coming. This heavy fire was maintained against us in consequence of the Duke and his Staff being two or three yards in front of the 92nd, perfectly seen by the French, and because all the reinforcements which

were coming up passed along the road in which we were. Here I had a remarkable opportunity of watching the sang-froid of the Duke who, unconcerned at the showers of shot falling on every side of him, and killing and wounding a number of his Staff, stood watching the enemy and giving orders with as much composed calmness as if he were at a review. The French cavalry were now beginning to advance in front of the 92nd . . . they tell me that eight pursued the Duke a good way. I wonder how he got off, for I saw him in front not five minutes before the charge.

Robert Logan described how his brother became a casualty:

George was wounded about threequarters of an hour before we went off the field, and I cannot describe to you my feelings when I saw him struck. I supposed his wound mortal, being given by a round shot, and having also heard of poor [Kynoch's] death, it made me desperate. I was hit by a ball above my ankle, which luckily did not injure the bone.

Scott and Haydon had become close friends, sharing the general patriotic fervour over Britain's role in defeating Napoleon. Haydon's circle included the Hunt brothers, Barnes, Wilkie, and Lamb, but he said in his diary John Scott 'had more sound sagacity than most of them' and spoke admiringly of 'his sweet little wife'. His admiration probably increased when Caroline's father, Paul Colnaghi, offered him a £10 loan after viewing the Solomon painting, although declining to buy it.

Two undated letters from Scott to Thomas Hill may have been written about this time; as had happened before, John's duties prevented him accepting invitations. In the first Scott wrote from Colnaghi's premises at 23 Cockspur Street:

When du Bois gave me your invitation I told him a friend was to dine at my house today, whom I would willingly leave in the lurch—(if leaving him with my wife could be so construed)—for the pleasure of dining with you and him. On my arrival here I found myself haltered—for he is now by my side—in the act of setting off for Paddington with my Brothers-in-law. They denounce vengeance if I leave them—nay, swear they will be offended.

The second letter, dated simply Tuesday, said:

I must beg you to excuse me fulfilling my engagement tomorrow—I really cannot come to town if I mean to write an article for the Champion, for I have been occupied yesterday and today in writing & otherwise preparing for my journey—& on Thursday I have a very particular engagement.

If this letter was written in 1815, the journey to which it refers was Scott's second visit to the Continent. Accounts of Waterloo had fired him with the desire to see the battlefield, and revisit Paris. Longman's again agreed to publish the results of his travels, although in May they had written to him: 'We have just perused your letter with every attention & are sorry to say that your undertaking appears to us so full of speculations and uncertainty that we really must beg leave to decline embarking with you in your interesting project.'

Perhaps this was the *History of the Public Events of Europe* advertised as in preparation at the time of Scott's first book. It was never completed, although John did not abandon his intention to write on the subject for three or four years.

In Paris Scott stayed with a friend at 65 Rue Neuve des Petits Champs. From there he wrote to Haydon:

> Mon cher Haydon,
> That I am in Paris you may see by my French. Two words out of three in that language is a great deal for me. I am but just arrived:—at four o'clock this afternoon I entered Paris from Brussels, after two days and a half, and two nights, hard travelling in the Cabriolet of a Waggon Laziness—not Diligence. I *found* Renier, mon ami, *out*—as an Irishman would say, and have been dining alone in the Palais Royal, after my journey. . . . A letter from my wife (whom God preserve) was waiting for me on Renier's chimney piece;—yet it is to *you* that I first address myself! . . .
>
> I arrived at Ostend on Tuesday 12 O'clock, last, after a twentysix hours passage from Ramsgate. The impression caused by this place is nothing compared with that made by Dieppe:—it is perfectly English in its toute ensemble:—at the Coffee-houses, English Officers were lounging at Dominoes;—in the streets English Soldiers mounted Guard;—on the Quays English Cannon-balls were piled. That same afternoon I went up the Canal to Bruges, with an officer of the 82nd, a fellow traveller: it was a large Schuyt in which we took our passage, with elegant Cabins, fruit shops, & liquor shops below. The Country is flat, rich, & enclosed:—it is exactly Lincolnshire. . . .
>
> At Bruges . . . at the inn a book was kept, in which the host was compelled to enter, every day, the name, age, profession, domicile, place coming from, & place going to, of each of his guests, & send the same to the *Police* every night. The name inscribed immediately before mine was as follows "Paddy O'Rafferty, age 25, Profession Military, Domicile Ireland, coming from Cork, & going to the Devil". So much for the waggery of some of the numberless British Travellers (Good God, you are in for another sheet!)—This Book was full of the names of persons of every profession, age, sex, & condition, our Compatriots, all on the swarm from England to Brussels—but many of them, with their country's plumpness of declaration, had put down at once the object of their journey, in the word *Waterloo*.

Scott told his friend that in the boat which took him from Bruges to Ghent he squeezed into a cabin with a crowd of local people speaking their own Flemish dialect, and he thought of his family at home:

> What a change does mere loco-motion produce: At Maida Place, they were tranquilly sleeping—I pictured to myself their faces on their pillows—the

> garden was quietly basking in moonlight—I recollected the particular flowers—three days ago I was there and then I looked at myself packed up in the hold of a Flemish Schuyt, perspiring at every pore, & silently listening to coarse jokes uttered in gutteral german! But a man should, at the expense of certain inconvenience & regrets, put himself occasionally into such situations, in order to give his mind a filliping up, out of its usual jogtrot.

With the army officer he met on the canal journey, an aide-de-camp named Captain Edwards, Scott continued his journey to Brussels:

> We took up our Quarters at the Hotel d'Angleterre, in which there was not a soul that could speak a word of English, where the attendance is bad, the fare not good, the charges extravagant. We were put into bedrooms up four stories,—no bells in the room, and in the morning we had no chance for hot water, our boots etc, but by bawling Garçon down into the immense depth of the Court Yard,—and after thus exercising our lungs for half an hour it was probable that some of the servants, passing to and fro all the time within hearing, would deign to cast up their eyes, & cry '*Oui, Monsieur*' and, if we were lucky, in another half hour some of them would come up to us.
>
> The appearance of Brussels was most interesting: the streets were crowded with our Countrymen who had been in the jaws of death & destruction, all bearing about the hurts they had received in the terrible Conflict. Many of them fine young men, with arms in slings, or using crutches, strutting nevertheless with a gallant coxcomical air, suggesting the excessive versatility & variety of human nature. It was but the other day that they were in the heart of the battle, black with powder & sweat, fierce, manly, terrible, bleeding, groaning, dying. Now they were out on a fine day, in a gay park, after much careful preparation at the Toilette, leering at the girls.

In Brussels Scott met George Logan, convalescing after being wounded at Quatre Bras, and together they visited Waterloo. John told Haydon: 'On the field, though it has been searched until it was supposed that everything had been raked from it, I found a twelve pound shot, which had plunged from our guns into the heart of the French lines. This trophy I carried about with me for five or six miles, in a blazing day, & mean to bring it home.'

His letter ended: 'Have the goodness to let the folks at Maida Place have a reading of this: and as it is full of matter that I may work up for my Book, will you oblige me by leaving it with Kate for a day to Copy.'

Kate was Scott's sister Catherine. She seems to have spent some time with the family, perhaps to look after the ailing Caroline.

When he came to write his travel book, Scott said of his visit to Brussels he felt a little shame-faced as a civilian to be escorted by George Logan with his arm in a sling, and to be staring at others maimed in the battles. But it led him to suggest what became apparent forty years later in the Crimea, that all was not well with military medical services.

He toured a hospital and was given to understand the wounded had in general done very well, but Logan told him they had to thank Providence and not the Medical Board for survival. Many owed their lives to being nursed by the families on whom they were billeted. Scott commented: 'Complaints on this point were so numerous, that it seemed scarcely possible that they could be without foundation. . . . It is due to the meritorious and useful class of men liable to be affected by it, to press for its correction.'

During his stay in Paris the allies decided the art treasures looted by Napoleon's armies from conquered cities should be returned. Scott visited the Louvre, and watched the dismantling of the triumphal car on top of the arch in the Place Carrousel. He bought from a soldier a gilded ram's horn decorating this chariot, drawn by the Greek bronze horses stolen from outside St Mark's in Venice. It had been Napoleon's intention to place a statue of himself in the car.

When Scott returned to England early in October he landed at Brighton after a rough crossing and wrote to Haydon, who was at the seaside resort with Wilkie. John told them:

> Here I am,—again in Alma Mater—the Country deserves the name better than a College,—I go at one oc. today for London. Meanwhile I am at the Old Ship, with occasional absences. If you find this in time, come & try to find me. Between the hot baths, & my Inn you are sure to see me. Two nights & a day on board the packet!! I have brought no remains of French Cookery over. I told them at the Custom House, that I discharged all my French affairs into the Sea. . . .
>
> On Friday last, I made a Catalogue of every picture in the Louvre—a gigantic job!—but performed in $\frac{1}{2}$ an hour. 270 Pictures form the *whole* collection. . . . I saw the Horses go! I was most lucky in getting to the top of the Arch. I sat in the Car, I stood in the Car—I plundered the Car, & have brought with me a ram's horn from it—and with it I shall try to blow down the walls of the first Jericho at which I arrive. I have a chance of being sent there by You, when I bother You in busy hours!

The two painters were enjoying their holiday, and tried to coax Scott into spending a little time at Brighton. On 25 October he wrote from Maida Place:

> My Dear Solicitors,
>   It has taken me a long while to screw my courage up to the sticking place of a denial to your very flattering request. . . . My wife says your request is a modest one, considering that I have only been from home eight weeks, and have just returned: but I half suspect, that, using the privilege of her sex, she delivers herself according to the rule of contraries, & means that your request is immodest. . . . My new book, & my old Paper, alike cry out for unceasing labour; and the vacation I have enjoyed must be followed by a period of redoubled industry.

The Champion certainly required urgent attention. During his absence George Soane, a young and prolific writer, was left in charge. He pursued a political line at odds with Scott's views, and even abused his own father, architect John Soane, in its columns. They were a quarrelsome family, it is said John Soane declined a baronetcy to prevent his son inheriting the title. He was knighted in 1831.

When Scott returned he received a call from the angry architect, and *The Champion* published an apology from his son. The editor added his own regrets.

Scott sighed for the days when Hazlitt covered art for the paper. Having written more than three columns in the issue of 22 October about the removal of paintings, including *The Transfiguration* by Raphael, from the Louvre, he concluded: 'The worthlessness of what is called a general taste for Art was beautifully proved and illustrated in The Champion several months ago, by that masterly writer W.H., the loss of whose Essays we feel more sensibly than the French feel the loss of the *Transfiguration*.'

Hazlitt did return, but only after Scott gave up active editorship the following year. John was already trying to dispose of *The Champion*. Just before he left Paris he received a letter from William Eusebius Andrews, printer and editor, saying he had heard in the trade Scott wished either to dispose of it, or make some arrangements with any individual able to raise the paper's circulation. The projected partnership did not materialise.

Back in London Scott received a letter showing how serious the situation had become. Writing from Throgmorton Street on 6 November, Horace Smith told him:

> I was very glad to observe your return, not only on your own account, but for the interest of the Champion which must, I am sure, have suffered by your absence.
>
> As you wish to know what monies I have received from Longman & Co I append the particulars, as well as of the little account between us, by which you will see that the advertisement money is now insufficient to pay Hill and myself our weekly half guinea & of course will leave us no surplus to reduce the trifling claim I have on you besides.

Smith's claim was for £23 for his own contributions.

For a while Scott turned out the paper almost single-handed, switching from dramatic criticism to fine arts, reviewing Walter Scott's latest poem—'Scott, unfortunately, has fallen never again to rise in the *Field of Waterloo*'—and writing leading articles. While still supporting electoral reform, he suggested the rough and tumble of the hustings, then spread over several days, should be preserved:

> The mingling together of the orders of society by means of a common

principle of animation, is so politically useful, that any thing short of a positive violation of morality and honesty may be considered as cheaply purchasing it; and certainly some appearance of intemperance amidst these popular assemblages cannot fairly be considered as forming either of these exceptions. The sense of personal consequence which an individual of the middling or lower condition feels, when he finds himself of recognized and coveted consideration in the commonwealth, would not be so inspiring as it is on these occasions, if our parliamentary elections were not attended with something of a general licence, a temporary companionship of high and low, a respite of common decorums,—in short, enough to blend the air of a national festival with the exercise of a national right. Rome has her Vatican, and Paris *had* her pictures;—but England has a time when a butcher may kiss a duchess as the reward of voting for an opposition candidate! It is to be hoped that no plan of Reform will ever be adopted, that would reduce all this to a mere business of registering names by clerks, conducted quietly, like the booking of passengers in a stage coach office; and accomplished, over the whole kingdom, in the space of one day.

In writing on the fine arts Scott, prompted by Haydon, took up the question of the Elgin Marbles. Lord Elgin, while acting as Ambassador to the Turkish court, had removed these masterpieces from Athens and shipped them to London. He wanted the Government to buy the treasures to cover the expense of what he considered their rescue from the Turks occupying Greece. Scott supported him, and eventually a reluctant administration agreed, but not at a price the peer considered adequate.

In a second article published on 24 December, the editor praised Haydon for grasping the importance of the Elgin Marbles at a time when some connoisseurs suggested they were second rate. Scott said of his friend: 'He owned, with the instantaneous acknowledgment of genius, the perfection of genius,—and felt as Columbus did, when the morning rose, and put before his eye the solid and smiling land of a new world.'

It was probably through Haydon that Scott recruited John Hamilton Reynolds to his staff. This young poet and friend of John Keats took a steadily increasing share of work off the editor's shoulders. At first he concentrated chiefly on the drama, and in one piece praised Fanny Kelly's acting but asked: 'Is it indispensibly necessary that Miss Kelly should so often appear in male attire?'

Soon afterwards a deranged man, George Barnett, wrote to Fanny accusing her of abusing her sex by appearing in breeches and then sent her a proposal of marriage. If she refused him, she would have to accept his challenge, and he added he had seen her dexterity in firing a gun. When Fanny ignored his letters, he went to Drury Lane and fired a duelling pistol at her during a performance, but his aim was wild. Lamb, sitting with his sister Mary near the madman, must have remembered with remorse his facetious letter in *The Champion* two years before in the guise of a pistol-firing dog challenging Miss Kelly to a duel; if indeed he was the author of that joke.

During 1815 Scott's fierce attacks on *The Times* and *The Morning Chronicle* had been accompanied by more courteous but ultimately more significant differences of opinion with Leigh Hunt's *Examiner*. Their principal quarrel was over France. *The Examiner*, no doubt influenced by the pro-Napoleon views of Hazlitt, opposed renewing the war when the Emperor returned from Elba.

After Waterloo, the paper was noticeably cooler in its praise of Wellington than the increasingly John-Bullish *Champion*. When Louis XVIII was again installed in Paris, *The Examiner* ran a series of articles headed 'Gloomy State of Things in France'.

There were more personal reasons for John Scott to quarrel with his fellow-editor. When *A Visit to Paris* was published, two long extracts from it appeared in Leigh Hunt's paper in succeeding weeks, the last ending with the promise 'to be concluded next week'. But it never was. It may have been this omission which caused Haydon to say, six years later, that Scott 'assailed the politics of the Examiner, after having offered to write for it, and was wounded by rejection'. In his diary, written nearer the time of the break, Haydon gave another reason for the editors' differences. After talking about his own arguments with Leigh Hunt over religion, he went on: 'This was always, too, his conduct to Scott. Tho he knew Scott & he never could agree about politics, tho he always left off in agitation & was ill for two days, he always began by some indecent, improper joke, and did he expect Scott was to bear it quietly?' As always with Haydon, it must be remembered he quarrelled violently with both the men he thus abused.

Scott cannot have been pleased when *The Examiner*, on 3 December, resurrected the unpleasant squabble between the Soanes. An anonymous letter, which occupied more than a page of the paper, complained of the 'cruel and wanton attack upon the professional character of the first Architect of the present day'.

Whatever his problems with the newspaper, Scott's reputation as an author was growing. His first book had gone through several editions, and Longman's announced its sequel *Paris Revisited in 1815* was in the press. Scott wrote to his father in more cordial vein than usual, acknowledging a Christmas gift of salmon shared with his Colnaghi in-laws:

> Your present arrived, in very fine order, on Friday last, and was appropriated to its proper purposes on Sunday, in Cockspur St. where we all dined. I have the least reason to thank you, for it gave me the heartburn and headache,—nevertheless I join with the others in thanking you heartily for your attention. I have not been well since I returned from France,—and find that some things are too good for my bad digestion.
>
> You will be glad to hear that I have risen in value in my Publisher's

estimation. I receive £210 for the Revisit, which will not be so large a book as the Visit. This is a considerable increase. Messrs Longman's have also presented me with fifty guineas for the second Edition of the Visit, and fifty for the third. I do not know that they go on so, for the fourth, which is just now published. If I am equally successful with my second work, I shall never be in want of a competition for the future among the best publishers, to have my works. . . .

The Champion rises a little, but very slowly, and is a heavy concern. I am anxiously waiting to know what will be the sale next week, which is the first of a new Volume. With my books, however, I should be easy enough off,—but the Banking house at Boston, Sheath's & Son, that lent me the money to start the Paper £500, have failed, and the Assignees call in the sum. This plagues me,—but I must get time from them.

We are but very poorly among ourselves, with the exception of Kate and little Caroline, who are extremely well. Fanny has been ill, like Helen, with a palpitation at her heart, and Mr Darling bled her, which has been of much service.

Fanny was Caroline's young sister, Francesca. Dr George Darling was the medical friend of many artists and literary men, including Haydon and Keats. He was very popular; perhaps he was considerate in the matter of presenting his bills.

On 10 January 1816 Scott called on Haydon and found he had just painted the head of Christ in his *Entry into Jerusalem*. The artist said in his diary: 'It affected Scott deeply when he saw it. His taste is good, natural and sound. I have always found his approbation followed by the World's.'

Through Haydon, Scott renewed contact with Wordsworth. The poet had written a sonnet eulogising the painter, and others on Waterloo. Haydon asked if they could be published in *The Champion*. The battle sonnets appeared in the paper in February. In writing to John the poet said: 'I know not that the three following Sonnets, occasioned by the Battle of Waterloo will do any credit to your journal, but perhaps the subject may make up with your Readers (if it does not tell the contrary way) for the Deficiencies of the execution.'

John was irritated when Leigh Hunt sneered at these poems, in a leading article in *The Examiner* headed 'Heaven made a Party to Earthly Disputes'. This reminded Wordsworth he had held strong views of a very different sort in the first euphoria of the French Revolution.

On 4 February came the announcement in *The Champion*:

> Just published in 8vo price 12s. Boards
> Paris Revisited in 1815, by way of Brussels; including a Walk over the Field of battle at Waterloo; observations on the late Military Events, and Anecdotes of the Engagements; a View of the Capital of France when in the Occupation of the British and Prussian Troops; a minute account of the Whole Proceedings relative to the removal of the plundered Works of Art

from the Louvre, with Reflections on this Measure; concluding with a Chapter on the Political Temper and Condition of France, and the Character of the Bourbon Government

by John Scott

Extracts from this book began to appear in *The Champion*. Longman's had printed 3000 copies for the first edition, followed a few weeks later by a further printing of 2000.

Scott must have been proud that his books were known in his native country. Early in March he received a letter from James Hogg, the poet known as the Ettrick Shepherd, whose work had been praised in *The Champion*. Hogg thanked him for the gift of a copy of *Paris Revisited*, saying: 'I know its character here is very high.' He added: 'The truth is that you are the only editor of newspapers whom I love in Britain for though I am myself rather a violent tory why I never know but you are the only independent one that I ever met with.'

More surprising was a graceful letter to Scott from Hogg's friend, Walter Scott. Walter had read his namesake's first book while making his way to Paris the previous summer, and his visit had overlapped part of the time John was there. The results of his trip were the poem on Waterloo and a book, *Paul's Letters to His Kinsfolk*. This led to some comparisons being made between the work of the two travellers—Reginald Heber, a noted bibliophile who became Bishop of Calcutta, said: 'Who is Scott?—what is his breeding and history? He is so decidedly the ablest of the weekly journalists, and has so much excelled his illustrious namesake as a French tourist, that I feel considerable curiosity about him.'

In *The Champion* on 3 March, John Scott made a mild criticism of Walter's work. He said French people 'use the word *amiable* as merely applicable to the vivacities and accomplishments of the evening circle, and therefore reconcilable with the veriest poverty and profligacy of heart. This is worth noticing, when the able Author of *Paul's Letters to his Kinsfolk* seems to sanction this degenerate use of the word, by terming the French most amiable in comparison with the other nations of the Continent.'

Writing from his home at Abbotsford Walter Scott sent his letter to *The Champion* offices in Catherine Street:

> Sir,—I cannot refuse myself the pleasure of thanking you for the fair & true interpretation you have given of the word *amiable* as applied to the French people in Pauls letters. I certainly meant only that degree of the power of pleasing which arises from a scrupulous attention to the petite morale as they themselves call it & I was inaccurate in using the English word which certainly signifies deserving of love and affection. I am very happy to recognize in you Sir a politician on a broad & English system who ventures to square the opinions both of ministry and opposition by general principles of

right and wrong instead of party feeling of any kind. It is very rare to see such an independent spirit in a journalist who are usually the mere mouth-pieces of one or other political faction. In some cases I might probably disagree with you on the application of the principle but I think never on the principle itself. As this letter is for the individual not for the Editor I subscribe instead of the factitious name of Paul that of your namesake and reader
Walter Scott

The author of *Waverley* continued to take *The Champion* for a time, receiving copies through his friend, London actor Daniel Terry.

Scott's books on Paris were written hastily to make money. But his keen observation, and sympathetic approach to the human comedy, caught public imagination when everyone was curious about France. *A Visit to Paris* reached five editions, and *Paris Revisited* four, although one or two of these may have been just a change of title page to boost sales rather than genuine new printings. The books were also published in America.

In addition to Walter Scott and Reginald Heber, their readers included William Beckford of Fonthill, who made four pages of notes on the two volumes. Thackeray wrote about the same scenes a generation later, and called Scott's works 'famous good reading'. Perhaps he was thinking of the description of the Palais Royal as 'a vanity fair—a mart of sin and seduction'.

Both Scotts had been preparing reviews of *Emma* by Jane Austen. John Murray, publisher of *The Quarterly Review*, asked Walter to write about the book. Walter sent him a long review, but did not seem to relish the task. His final paragraph contained a wistful reference to his unhappy love for an Aberdeenshire heiress: 'We are quite aware that there are few instances of first attachment being brought to a happy conclusion.'

John Scott devoted more than two columns of *The Champion* to analysing the quiet charm of the authoress:

> Lively sketches of comfortable home scenes—graphic details of the localities of provincial life—pictures of worthy affections, unassuming amusements and occupations, and most spirited and racy touches of the grotesque peculiarities which diversify human character, are the claims which our authoress puts forward to popularity. She presents nature and society in very unadorned hues; and yet, so strong is the force of nature, that we will venture to say, few can take up her work without finding a rational pleasure in the recognition which cannot fail to flash upon them of the modes of thinking and feeling which experience every day presents in real life. Her scenes have the advantage of being of that middling stamp, which comes within the observation of a very large proportion of readers....
>
> Our authoress possesses a peculiar felicity in measuring a character—and has a nice eye and a facile pen for arresting and embodying oddities—a species of light satire for which the delicate tact of female minds is admirably adapted.... We must shut up these amusing volumes, which plainly

manifest the author to be a woman of good sense, knowledge of the world, discriminating perception and acute observation.

John Murray, who published *Emma*, probably felt this review was compensation for a less agreeable one some weeks earlier. John Scott had asked for an advance copy of Byron's latest volume, containing *The Siege of Corinth* and *Parisina*. But *The Champion* poked fun at the peer who had produced a string of poems since the success of *Childe Harold*, while protesting disdainfully that he would abandon poetry. Scott commented:

> So long as an author's faithlessness to his views, 'to write no more,' leads to what are called, in the common phrase, *agreeable disappointments*, he will not be harshly treated for breaking his word;—although a frequent quarrelling with one's bread and butter,—quickly and constantly succeeded by an eager taking to it again, may be an amusing, but is by no means a dignified exhibition. *She would and she would not*, is a pleasing comedy, when performed by a lovely woman; but a change of gender converts it into a farce....
>
> *The Siege of Corinth* and *Parisina* are his two worst poems,—and the unfortunate word, worst, conveys all that they have of novelty. They are mere repetitions in style, and personages, of what he has done before.

The continuing failure of *The Champion* to show a reasonable profit, made John restless to try something new. He turned his thoughts to poetry; the epic poem, like the three-decker novel, was the fashion, and Moore, and Walter Scott received thousands of pounds for their works.

John Taylor, partner with James Hessey in the Fleet Street firm of booksellers later famous as publishers of Keats, told his brother James in a letter on 6 February 1816: 'Yesterday I accidentally met with Scott of the Champion. His engagements with Longman's are now at an end, Paris revisited having just made its appearance. We had a good deal of conversation about future undertakings & next Spring I hope he will have another work ready for the press.'

By this time Scott and his family had moved from Maida Place to 14 Park Place, Upper Baker Street (now No 27 Park Road) and on 2 March Taylor wrote again to his brother:

> Hessey and I went to see Scott at his House facing the Regents Park (nearly four miles from Fleet Street) on Tuesday evening last. His profession is that of an Author. The newspaper brings him in something regularly, & he depends upon his other works for extra supplies.—By Paris Revisited he has gained £300.—He read to us portions of a Poem on the Battle of Waterloo, with which we were much pleased.—It will be finished in 8 weeks, and then I hope we shall publish our first successful poem—Its length will be about 1,800 lines—I very much approved of his Review of the Siege of Corinth: it appeared before that poem was actually published—I think him a very well-principled, moderate, candid young man.

On 7 February John mentioned the projected poem in a letter to Wordsworth thanking him for the Waterloo sonnets: 'To have the country's finest Victory celebrated by her finest poet in my Journal, I certainly regard as the most honorary thing that has happened to me, and as a reward quite beyond my natural chances, and fair expectations.' He offered to send Wordsworth *The Champion,* but added: 'I am becoming more and more engaged with the Booksellers, & the Champion is neglected in consequence. I feel it a drudgery.'

Scott asked Wordsworth to do him the favour of reading the portion of the poem he had written and giving his opinion of it. Surprisingly, Wordsworth encouraged Scott's ambitions, telling him, 'I am convinced that you have the eye, the heart, and the voice of a Poet.' But he did counsel caution to one who had not practised the art, tactfully saying Scott was a master of prose.

In the end the poem was not completed, nor did Scott send what he had written to Wordsworth. His design for the work sounded well beyond an inexperienced poet, or even an experienced one.

Writing to his friend on 2 April, John said:

> You will find the undertaking includes endeavours at different kinds of style: in this I have acted on a principle—good or bad—which I have taught myself to harbour. I have thought that Poetry naturally includes the burst, the break, the shift, the pause, the swell and fall of music; and therefore that a battle-piece *might,* at least, be legitimately constructed on this method equally in both Arts. I am not here alluding to the varieties of the Ode: they fall into my plan as forming one style of measure: to this I have added the ballad quatrain,—and the eight & ten syllable couplet, according as my subjects change. Perhaps all this is babbling.

It was not diffidence that caused Scott to abandon his poem, but a sudden family crisis. The freedom with which he discussed his cares with Wordsworth, and the poet's ready response, show how deep their friendship had become. In the same letter he wrote:

> Your kind & esteemed letters have been the most pleasant things that have happened to me in a time of considerable domestic anxiety and distress, caused by the extreme illness of Mrs Scott, whose state of health for some period past kindled our fears. The disorder partakes too much of the nature of that, the name of which one trembles to write, while it is not possible to shut out its appearances from the alarmed observation. Yet the medical friend whom we consult, is, I believe, now of better hope than he was, that the fatal stage of consumption may not be arrived at. Speculation, however, in so touching a case, is sad; but a few weeks, which must bring on childbirth, will, I understand, decide all.

Scott's letter broke off abruptly, and was continued eight days later:

From finishing the first sheet of this letter, while my pen was yet on the paper, I was called to my wife's bedside by her increased illness. I found that violent pain had suddenly been added to her other afflictions. This was of all the others most insupportable to her friends, and seemed to be fast breaking down the admirable strength of her own mind, which had been so signally displayed during the trial of her previous illness. It so continued, night & day, for some days, when the results of a medical consultation was, that Nature should be quickened by Art, to produce Labour. She submitted, though warned that the measure was most critical, & while it formed her only chance for recovery, would expose her to the chance of immediate death, in the exhausted state of her strength. At this very awful posture of affairs, when She had but a few hours to reckon upon to be with us, Nature herself came to our assistance, & she was delivered without any violent means being used, and with tolerable ease. This was indeed a most fortunate event, and spread a joy throughout our dwelling truly heartfelt. Since this event, she has been lying in the quiet of half-life, but with favourable symptoms, & I am now bidden to hope, by him who warned me before that I could scarcely with safety allow it to speak even in a whisper.

The child is well, unexpectedly; he seems to have thriven on his mother's weakness.... To most other persons I would apologize for the freedom of this domestic disclosure—but I think I am safe with you: you know the best & deepest interests of the heart, & I am sure that he who can so well excite sympathy with them, cannot be without it.

Since Caroline Scott lived to be eighty-eight, her strength of mind must indeed have been admirable. The boy born in such harrowing circumstances, John Anthony, was not strong, but reached middle age.

Wordsworth responded warmly to the confidences offered to him:

If sorrow is to be your portion, be assured that under this roof there is more than one heart that will feel for you in a degree which is rare where personal intercourse unfortunately has been so inconsiderable.

Against the background of his own trials, Scott plunged into the affairs of Lord Byron. After little more than a year of marriage Lady Byron, the heiress Annabella Milbanke, left home in Piccadilly, taking their infant daughter with her, on 15 January 1816. She went to live with her parents, and never returned.

Almost immediately rumours circulated that the separation had been caused by Byron's treatment of his wife, and even that he was mad. Her family denied being responsible for these reports—some originated with Lady Caroline Lamb, the poet's discarded mistress. But Annabella's legal advisers, who included Henry Brougham, did nothing to discourage them.

Byron hit back at his accusers as only he could—in verse. First he wrote a poem addressed to his wife, *Fare Thee Well*, a plausible plea to her for reconciliation. He later composed *A Sketch from Private Life*, a virulent attack on a woman called Mrs Clermont, who occupied a confidential

Paris Revisited and a Row with Byron 81

position somewhere between a servant and companion to Lady Byron. Fifty copies of each poem were printed by a reluctant John Murray, and circulated or shown to people who might counteract the flood of rumours.

Although not prepared to publish the poems openly, Byron should have realised they would be leaked to the press. This had happened to previous verses he put about in a similar way, and in 1814 he was embarrassed by *The Champion* printing, with his name, some satirical lines on the Prince Regent.

At the height of the scandal Scott called on Brougham, who lent him copies of *Fare Thee Well* and *A Sketch from Private Life*. The following Sunday, 14 April, both appeared in his newspaper under the heading *Lord Byron's Poems on his own Domestic Circumstances*. Scott accompanied them with a long and skilfully argued attack on Byron's behaviour. It was plain his views were expressed all the more strongly because he was uneasy about the propriety of taking sides in a matrimonial dispute. Scott wrote:

> His lordship, then, is determined that nothing shall stand between him and public animadversion.—He will compel that notice which an honourable sense of delicacy would have withheld, if he had been content to offend in silence. The better part of the Press will always be cautious of engaging in the dangerous and disagreeable task of interfering with the vices of private life,— for the principles on which the safety of society rests, will usually be more injured by such intrusion, than improved by any correction that is thus applied to the violation of virtue. . . . It is a rather singular fact, that Lord Byron, of all the writers of the present day who occupy respectable stations in society, and possess a high order of literary talent, has been least scrupulous about encroaching on the gentlemanly restriction in question. His satires have not been more distinguished by a looseness of aspersion, exposing him to the necessity of unnumbered apologies and disavowals, than by a vindictive keeness in their application to the tender points of personal foibles, and private circumstances. . . .
>
> Lord Byron will not pretend that these poems were not designed as an appeal to the public, to throw the blame of his early separation from Lady Byron on the weak and defenceless party. Though not sold, they have been very generally distributed by his respectable bookseller Mr Murray.

So scornful was the attack by Scott it seems strange Byron did not challenge him to a duel. William Jerdan, later editor of *The Literary Gazette*, but at that time working for *The Sun* newspaper claimed Byron demanded satisfaction over remarks in that publication on *A Sketch from Private Life*. But Douglas Kinnaird, brother of Lord Kinnaird, was deputed to deliver the challenge, and sensibly failed to do so.

In fact Scott's onslaught did not damage permanently his relations with Byron, but did complete the breach with Leigh Hunt. In the newspaper outcry which followed publication of the poems, *The Examiner* and *The*

Morning Chronicle, almost alone, supported Byron, James Perry's paper going so far as to talk of a conspiracy against the peer. Leigh Hunt wrote in a manner calculated to add to his rival editor's fury. He accused Scott of hypocrisy in publishing the verses, while attacking Byron for writing them. 'We have the honour of knowing the Noble Poet', he said, and went on obscurely to say of Scott's comments: 'We told this writer on one occasion that he had every advantage over us, precisely because he had none, and we hoped the observation would have done him some service.'

If Scott had forgotten the snub administered to him by Byron in Leigh Hunt's cell three years before, the smug reminder that his rival enjoyed the peer's friendship reopened the wound. Later in the month John reprinted some of the hostile comments by *The Morning Chronicle* on himself, and dismissed James Perry as an imbecile, a meddler, and a simpleton.

In dealing with Leigh Hunt, Scott reminded him of the times when they agreed on public affairs. Referring to the court case in which the Hunt brothers were convicted of libelling the Prince Regent, he said they had then fought side by side against 'a husband's cruelty and licentiousness'.

In an almost line by line response to Leigh Hunt's remarks, Scott landed one telling hit when he accused him of 'coxcombical uppishness'. Scott alluded three times to Leigh Hunt's remark, 'We have the honour of knowing the Noble Poet.' Fortunately, we do not know his feelings when he opened *The Examiner* on the same date, 28 April, which contained a long poem by the editor bidding 'Dear Byron' farewell as he left for the Continent.

Leigh Hunt did much for journalism, literature and reform: he revolutionised dramatic criticism, was a charming host who encouraged Keats, Shelley and Reynolds in their poetic careers; he fought bravely for the freedom of the press and against political corruption; he poured out words to keep his family solvent. But he seemed fated to exasperate his friends, in much the same way that he irritates readers by his unbuttoned style of writing, and his habit of button-holing them while unbuttoned.

Some of Byron's friends suggested it was the furious attacks led by *The Champion* which caused him to leave England, an exile lasting until his death. But more potent reasons were the bailiffs, who moved into the Piccadilly house soon after he went, and the poet's preference for living in countries which did not impose on his behaviour even the feeble restraints of Regency London.

Haydon writing about the affair eight years later, said:

> Scott by accident called on Brougham & he had got a copy of 'Fare thee well'. He asked Brougham to lend it to him—Scott called on me as he returned—I was then on Jerusalem—he read it to me and both admired him excessively—Scott said By G–d I'll publish this—If you do I said you will be guilty of great dishonour: It will make the paper sell, said Scott. I replied it is a private

business and no business of yours—I saw it was no use. Scott left me, I saw he was rankling, and longing to be at Byron. . . . He sold on that day 7,000 papers at least he told me so . . . at the very time Scott was doing this as he *affected* from principle, he was ill using his own wife & before or after I *know struck* her, on some dispute about a Carpet & its colour. John Scott was the most malignant being I ever knew.

Scott was an irascible man, like his father, but if he ever struck his wife, it is unlikely to have been when she was desperately ill. From what is known of her she would have emulated Lady Byron and walked out.

However Haydon may be right in saying Scott's motive was principally to raise circulation, though scarcely to the figure suggested; most of the contents of newspapers are designed to sell them. The editor-proprietor would be anxious to increase sales when trying to dispose of the paper.

Yet Scott was influenced by other considerations. Himself a loyal family man, whose writings showed repugnance for licentious behaviour and reflected his Presbyterian upbringing, he was genuinely shocked by Byron's treatment of his wife, as retailed by her supporters. With other journalists of the day, he had much space to fill, and it is easier to abuse another newspaper or another man than to compose an original article. When Hazlitt was chided for making use of private confidences in his articles, he replied: 'It may be indelicate, but I am forced to write an article every week, and I have not time to make one with so much delicacy as otherwise I should.'

Scott's own domestic crisis did not improve his temper, and he explained in a letter to Wordsworth on 29 April that he himself was ill during the battle with Byron, Perry and Leigh Hunt. He wrote:

> I was taken ill the day after I wrote you my last letter, and have been confined to bed the greater part of the time since. My illness originated in a cold, caught by leaving Mrs Scott's warmed bedroom where I had passed my nights for some months, to sleep in an upper & cold room, after her delivery.

Fortunately Scott had at last found, in Reynolds, someone who could deputise for him without upsetting readers. He went on:

> I am glad you have lately liked the Champion, because it proves that I have been lucky in lighting on respectable coadjutorship. I have done nothing for the Paper for several weeks past, but Lord B.'s business. I sat up in bed to write these articles because I was warmly indignant at his baseness. . . .
> My hand, My Dear Sir, trembles; and even to think these loose sentences makes my head ache. But your Letters are cordials to me in my distress, & I must make you some return. I thank your family for their kind sympathy: I am not out of the need of it. Everything is still very threatening, & I am afraid I have more chances against me than for me. If she can but get strength enough I mean to take her to the South of France,—but it is doubtful whether her strength increases at all.

A month later Scott wrote to say Caroline was much better:

> Within these very few days, she has burst out upon us something like the fine weather.... I also have lately (that is within this last week) worked my way out of the encumbering & enervating pains and lethargies by which I have been annoyed,—and our house, that has been so long the abode of dullness and dismay, has acquired a cheerful air, which a little while ago, I thought it was never likely to obtain.

Wordsworth had sent Scott a copy of his *Thanksgiving Ode,* and John described it in his letter as 'the hymn of a high & well-tuned Soul, the poetic harmonies of which have been called into play by the ardour of patriotic affection'. He also spoke of 'my antagonists in the Examiner—one of whom is Mr Hazlitt—a powerful writer,—but an inconclusive and dangerous one'.

When Lady Mackintosh heard Scott was setting out for the Continent once more, she wrote to him from Weedon Lodge, Buckinghamshire, where she and Sir James had moved to avoid the expense of a London home. She told him how sorry she was to learn he found it necessary to go abroad 'on account of your health. If you have made any decided plan & chosen your Place, you would do me a favour by letting me know, under cover to Sir James at Holland House where the medical people have advised you to go at this season with any other particular about accommodation & expense.... I am unfortunately very much interested to obtain these on account of a Sister of mine who is advised to take her eldest boy immediately abroad for a very similar complaint in his lungs.'

This letter suggests Scott's recurring ill-health was caused by consumption, although Lady Mackintosh may have been confusing his illness with that of Caroline or with the delicate constitution of their elder son, Paul. If John was consumptive it would explain some of his bad temper, and his feverish bursts of activity followed by bouts of idleness. In his second travel book he wrote: 'The summer air of Paris is an object of enjoyment, valuable beyond description to an inhabitant of these islands, who has constitutional susceptibilities that are unpleasantly affected by a humid and inconstant atmosphere.'

No buyer had been found for *The Champion,* so Scott had still to play a part in its affairs. But Reynolds was now the mainstay of the paper, and Horace Smith offered to help. He wrote to Scott:

> Can I be of any service to the Champion in your absence? If so I shall be very happy to lend a helping hand, tho I am much afraid you will be sadly missed in that quarter—The Lord deliver us from a second Soane!—if not you may expect to meet only the ghost of the Champion at your return.
>
> I have been two or three times on the point of writing to you to express, in common with all my acquaintances, my delight at the admirable way in

which you have trimmed Byron and his besotted defenders. It does you infinite credit & it must have assisted the paper in the most honourable way. You have beaten Hunt to a . . .

Although Scott was a seasoned traveller, he left his arrangements for going abroad so late that Haydon had to come to the rescue and forge his signature on a passport application. In his diary for 21 June 1816 Haydon wrote: 'Scott forgot his passports until the last. I went for them yesterday and on receiving his note the evening before, I practised copying his name till I am quite an adept, J. Scott, J. Scott, J. Scott.'

Chapter 6

TRAGEDY DOGS
THE CONTINENTAL TRAVELLER

Scott embarked from Southampton on his third Continental journey, accompanied by Caroline, eight-year-old Paul, and his wife's sister, Francesca Colnaghi, then sixteen. They sailed to Jersey, where the climate was gentle and food and wine cheap and good, he reported, but before long they crossed in a small fishing vessel to the mainland. Scott described their landing, an account which later formed part of his third travel book:

> I have never seen anything more magnificent than the approach from the sea to Saint Malo. Several rocky islands, some of them strongly fortified, stand out in the opening to the great basin that forms its harbour. This at full tide, which it must be to carry vessels up to the town, is a most noble object. The tide sets in with a rushing impetuosity, that gives to the ocean the appearance of a tremendous torrent. It returns in the same grand way. The town, though in reality mean and gloomy, is hid on entering the harbour behind the lofty and superb walls of the place . . . the battlements form the promenade, and the arrival of a cargo of passengers from England or Jersey always brings out hundreds to look down from the stony height on the newcomers. . . .
>
> The boat that took us to the shore from the packet, having only a few yards to row, no one seemed to care how it was crowded; men and women, and trunks and bandboxes, were heaped upon each other, clinging together for the sake of mutual support, Ladies holding by the shoulders of gentlemen, and gentlemen compelled to steady themselves by trespassing on their fair companions. On the inclined pavement that formed the point of disembarking, there were collected at least a hundred ragged boys, all of them bare-legged and bare-footed, most of them without coats, and many of them without breeches. They were crowding and clamouring, and looking hope and fear, both together, from their wild but fine faces, as we advanced towards them. The important object was to get hold of some package to carry it to the custom-house. . . . The moment the boat grounded, a yell broke out, and a struggle ensued, which intimidated the most dauntless among us. It

seemed, as if we were landing amidst a flight of harpies, and the spirits are never very vivacious at the conclusion of a sea voyage. The scramble defeated its own ends; no one got hold of a trunk, because every one was trying. I believe, from all I could hear, that, notwithstanding the tumultuous and needy character of these porters, property is always safe in their hands, yet it was not easy to be assured of this, when we saw so strange a set combating so violently for our things. We stood on the defensive, and they redoubled the energy of their attack. The confusion now in the boat equalled that without. Men and women tumbled over each other, and got jammed and overwhelmed. The boatmen stormed in nasal French; the boys fought, and the numerous spectators on the walls laughed and shouted; for the space of ten minutes, not a soul could land from the boat. At last the douaniers lost all patience, and began to lay about them most unmercifully with the flat of their swords. The boys still looked forward to the trunks, as if they were totally insensible to the blows inflicted from behind.... It seemed as if four sous, the most that any of them could hope to receive, were sufficient payment for a severe scourging, and a heavy burthen to boot. At last, however, they flinched a little under the application of the swords, and our things were landed while they made a momentary retreat.

From St Malo the party sailed up the river Rance to Dinan, then on by road to Angers, capital of Anjou. The town, with its almost perpendicular streets, reminded Scott of Edinburgh.

He addressed a letter to 'Most Glorious Haydon' on 18 July:

Here we are at Angers,—& there you are in Marlboro' Street. How I pity your untravelled littleness! Last night a Centinel shot at a Waggoner close below our window, when Mrs Scott was undressing to go to bed, because the poor man, deafened by the noise of the wheels, did not hear the *qui vive,* thrice repeated. This is fact—simple fact! The bullet was sent to find its way, either into the man's brains, or into any of the neighbour's houses, just as it might happen....

This the country, & such are the people, to visit which we are all crowding for Passports in a way which you know to Your cost. I hope, my dear fellow, Heaven will reward You for that act of generosity—for to do so is beyond my means. Your trouble however has not been wholly thrown away: Mrs Scott certainly mends much in health, and this was the first great object to which we looked. We have been all of us much amused & interested by what we have seen; and I hope I shall be able to make something of the various circumstances and appearances that pass before me. The French every where, where we have been as yet, are precisely the same race which You found at Paris.—I asked a man yesterday, who professed great skill in angling, what bait they used in this river? '*A thousand little drolleries,*'—was the reply. The effect of such a response on the mind of a sedate, regular, & practised English Angler, deeply read in Walton and the Guide to Flyfishing, can scarcely be imagined by one who like Yourself is uninitiated:— but you will take my word for its being supremely ridiculous. On further

> inquiry I found that here they actually fish for Pike with *cherries!*—The Pike, the fresh water shark!—the voracious cruel monster of the lakes and rivers,—whom in England we decoy with baits agreeable to his nature—frogs, small fish, young birds, &c: here they bob for him with cherries! . . .
>
> At Lavalle we were cheated by a Postilion, & sent for Gendarmes. The two men who came said we were quite in the right; but they could not decide,—we must go to the Commissary of the Peace. He came down stairs more like a low turnkey at Newgate, than a Magistrate. He behaved with marked rudeness to Mrs Scott, & in the teeth of facts & reason, decided in favour of the scoundrel Postilion.

While at Angers Scott visited the half-ruined riding school where, thirty years before, the young soldier who became the Duke of Wellington studied and trained with other sons of noblemen.

Scott seems to have preferred travelling by river or canal wherever possible, perhaps because of the discomfort caused by rough roads and lumbering vehicles, and to avoid rascally postilions. But the next stage of their journey sounded hazardous for a group scarcely one of whom was in robust health:

> We thought to proceed to Tours from Angers by water, up the river Loire. The ascent of the river is not often attempted by passengers, the current rising so very strong that there is no rowing against it; the boats therefore are dragged by men with ropes, or pushed along with poles, unless when the wind is very fair. . . .
>
> As it was flooded very much when we embarked upon it, we had an opportunity of seeing it in all its splendour.
>
> The first view of its mighty stream, pouring down with great rapidity, gave us some alarm as to venturing ourselves upon it in the very awkward boats that are here used. The wind, however, was fair, and the boatmen assured us that we should reach Tours in two, or at most three days; the distance being about ninety miles.

Scott said the boat was flat-bottomed, shapeless, and fit neither for sailing nor rowing. A wooden shed was built in it for the passengers, although they slept at inns along the route: 'The sail was an immense square one, that enabled us to derive little or no advantage from any wind that was not directly fair. . . . Our progress for the first eight miles gave us a very favourable idea of the plan we had adopted, and we complimented our own sagacity in disregarding the advice of the good people of Angers, who were all mightily shocked when they heard us speak of encountering the perilous Loire.'

The journey produced one crisis, when a squall threw the boat on its side, and water poured on board. But they suffered no more than a fright. Evidently Caroline's health had improved so much that the idea of going to the South of France was abandoned, since from Tours Scott and his companions went to Paris, a city which seemed to draw him back again and again. He was still editor of *The Champion*, and on 11 August 1816 the paper published the first of a series of articles from him by-lined 'The Itinerant'. It was blunt about the passion for travel:

> The British who have ventured on the momentous proceeding of a *family visit* to France, Switzerland, or Italy, from whatever motive, or with whatever object, eight out of every ten regret in their hearts the step they have taken; and, when they choose to speak sincerely or without reserve, describe themselves as disappointed in their favourite expectations and chief designs. None have been so seriously chagrined as those who have emigrated from motives of economy; except that other class whose sole object in leaving their homes was to enjoy perpetual vivacity. . . . It is a great error but a common one to fancy, that because home is dull, to be abroad must be enlivening. . . .
>
> On one of the very worst roads of France, we lately met three of the hard-running carriages of the country, in each of which there was a couple of British travellers. The jolting was almost insupportable, under the suffering caused. . . . When these travellers would arrive at the place of their destination, which we had just quitted, they would find the hotels full, the servants negligent, and the beds dirty.

The same issue contained the start of another batch of articles by Scott, entitled 'Small Talk from Paris', describing social customs in the capital, and theatre-going.

A week later The Itinerant continued the account of his travels, and indulged in some gentle fun at his wife's improved nerves:

> Rough roads, dirty rooms, and even damp sheets, though joined as if in a conspiracy against the welfare and happiness of the traveller, do not hinder him from soon finding that he rises with an appetite for his breakfast, and goes to bed with an assurance that he will not much discompose his pillow. The body seems to thrive, like a snow ball, in proportion as it is flung about from place to place; and the spirits, though fretted by the friction of disagreeables, are preserved by it from that melancholy stagnation which causes life to rot away under the foulness of a surcharged state. The fact is, travelling forcibly imposes on the rich and lazy many of the necessities and habits of the poor and industrious; and nature orders it in kindness that the benefit shall always accompany the smart. Persons, male or female, with a constitution nervously debilitated, as the phrase is, will undoubtedly derive great good from travelling: They will unconsciously steal into all sorts of coarse, healthy capabilities and accomplishments. It is probable that at the end of the first week, they may find themselves strong enough to stand the sudden shutting of a door without starting; by the termination of the second, if their letters have not miscarried, which is sure to throw them back, they may fairly attempt a stage before breakfast, and will be able to do without their tea of an evening, when none is to be procured;—before the month is over, they will be recovered enough to finish a plate of soup after detecting a

hair in the introductory spoonful, and bear a shower of rain, even though the umbrella has been forgotten, without taking to bed in consequence.

John was preparing to visit Switzerland and Italy. In a letter to Haydon from 10 Rue Neuve des Mathurins, he said he was studying languages, reading and writing: 'In the intervals, such as they are, I walk on the Boulevards and look at Punch.'

Caroline's health was considerably better than when she left London, although there was still room for improvement. As for Scott himself, the French capital, for all his carping at its inhabitants, had the usual exhilarating effect:

> At this time certainly Paris is a superb exhibition: the public walks are crowded with genteel people: the weather has become fine: the trees, buildings, dresses, & amusements form a melange stimulating, intoxicating, & subduing. The greatest enjoyment in life is active thinking,—& Paris occasions to me more of this than any Place I have ever been in. Rome will do it still more, & in another way: and I expect to have my machinery put into rapid motion by the silent vastness of Switzerland.

Scott gave *Champion* readers an example of the city sights in a Small Talk article:

> On the day of the king's fete, an orchestra was struck up in the *Champs Elysées*; it had five old fiddlers, and one fat woman, without a tooth in her head,—but then her cheeks were rouged. She had a bunch of lilies in her immense bosom, and as the priestess of the jubilee, she held in her hands a quantity of tender songs and couplets, which she dispersed amongst the crowd, and which told them, that their hearts were touched, that the heavens were pleased, the king good, and the world at peace! She advanced to the front, and sang one of those about loyalty and love; she heaved and felt about for her beating heart: the old fiddlers played up to her for dear life;—the leader, who sported a cocked hat, but enjoyed but one eye, marked the time to the others. . . .

Early in October Caroline Scott wrote a lively letter to Haydon. She teasingly suggested she was losing her looks, but hoped to make up for it by the polish she would acquire in Paris, Rome, Venice, Naples, Vienna, and other cities. Like her husband, she was critical of French society:

> In the few visits I have paid here I have been surrounded by Marquises, Viscounts, Counts &c but as far as my powers of observation lead me I am sure my old friend Mr Cowan the waxchandler opposite Mansion house, is a really more well bred and polite person than most of the Gentlemen I have the honour of speaking with, though Dukes have been of the number. . . . The other evening at the Viscount de Luppé's, the Duke de . . . some terrible name or other, was announced, and I was big with hope and expectation when to my utter dismay and astonishment in pops a little black fellow somewhat like the tailor in Catherine and Petruchio, who after a thousand bows and skips gently slid behind the door and was forgotten. The Viscount

de Luppé, with the exception of a little freedom in conversation not very agreeable to English ears, is a very honest handsome pleasant gentleman, the Viscountess his lady, I can scarcely tell what *she* is, I think, though, if one wished to paint Mrs Grundy, the lady spoken of in Speed the Plough, she would be the model for her; but they have a daughter! a little delicate sylph! a little pearl! . . . My lord is just come home from spending the evening with this enchantress—he is impatient at my being occupied by any thing save himself, therefore fare well for the present. He bids me just add, that she was tonight more lovely than ever, and that he had the pleasure of her arm home.

I thank you a thousand times for your kind promise of a sketch of my boy— I am a bold woman to ask such a favour, but you are a kind hearted friend, and will forgive a foolish mother.

Perhaps Caroline had a foreboding of disaster, for on 19 November Haydon said in a letter to Wordsworth: 'Poor Scott is still at Paris, and at present weighed down with family afflictions—his eldest son on whom he and his wife dote has been attacked by a severe complaint on his liver and when heard of last, there was little or no hope of his recovery, his wife's sister is also ill, and Mrs Scott from her anxiety in attending her son will most probably renew her illness to get rid of which she principally accompanied her husband—the winds having been unfavourable there has been no letter for a week—I really feel for Scott I really believe no man has been more afflicted with sickness and I have often wondered how he found time to think a moment harassed as he has always been by the continued illness of those so nearly allied to him—to aggravate it, the increase of his Son's complaint was owing to the ignorance of his medical attendants. Heaven have mercy on all who expect relief from French physicians!'

Paul was already dead. He was buried in the great cemetery of Père Lachaise, eastern Paris. A broken stone pillar erected over the grave bore the inscription:

> Paul Scott,
> An English Child,
> Aged eight years and a half,
> The son of John and Caroline Scott.
> Died at Paris, Nov 8th, 1816
> He was buried here by his
> sorrowful parents

John added some lines adapted from an epitaph written by Wordsworth:

> Not without heavy grief of heart did we,
> Sojourning homeless in this foreign land,
> Deposit in the hollow of the tomb
> Our gentle child, most tenderly beloved,
> Around his early grave let flowers rise,
> In memory of that fragrance which was once
> From his mild manners quietly exhaled.

The grave was surrounded by low rails and shrubs. What appears to be his resting place can still be seen in the cemetery, although the inscriptions have worn away. Curiously, the records there state interment took place on 7 November.

A brief announcement in *The Champion* described Paul as 'a simple-hearted, affectionate, and pleasing child. His life was the daily and sufficient consolation of his parents under trying circumstances, and his untimely death has cast them into the lowest state of unhappiness.'

Fortunately they were not without friends in Paris; Thomas Hill and Joseph Ritchie were at hand. An undated note from Scott to Hill read:

> Caroline in some respects would seem to mend a little—but it is only evident as yet in her mind becoming more alert & active under the feeling of deep mental pain. . . . I am much afraid of her health. Her cough has come on a little. Altogether we are in a very low black-looking way, yet on that account the more sensible of friendly sympathy and attention.
>
> My best regards to Ritchie; in a day or two I should be glad to see him. My wife often mentions his name as one who takes a kind interest in our misfortune.

It seems the authorities ordered the destruction of furnishings in the Scotts' lodgings, probably because they suspected Paul's death had been due to an infectious disease. Scott wrote again to Hill:

> The immediate expenses of my poor Boy's illness & funeral are upwards of 600 francs; to these I have had to add the payments necessary on leaving lodgings. I have written to Mrs Scott's friends, or at least she has, for some assistance to meet this most unexpected and forlorn expenditure, & it will arrive, but in the mean time we are *quite out of money*.
>
> I have no one here to ask such a favour of but *you*. If you could accommodate us with 150 francs for *a week* or 8 days, you would relieve us from one of the perplexities of our present very sad situation. We can rely, in *present circumstances,* on Mr Colnaghi's aid. I have some immediate calls to satisfy. I had 1,000 francs but the other day!

In contrast to these businesslike notes Scott poured out his grief in a letter to Haydon from the Hotel Mayence, in the Rue St Honoré, on 1 December. It showed the tenderness of his feelings for Caroline, and their absorption in Paul to the seeming exclusion of their other children:

> We have at last been overtaken by an overwhelming event; and You sympathise with us. There is this much in it however,—that the cards are not worth the playing now, for we have lost that on which all our hopes were placed. 'The garland of our War is withered';—success can have no trophy,—defeat will bring with it no loss. Three weeks after his death I write You this; because three years after it, if we both live, you will see me act it. I had my own peculiar notions of the utter wretched emptiness of things before;—but now my Soul emits nothing but the words 'Weary, stale, flat

and unprofitable'. And my poor Wife: she is now sitting opposite me: she does not know I am writing You. I begged her to read the Article in the last Edinr. on Dugald Stewart: She consented, & the Review is before her; but this very instant she clasped her hands, and ejaculated—'*To take away our good child!*' Oh, Haydon, it has been a fearful trial for us in our lonely, & otherwise tried state. On me the thought of my loss comes in gusts that break me down;—with her it ever reigns in a still severity. She never will be again what you have known her: Lovely in a chaste gaiety,—happy in her disposition under all circumstances,—giving grace to my home in the estimation of every one,—& pride to my heart through the consciousness that intrinsic worth never had so beautiful a setting as in her manners & form. She is now, & always will be, darkened & subdued by sorrow. Our boy was the light to lighten her steps. He was worthy of her, for she had made him all he was. You did not know him; in some respects you mistook him. I speak from observation, quickened, not blinded, by my fatherly anxiety when I say, that in all the qualities that twine round the heart in the secret development that the warmth of the innermost recesses of home occasions, he was a *matchless child*. Superior powers than fell to his share I have seen:—but in *kind obedience, cheerful respect, silent tenderness, native modesty giving a simple self-possession,*—he was unique:—and in him I have lost the *only* child I have, or can have. Every day was increasing his value to me: since we left England his conduct has been such, that I have felt him always wrapped round my heart,—his limbs folded round it,—& with one hideous clutch of an unseen hand he was torn away.—He is to lie in France too! England that I do so much love is not to have his bones. The Years that pass over my Country will never find him:—he is lying among strangers with whom we have no sympathy,—for whom we have not a single cordial feeling. His life was becoming brighter every day of late: we had forgot our fears; how we lost him God knows,—but we dread much! In short, every attending circumstance adds to our misery. I resolved to bring Mrs Scott to England, & had taken places for last Friday. On Thursday we visited his grave, and both his Mother & myself felt it would be base ingratitude & desertion to leave him, at least so soon. He is not yet, poor, dear fellow decayed. Oh, he would have deemed it unkind if he had been told that we could have thought of leaving him so soon. We are here then for some months—& where for next is as maybe.

In my first state of mind after his death, I quite resigned the idea of going again to disgusting politics: but I feel differently now. The drudgery being stated,—& the subjects not inviting, I will go through them with a labourer's punctuality. The whole matter here is a farce, & I will go through my part. I have no earthly consolation but in indifference: I am in agony always but when I fix my mind on misery, & then I am relieved, for then I say he has escaped. We have met much kindness, as the forms of it go,—from various persons here. But ah we are cold, cold, cold. In the very midst of the race, when I was at the push, & straining my strength even to torture, the plate has been suddenly taken away. I had been telling him a few days before his illness of Naples, & Mount Vesuvius, & Rome:—& in a fortnight's time I followed his body to a hole in a French Churchyard. Good God, when I saw the earth thrown in! On *his* body.—I had run about with him not many weeks before, over the graves & tombstones, in this very place. He & I together alone had still more lately spent a whole day at the Jardin des Plantes, & I was delighted with him:—not more than a month elapsed, before I stopped the man who came with the Coffin, & lifted him myself out of the Bed, wrapped him in a sheet, kissed his feet & mouth, & put down the lid on the face that had for years shone upon me in the changes of fortune,—but he was always sunshine. He was our anchor: his unconsciousness of evil was our refreshment under all accidents. It is not a wound that is made in our hearts, but a hole that is cut in them: it is not that we are unable to possess pleasure more, but that we must ever loath it, & turn from it, & abhor it.—I only laugh aloud, at the thought that now nothing more can happen. I have closed all my accounts—shut up the Ledger,—what is due to me I will not claim, what I owe will not be paid. Days go & go, & nothing goes with them, nor do they bring anything. People come & see us & we talk with them,—for that is part of the Farce.

You are the only one to whom I have outpoured in this way—the only one with whom I could take the liberty—& I have eagerly availed myself of it. I have given vent to Lamentations merely, for in the sincerity of my soul nothing else will come from it. My afflicted wife sends you her love; she shed tears over your letter—& it therefore had a good effect, for she seldom cries— We are indeed very unhappy. Write us again in pity.

Scott did write another Itinerant article for *The Champion,* and more were promised, but this seems to have been his last contribution of any substance. His name continued to appear in the imprint for another eight months, but conduct of the paper was in other hands.

In spite of reluctance to desert his boy's grave, Scott was in London a few days after writing to Haydon; the need to raise money probably made this essential. Caroline remained in Paris with her sister. She wrote to Haydon on 13 December 1816:

I used to think of my Paul as the Ascanius of Eneas—the star that led us through the world—and would shine upon us in our old age. . . .

John's absence has deprived me of the consolation of talking continually of my child, and of being soothed by him when my mind became overwhelmed—but his absence was necessary—I was happy to see him go, for he required a change of scene.

On the last day of the year Haydon wrote to Wordsworth:

John Scott has been in town for a short time, dreadfully cut up by the loss of his boy. He brought over a poem written in all the fury and agony of despair, which I assure you, I think will affect you deeply and give you a higher idea of his powers than anything he has done. There is a want throughout of pious dependence, but for a feeling, as it were of hugging misery, and banquetting on sorrow with fierce and daring defiance, I never read anything so dreadful.

The poem, entitled *The House of Mourning*, was sold to Taylor and Hessey. In addition to relieving Scott's grief, it helped his finances. An undated note from him to Taylor said, 'I enclose you the bill for acceptance—as I am obliged to be *quick* about my affairs in London.'

Just how entangled his finances were emerged from a letter to him in Paris from Longman's recalling his commitment to write a three-volume account of his European tour. Dated 30 January 1817, it ran:

> We have as you desired sent the books you ordered to Mr Colnaghi. In our arrangements with you we quite overlooked our account against you for books (which we now enclose) and it far exceeds any idea we had of its amount. This added to the sums of money which we have paid you makes our advances nearly £860, a sum beyond that which we were to have paid you altogether for three volumes. So situated we trust you will be enabled to manage without drawing further on
>
> Longman & Co

The progress of the mourning poem can be traced in letters from Taylor to his father. On 1 March he wrote: 'There is just come a violent letter from Scott at Paris on account of some changes he thinks we have improperly made in his Poem.'

Ten days later he declared: 'I have written Scott a most trimming letter exposing all the faults of his Poem, and setting his ridiculous conduct in the plainest light. It will make him sensible I hope of his error in not attending to our Suggestions, but I daresay that he will pretend we have made too free with the Dignity of Authorship.'

By the end of the month John Taylor could report: 'We have sold sufficient of Scott's Poem to reimburse ourselves. . . . It is not, perhaps, worth reading as a poem; but in its way, as an Expression of excessive, miserable feeling, I think it will find Readers, and even Admirers.'

He later told his father: 'Scott's poem has been praised, Murray tells us, by Gifford, & I have seen a letter from Sir James Mackintosh to my Doctor where he speaks highly of its Feeling & poetical Power, though he finds fault with its length.'

The editor of *The Eclectic Review*, Josiah Conder, who devoted six pages to the work, summed up fairly when he said: 'Mr Scott is assuredly possessed of genius, although his genius has evidently not been trained, by the habit of poetical composition, to correctness or facility. He has more force of thought than skill in expression.'

Too frequently *The House of Mourning* descends to the level of

> In overflow of soul then, let me say,
> That ever since this precious charge we had
> Our ways have all been rough, the weather bad.

But there is real pathos, as well as bathos, in its 842 lines, and it throws some light on the all-embracing role Paul played in the lives of his parents.

The volume, which contained some shorter poems, and sold for 5s. 6d., had a preface addressed to Dr George Darling. It began:

> It is another's wish, as well as my own, that the following Poems should be dedicated to you. We believe that your ability, and zealous friendship, were the immediate means of prolonging the life of that dear child, whose untimely death, when at a distance from you, has drawn from me the principal piece is this small work.

The preface concluded with a tribute to the doctor's skill during Caroline's illness the year before: 'It is directly to be traced to a long course of laborious, anxious, courageous, and judicious exertion of your knowledge and talent, that I have now a partner in this acknowledgment of your very disinterested, and much valued friendship.'

Scott told readers one reason for making such personal grief public was regret their son should be buried away from England, 'he lies in nook of foreign ground; mute, cold, and lonely'.

At the heart of the poem was a picture of the Scott family life in good times and bad:

> Life must run on, and wants must have their means,
> But we will walk the field like one who gleans
> After the sheaf is carried,—stooping low
> For little; without heart or power to sow,
> But picking what is scatter'd, as we downward go,
> Life must run on,—but it will be through weeds . . .
>
> He was a presence never out of sight,
> First object in the morning, last at night . . .
> Unconscious of each foul and evil thing,
> He drew around our lives a hallow'd ring,
> Within whose bounds, when grief or want assail'd,
> We stood, and found a charm that never fail'd . . .
>
> When our looks darken'd, and he saw us tried,
> Closer than usual to his mother's side
> He quietly would creep, and then would wait;
> Watching with meek and patient looks the while
> When he might break the cloud with sunny smile . . .
>
> And when, not oft, our plans had won success,
> He was a reveller,—in delight he'd swim . . .

The end was simply depicted:

> He was too gentle even to fight with death,
> But hard it is to draw the dregs of breath,
> And hard he drew them.

The remaining poems in the book did little to remove the impression Scott's excursion into verse was ill-judged. One, entitled 'England, written in October, 1815', may have been part of the abandoned epic discussed with Taylor and Wordsworth, to judge from its varied pattern.

Longman's took 100 copies of *The House of Mourning*, but in a letter to Scott on 14 April they reported only 65 had been sold. They discouraged him from writing 'another work of the same kind', and urged him to proceed on his travels.

The firm's letter book throws some light on Scott's relationship with *The Champion* at this time. The first draft of the 14 April letter says: 'We have, whenever we have had opportunity stated that you had now nothing to do with the Champion', but this version was broken off and the substitute letter read '. . . nothing to do with the writing of the Champion; and we shall as you desire continue to do so'. It would seem that although Scott was no longer editor or even a contributor, he had not disposed of the paper entirely.

Nevertheless Sir James Mackintosh wrote to his wife on 17 March: 'The new proprietor of the Champion is a Mr Jennings whom I have known for many years.' Joseph Clayton Jennyns had held a minor official post abroad, and used the paper to attack the Government over what he considered unjust treatment. His editorship was brief, but the following year Jennyns appeared in another quarter associated with Scott. Passing through Stamford on business he was persuaded to stand in the general election in what the reformists called the popular interest. Only a handful of voters supported him. The candidate for whom Scott had voted six years before, now Sir Gerard Noel, had to give up his political ambitions when a bank in which he had an interest got into difficulties.

Haydon kept up his correspondence with the bereaved Scotts, and succeeded in diverting John's mind, to some extent, from his grief. Perhaps the fact Caroline visited London did something to loosen their bond of woe. On 10 April Scott wrote to the painter from 296 Rue Chaussée de Belleville, on the outskirts of Paris, but within walking distance of Père Lachaise cemetery; his letter showed some of his old spirits:

> I thank you very heartily for Your kind Letters. . . . When Mrs Scott was in London, I sat up reading Rousseau's Confessions till 5 & 6 o'Clock every morning—I had never looked into them before. I can now easily account for Hazlitt's enthusiasm in regard to Rousseau, expressed in the Round Table. I have just had this last-named work sent me over from England, & I am perfectly amazed by the genius of that extraordinary creature. His Essays, as *specimens*, are the finest things of the Age. Never before was the truth, so beautifully expressed by himself, so exquisitely illustrated—'Our virtues are built on our vices; our strength lies in our weakness; our faculties are as limited as our being; nor can we lift man above his nature, more than above the earth he treads.'

> He is like the House dog we have here; who growls, bites, & barks when chained to his Kennel,—but let him loose, & his temper becomes kind, he springs upon You, flees over the fields, & is out & in your sight in a twinkling. Hazlitt is just as ferocious & surly when confined to the things which form his daily dwelling-place—but let him loose into the expanse of imagination—get him to course after the Poets, to run down their beauties, to try 'what the open what the cover yields',—to revel & bound amongst the solitudes & charming places of nature, & he is at once faithful, fond & graceful. His Book is an extraordinary production; it is one of those things that one is well-contented to take as they are;—because they are beautiful in their nature, even when they are mischievous & inimical in their effects.
>
> The Poems of Keats, *I believe,* are also extraordinary; but I have not so strong a turn to matters of his sort. I see in them prodigious *gusto*: I see that he has a genuine impulse to do that, which some whom we know, attempt to do in affectation of a feeling which does not properly belong to them I see that he is really inspired;—that he writes Poetry as one desires a fine Woman;—and therefore I see all that even he would wish me to see—for what is still wanting is wanting in my relish,—& he will not blame himself for that ... by & by, I expect, we shall have him reflecting in his passion, & developing a meaning more distinctly than he does at present. . . .
>
> Will you take the trouble to convey to Mr Keats the enclosed packet. I send him my Poem in acknowledgment of the gift of his.

Scott said he had declined to answer a very insolent letter from John Taylor, presumably the 'trimming letter' of which the publisher spoke to his father. 'To his *criticism,* you may suppose I am not inclined to pay much attention, either in the way of respect or anger,' Scott commented. Taylor befriended many authors, including Keats and John Clare, but his ideas on editing roused the anger of others beside John Scott.

Keats did not appreciate the gift delivered by Haydon. In a humorous sonnet written apparently in 1819 but not published until 1936 he included 'The House of Mourning written by Mr Scott' among a list of things of which he said, 'All these are vile.' But he was clearly writing for amusement and Coleridge, Haydon, and Wordsworth were included in the castigation.

During the summer of 1817 the Scotts left Paris for Thomèry, a riverside village about four miles from Fontainebleau. Caroline described 'the view directly opposite the window of the room in which I am now sitting' in a letter to Haydon on 19 July:

> The river Seine, which is by no means narrow here, runs gently by close to the pathway before the door, making a constant rippling sound; which with the distant tinkling of bells round the necks of the cattle upon the hills, causes the most melancholy music I ever listened to. At night when the moon and stars shine brightly and the wind gently moans in the trees upon the hills that rise abruptly on the other side of the water, the most lively imagination would scarcely conceive of anything more beautiful. . . . At one time, I

thought of futurity as a period when the spirit would be master of infinite space exulting in all the wonders of the universe, but now I must confess I have so deep a feeling for the quiet of hills and vales, that I could be almost contented to become a part of what is so beautiful!

She had been ill, perhaps the cause of the move to Thoméry. Even today this resort, with an ancient church and weekend cottages, retains much quiet charm, except when freight trains thunder along the opposite bank, or barges chug up the Seine.

A brief note from Scott accompanied his wife's letter: 'I am terribly incommoded by my wife's illness, & my own: she has had another attack, but not so bad as the former one. It took her on the road.'

In September Caroline returned to London, leaving her husband once more at Belleville. Keats' younger brothers, George and Tom, were in Paris that month, and met Scott and Joseph Ritchie. Tom left with John a notebook containing transcripts of some of Keats' early poems, now preserved at Harvard University. Towards the end of September Scott wrote to Haydon, thanking him for what he called a kind and lifting letter, and went on:

> I am now quite alone: you have got my Wife with You,—and under circumstances of no very cheerful or encouraging kind. I have not yet heard of her arrival, so that I am in a state of great anxiety as to how she stood the journey, & what opinion may be formed in London of the nature of her complaint. It seems hard I could not keep her,—for really I am very unfit to be quite alone.

Money was still short and Scott entrusted Haydon with the task of trying to place a long article on French literature with John Murray's *Quarterly Review*. Scott's friends in the Whig Party and in radical journalism would have been surprised at this flirtation with a Tory publication, and he seemed uneasy about it himself, for in a letter addressed to Murray with the article he said:

> If the present specimen intimate that I could be of any use to the Quarterly, I should be glad to hear from you whether your Publication be open to such articles from my Pen, once a quarter, or so.—I have had in view to put together some remarks on a question of considerable interest—namely, how far the French Revolution and Buonaparte's influence as a ruler, were of advantage or disadvantage to the *Cause of Intellect,* as it is commonly called,—considering little or nothing else. On this question, I believe, I should have nothing to say but in perfect unison with the tone of the Quarterly—yet in many respects my Politics, I must confess, are tottering & timid, compared with your perfect confidence, & firm footing.

In his letter to Haydon Scott was less diplomatic: 'I am inclined to make very little advances to Murray, for his last Quarterly Review, which I have just glanced over, gives me considerable distaste to appear in such bad company. Yet the Edr. Review is as far from me on the other side. I have still a leaning to Baldwin, though he would not probably pay so well.'

The firm headed by Robert Baldwin published *The British Review*, satirised by Byron as 'My Grandmother's Review'. It was this journal which finally published the article, establishing a connection which was to be important to Scott. John Murray's answer to his proposition is not recorded.

Haydon had chided Scott on his lack of Christian faith, drawing from him an impassioned letter on 27 October in which he said:

> You do me great injustice when you say that I am fighting against Providence. In what respect? Since I have lost my child, I have *more than ever I was before,* inclined to 'jog on' industriously & sedulously, & patiently, *'till my day be done'*. Before, I was all for *here*: I held in my trembling hands twenty slender strings, to each of which was attached a precious hope; and over-anxiety occasioned fretfulness, & intermissions, & disgusts, & givings-up; & the fear of not attaining to what I wished made me often disregardful of what I could reach:—but now I have nothing to do but to pass the time; I have not a single distraction from all which can fairly be required from me by anybody—namely the fulfilment of the duty of performing the business of life as my family have claims upon me to consider their interests. I have never done more in the way of *work,* than during the last blank, dark, dismal year.

Back in London Caroline Scott had again become a popular member of Haydon's circle of friends. She is mentioned both in his correspondence and in that of Keats, but her health remained delicate. In February 1818 she wrote the painter a note declining an invitation to accompany his pupil, William Bewick, to hear Hazlitt speak:

> I shall be very much obliged to you to make my Compliments to Mr Bewick, and at the same time to tell him that I am very sorry I shall not be able to go to Hazlitt's Lecture with him. I caught cold the other night from being out after dark, and Mr Darling has laid his commands upon me, not to attempt such a thing again till the weather be fine and warm. . . .
> Mr Ritchie took leave of us last night. *You* do not like to say goodbye I think, neither does Mr Ritchie, for he only said 'good night', as usual.

Ritchie went on a journey of exploration in Africa, from which he did not return.

Scott's article on 'French Literature and Criticism' in *The British Review,* was followed by other contributions, but the relationship was not always smooth. On 12 March 1818 he wrote to Robert Baldwin, of Baldwin, Cradock and Joy, of Paternoster Row:

> You say that *you believe it to be consistent with the spirit of my proposal that if the Editor should find it necessary to reject any of my articles, the Articles so*

rejected should not be paid for. By returning to my Communication you will discover, that this is in direct contradiction to its letter! I stated in my last, that *it was necessary it should be fully understood between us, that when the stipulated quantity of Ms. was furnished on my part, & received on yours, the Sum of Fifty Pounds for the Quarter became due to me as a matter of course*. . . .

It was, I may say, the principal object of my Letter to explain to you that I required to be secured in the receipt of a certain Sum for a certain quantity of Ms., without being liable to loss in consequence of such curtailments & rejections as the Editor in the exercise of his functions might be pleased to make.

Articles on French topics appeared in subsequent numbers, but it is not always easy to trace the hand of Scott in them since the editor, barrister William Roberts, altered his contributors' copy freely.

John's need to secure a steady income was more urgent than ever, for he had at last left Paris. After visiting Lyons he reached Geneva, and it was from there he wrote to Baldwin. He had exhausted the patience of Longman and his partners. Not only did they refuse further advances, they demanded life insurance and other securities to cover the money already paid. They may have heard of the letter to Baldwin, for they too had premises in Paternoster Row. Six days after Scott sent it Longman's wrote to tell him:

We were greatly concerned to learn a few days back that you were then at Geneva & had not been in Italy, Whereby, according to your promise in your letters of May, June & July last, you were then to have proceeded directly to the North of Italy, and to have completed two volumes by the end of the year, and a third in three or four months after.

Instead of going to Italy, Scott returned home. His about-face was presumably caused by the death of his father, Alexander Scott on 24 March, although there is no evidence John went to Scotland.

Alexander's will showed the same attention to detail that marked the Aberdeen upholsterer's other business transactions. It was dated 1810 but was altered less than a month before he died. All his possessions were left in trust to his widow, Catherine Scott, for life. On her death, £100 was to be paid to John. The original will left £500 each to the other nine children, Margaret, Nancy, Catherine, Jane, Marion, Helen, Eliza, Hannah, and Alexander Dick; but this was changed in the 1818 provisions so that, apart from John's £100, his brothers and sisters were to share the estate equally between them. This discrimination against him was clearly because he had already received financial help, for the will provided that 'on my Son John Renouncing any claim he may have to any further share' the executors were 'to discharge him of all advances of Cash made by me to or for him'.

Alexander Scott's estate was valued at between £4000 and £5000. But more than half the assets were stock in trade, upholstery goods, and 'wood

& sundries in the cabinet shop'. Nearly £1300 consisted of book debts owed by customers—and Regency gentlemen were as reluctant to pay their upholsterers as Edwardians were to pay their tailors. The post-war years were a time of recession, and Aberdeen and Glasgow suffered an unprecedented wave of bankruptcies in this decade.

Catherine acted swiftly; on 22 April the *Aberdeen Journal* carried the announcement:

> Mrs Scott
> with grateful acknowledgements for all the favours conferred on her late husband, begs leave to intimate that it is her intention to continue the business in all its branches. . . .
> Alex. D. Scott sets out for London in a few days, and will return in about three weeks with a selection of New and Fashionable Articles in the Upholstery and Cabinet Lines.

By this time the business had moved to Queen Street. Two months after her first announcement Mrs Scott told customers her son had returned with a handsome assortment of goods.

Whatever John Scott's role in this family crisis, by 23 November 1818 he was again on the Continent. Landing at Calais, he passed swiftly through France to Switzerland and on to Italy.

Scott spent five or six weeks in Milan, sight-seeing, learning Italian, and using its libraries. He stayed at a modest hotel, for he commented: 'Among the commercial travellers at the table d'hote, there were evident signs of great hatred to the English. I cannot forget the singular effect produced on my mind, by hearing these men talk of Rimini, Piacenza, Bologna, and Rome, with reference to cotton threads and silk stuffs as one may hear travellers in England talk of Manchester, Sheffield, Birmingham, and Coventry. So different in my mind were the ideas, associated with those renowned Italian names.'

Like so many men who abandon the practice of their own religion, Scott was drawn to the ceremonies of the Catholic Church. He described Santa Maria del Carmine, famous for its music:

> The church was crowded . . . whole families, fathers, mothers, and daughters; young companions coming in together, under the influence of mixed motives, but so far impressed with religious sentiments as, in the more sacred parts of the office, to follow it closely; I could not help feeling, that, by effacing all this from the internal surface of the human heart, a connecting link of social intercourse was broken away. Reduce man strictly and closely, according to the principles of our philosophical economists in morals, and what is he to his fellows?—a power to act drily and strictly according to such and such definitions. You may put in generous, cordial sentiments as you will, among the class of utilities; but this will answer for nothing but in enumeration, after their sources are dried up. The preference for country is

1 Catherine Scott by John Phillip   2 Alexander Scott (artist unknown)

3 Helen Kidson Scott (left) and a sister in 1815 by John Boaden

4 Caroline Colnaghi before her marriage to Scott (artist unknown)

5 John Scott at 19
Miniature by Joseph Pastorini

6 John Scott at 30 by John Boaden

7 John Scott at 34. Pencil sketch by
Seymour Kirkup

8 Scott's second son, John Anthony
Scott at 45. Drawn by John Horrak

9   Frederick, Duke of York and Albany by David Wilkie

ridiculed; religion is ridiculed. . . . When it shall become ridiculous to rise at the sound of God Save the King in a foreign land, and contemptible to go into a church, shall we have made an advance in extent of imagination and height of sentiment?

Of the climax of the Mass Scott said: 'These grand forms are very striking; when the incense rises, when the host is elevated, as actually the Deity among the people, while all bow the head, and floating sounds of solemn music roll with the clouds of smoke and perfumes, the effect is prodigious on the heart of him, who, without belief in facts, believes the reality of the source from whence such sentiments come.'

But he added: 'There is an invisibility about the tenets of the Methodists and the Scotch church which still more forcibly strikes the imagination of the votaries than the organ and the surplice.'

From Milan Scott went on to Venice, arriving there early in February 1819. He found this city on the Adriatic beguiling, as have so many other writers:

> What Lady Mary Wortley Montagu said of the Turkish dances, which she saw performed to the fair recluses of a seraglio, may be said of an excursion in a gondola: it inevitably suggests voluptuous ideas. The lounger going to pay his visits, and the merchant to look after his affairs, glides along reclining on cushions soft as eiderdown, and buried in a curtained twilight. The affect of this mode of common communication on the disposition, is very different from that of a walk along the Strand, through Temple Bar, to Fleet Street and the Royal Exchange!

It was in a gondola he made his peace with Byron. The scene was described later by Scott to Peter George Patmore, who wrote in his book *My Friends and Acquaintances*:

> Until their meeting at Venice, there had been an estrangement between Byron and Scott, in consequence of the part the latter had taken in the 'Champion', relative to the publication of the celebrated 'Farewell', but they were now reconciled, and were on the water together in Byron's gondola, under circumstances which led Scott to express a strong sense of danger as to their position. 'Oh!' said Byron, in a tone of perfect seriousness, 'you need not be afraid of anything happening to you while you are with me, for we are friends now.' And Scott explained that Byron had the most intimate persuasion, that any of his friends who had quarrelled with him were never safe from some strange accident, until they had made it up.

This meeting required courage on the part of Scott and magnanimity on that of Byron. According to Haydon, who gave Scott a letter of introduction to Richard Belgrave Hoppner, British consul at Venice, Byron sent for Scott and they passed several days together. 'His great weakness seemed to be, Scott said, a belief that every woman was mad after him and with an affected contempt as if he seemed to despise it, he coquetted about you, till you seemed to believe it, and then he was pleased', Haydon wrote in his diary.

Byron did not entertain many guests in Venice. Writing in 1821 he said:

> I have invariably refused to receive any English with whom I was not previously acquainted, even when they had letters from England. . . . Except Lords Lansdowne, Jersey, Lauderdale; Messrs Scott, Hammond, Sir Humphrey Davy, the late M. Lewis, W. Bankes, M. Hoppner, Thomas Moore, Lord Kinnaird, his brother, Mr Joy, and Mr Hobhouse, I do not recollect to have exchanged a word with another Englishman since I left their country: and almost all these I had known before. The others, and God knows there are some hundreds, who bored me with letters or visits, I refused to have any communication with.

This was not a comprehensive list, but it indicates a strong motive, if only curiosity, impelled the poet to see the man who had assailed him.

Thomas Moore said in his biography of Byron, 'to meet with an Aberdonian was, at all times, a delight to him', forgetting this was the reverse of the case when he encountered Scott during Leigh Hunt's imprisonment six years before. Byron himself wrote of Scott:

> I knew him personally, though slightly. Although several years my senior, we had been schoolfellows together at the 'grammar-schule' (or as the Aberdonians pronounce it, 'squeel') of New Aberdeen. He did not behave to me quite handsomely in his capacity of editor a few years ago, but he was under no obligation to behave otherwise. . . . I met him at Venice, when he was bowed in grief by the loss of his son, and had known, by experience, the bitterness of domestic privation. He was then earnest with me to return to England; and on my telling him, with a smile, that he was once of a different opinion, he replied to me that he and others had been greatly misled; and that some pains, and rather extraordinary means, had been taken to excite them.

Byron's forbearance was not shared by his friend Hobhouse, who had travelled in Italy and written about it. He said in a letter to John Murray:

> If anyone writes a book of travels without telling the truth about the masters and subjects in this most unfortunate country, he deserves more than damnation and a dull sale, and I trust you will take care he has a niche—forgive the word—in your temple of infamy, the *Quarterly*. I heard that Champion Scott was collecting five hundred pounds worth of news for Longman in these parts. If any but a gentleman and a scholar, and an accomplished man in every way, presumes to hazard such an undertaking, be ready, Mr Murray, with all your thunderbolts: dash him to pieces.

Perhaps it was due to Byron's benign influence that Scott suddenly found his future brighter than for many years. Just before leaving Milan he received an offer from Robert Baldwin to edit a new monthly magazine in

London. Scott expressed interest in the venture, although it was likely to interfere with plans to stay on the Continent and pursue his old project of an historical book. He wrote saying he proposed visiting London in September.

In his journey from Milan to Venice Scott was pursued by a letter containing an even more tempting offer. It came from Sir James Mackintosh, who had added to his political activities the post of professor of law at the East India Company's staff training centre in Hertfordshire, which later became Haileybury College. To be near the college Sir James had moved to Mardocks, outside Ware, and from it on 15 January he addressed Scott:

> Though several years have elapsed since I have had the pleasure of intercourse with you I have not forgotten your merit nor has the impression made on me by your understanding and your character, been weakened. A circumstance has lately occurred which I think it my duty to communicate to you. . . .
>
> A Director of the East India Company authorised by the chairman has informed me that the directors are in want of a Man of Talents to write their Dispatches. He has desired me to enquire if I could find any able man disposed to accept such a station. He would not name the terms in the first instance but a Mr McCulloch who does part of the same business has in a few years had his income raised to £2,000 a year—It is respectable employment which would probably leave you leisure for literature & Society & which would be provision for life. It is far beneath your merits or my wishes for you. But it is above the ordinary chances of the success of a man of letters in the pursuit of fortune. It is also politically independent.

This letter did not reach Scott until 9 February, and he hastened to reply:

> Your Letter of the 15th Jany has unfortunately rested eight days longer on the road than is usual: It only reached me yesterday, which was no post day from Venice, so that, although I lose not an instant in replying to Your truly kind communication, I am afraid you will have found the interval longer than you had anticipated. . . .
>
> The sight of your hand-writing here, and the assurances of friendly interest which it conveys, produced no trivial effect on my mind. Such remembrance I had no right to calculate upon—it has reached me unexpectedly—permit me therefore heartily to thank you for it, as a new, and perhaps a needed animation, as well as a satisfaction extremely grateful to my feelings.
>
> My present situation I can have no difficulty in stating to you. A proposal has, within these few weeks, been made me by a London Bookseller, to undertake the management of a publication which would require my presence in England before the close of the present year. We do not, however, as yet, accord exactly as to terms,—nor am I very well-disposed to

recommence the avocations of an Editor. Before receiving this proposition, I had settled to rest in the neighbourhood of Paris (Fontainebleau) for some years, employing myself on a work of a mixed nature on the public events of Europe that have occurred since the French Revolution. My aversion to plunge myself again in the turbulence, presumption, heats, and regrets, that form the atmosphere of an Editor's work-room is strong; and I have only been induced to contemplate renewing such an employment, for which I am now very unfit, by a circumstance of a peculiar nature. Mrs Scott, during her present residence in London, has become necessary to the happiness,—and I believe I might say to the life,—of a brother,—a fine young man, who has been suddenly struck with what appears to be incurable blindness. Her representations, and my own feeling of what humanity requires, have induced me to lend an ear to an offer, which, altho' not presenting a prospect very desirable in itself, would at least prevent the necessity of making a separation in the case alluded to, by affording me an opportunity of returning to England.

The situation which you describe in Your Letter, would put this in my power in a manner much more agreeable to me. It is my earnest desire to withdraw from the anxieties of Literary gladiatorship. I have lost the spirits necessary to maintain such combats.

In spite of Byron's kindness to him, Scott could not resist including in his letter to Sir James this waspish anecdote:

I saw Lord Byron last night at one of the common masked balls of Venice, the price of admission to which is *twenty Sous*,—alone and unnoticed—grown very fat—and going through the rooms performing practical pleasantries with the Ladies who were there in the discharge of their professional duty.

It was a lighthearted John Scott who set out for Rome, travelling once more when he could by canal and river, and stopping on the way to admire Bologna and Florence. In Rome however, the dark clouds that followed him through life returned, and he must have felt a fellow-feeling for the Lenten penitents. For a letter from Lady Mackintosh, dated Mardocks, 28 February 1819 told him:

Sir James received your letter of the 10th this morning and as he is at the moment overwhelmed with Parliamentary business he has desired me to tell you on the subject of his letter to you what I am very sorry to do, that the situation which he was in hopes you would have found it suitable & agreeable to accept has been already filled up during the necessary delay which has occurred.

The letter was forwarded to Scott from his wife in London, who added a note to it: 'It will gratify you to find that you are still remembered by Lady Mackintosh—Fanny often talks of the way you used to describe your visits to this lady to her.'

Sir James must have been glad to pass over to his wife the task of explaining things had gone wrong, particularly as the company did appoint three assistants to Mr William McCulloch, Examiner of Indian Correspondence. They were Edward Strachey, an experienced Bengal civil servant, James Mill, author of a monumental history of British India, and Thomas Love Peacock. In his book *The East India House* Sir William Foster suggested Peacock may have owed his appointment to the influence of his friend Peter Auber, the company's secretary. Auber arranged for the satirical novelist to take temporary employment in the Examiner's department in order to groom himself for the post of assistant.

There may have been other reasons for Scott's failure to secure an appointment. *The Champion* had, in the past, criticised the monopoly powers of the East India Company; as editor he had also attacked Lord Kinnaird, one of its directors, and George Canning, the Government minister responsible for its affairs.

However, there remain grounds for suspecting Peacock was given the job Sir James intended for John Scott. Otherwise Peacock might have written more novels, and John would not have scaled the literary peak which now rose before him.

Peacock had written to Percy Bysshe Shelley in Italy explaining he was studying at the East India House, and Shelley asked questions about his friend's new career. In view of Scott's troubles with delayed letters it is ironical that Peacock should tell a friend that although he had done his best to satisfy Shelley's curiosity 'it was in letters to Naples which he had left before they arrived, and he never received them. I observed that this was the case with letters which arrived at any town in Italy after he had left it'.

Freed from the need to hurry home, John followed Shelley's path from Rome to the south, where he seemed in better spirits than the poet who composed *Stanzas written in dejection near Naples*. Scott noted: 'In the Hermit's Album of Mount Vesuvius, I observed that the Germans were the longest, the French the most particular in regards to their own conduct at the crater; and the English divided between the simple inscription of their names, and of coarse jokes. The Americans were mean.'

He spent Easter on the island of Ischia and in the same month of April returned to Rome. From there he wrote to his mother in wistful vein, but including his congratulations on the wedding of his youngest sister and an Aberdonian merchant named Peter Macfarlane:

> This letter must travel a long way to reach you—(not much less I believe than two thousand miles)—and its safe arrival is very uncertain—for these things here are very badly managed. I am not willing, however, to let longer time elapse without thanking you for your kind letter of the 1st January and its enclosure—which I received at Venice....
>
> It is far to look back now—both in point of distance and in point of time, to those earlier scenes which you say the New Year suggested to you, and which

your letter brought forcibly on my mind. The vista between them and the present moment is beset with much that appals and occasions regret—but the affections may even strengthen under what depresses the spirits, and saddens the general temper. I received with gratitude and much pleasure this last token of your remembrance—and *think I am likely* to be a more punctual correspondent for the future, than I have been during past years. I am here surrounded by much that forces the mind into retrospection, and which is calculated to beget resignation under earthly vicissitudes. The things of this world do indeed pass away, and nowhere is the truth inculcated in so impressive a manner as at Rome. The very atmosphere of the place seems charged with a calm melancholy influence: the living and the dead seem here joined in a more intimate connection than elsewhere; the step from the one state of existence to the other seems here short and easy. When at Rome one feels to have travelled as it were to the waterside,—to the embarking place for another world,—and all about one lie what have been left by generations that have preceded us in the passage. Amidst these accumulated proofs that the sublimest productions, and the greatest characters are but here to go onward, a more practical reconciliation with the system of Life and Death takes place, than the mind can easily form elsewhere. Our own losses by this general law couple themselves with others in the vast scheme and order of events,—and thought, embracing an extensive period of time as circling round one centre of interest, attaches less importance than usual to the interval of a few years that may possibly separate us from those whom we wish to be with.

Give my love to Kate, who is now with you on the occasion of Hannah's marriage, and my congratulation and love to the latter.

While in Rome Scott met two lively artist friends of Haydon's, Charles Lock Eastlake, who later became Sir Charles and director of the National Gallery, and Seymour Kirkup. Eastlake was recruited as a contributor for the magazine to be launched by Baldwin. Kirkup drew Scott, a head and shoulders portrait now in the Scottish National Portrait Gallery. It shows a handsome sensitive face with questioning eyes, but is probably a flattering likeness of the man of thirty-four bowed down with sorrow.

When Scott reached Paris he encountered another artist, Frederick Nash, a specialist in architectural and landscape subjects. It was agreed John should write the text to a series of paintings of the city and its suburbs on which Nash was working, to be published as engravings.

By August 1819, Scott was back in London, three years after setting out with his wife and son to write a travel book about France, Switzerland, and Italy. The book was still incomplete, but he was to take up a bigger challenge, the editorship of *The London Magazine*.

Chapter 7

THE LONDON MAGAZINE: INTRODUCING TABLE TALK AND ELIA

Before returning to London Scott had reached broad agreement with Robert Baldwin on his engagement as editor of the new magazine. His starting salary was £600 a year; he would contribute some 48 pages out of the 120 each month, as well as supervising the rest.

The London Magazine was to be wide-ranging, intended to entertain and inform its readers on many topics, from painting and literature to politics. It was designed as the capital's answer to *The Edinburgh Monthly Magazine* published by William Blackwood since 1817. This had proved highly successful. Known as *Blackwood's Magazine* or simply *Maga*, its politics were Tory, in contrast to the prevailing Whig principles of contemporary Scottish society and the all-powerful *Edinburgh Review*. Good criticism, particularly of poetry, patriotic and amusing essays about Scottish life, and clever satire were the main features of *Maga*. But its pages were frequently marred by intellectual arrogance and vulgar buffoonery. In speaking of political opponents and Blackwood's rival publisher in Edinburgh, Archibald Constable, it sometimes descended to coarse abuse and scurrilous innuendo.

In particular the Blackwoodsmen, as the magazine's writers came to be known, attacked Hazlitt and Leigh Hunt for their radical views, and John Keats for his friendship with Hunt, and for daring to write poems on classical topics without having a classical education. In the case of Leigh Hunt, some abuse arose from jealousy of the success enjoyed by his poetry. One of the most distasteful aspects of the articles on him and his friends was the blatant attempt to discredit them with booksellers and so take away their livelihood.

Editorship of *Blackwood's Magazine* was deliberately veiled. In after years it was stated William Blackwood was his own editor, and in the sense that he took the final decision about suppressing or leaving in the more obnoxious articles this seems to have been so. But when people who had been insulted applied for redress, Blackwood shuffled off the responsibility, regretting his inability to restrain his unnamed editors.

What is beyond dispute is that the guiding lights of the magazine for several years were John Wilson and John Gibson Lockhart, two inexperienced and underemployed advocates at the Scottish Bar. They had several helpers, including James Hogg, and later a wild and witty Irishman, William Maginn, but Lockhart and Wilson took it in turn to superintend assembly of material for the early numbers. Lockhart once boasted he could, if necessary, write a whole issue himself in a week; there were occasions when the magazine read as if he had.

Walter Scott contributed at the beginning, although keeping aloof from satire and horseplay. He had no doubt of the editorial control when, in December 1818, he wrote to a friend: 'Our principal amusement here is Blackwood's Monthly Magazine which is very clever, very rash, very satirical, and what is rather uncommon nowadays when such superlatives are going in:—very aristocratical and Pittite. The conductors are John Wilson and John Gibson Lockhart.'

It was a dangerous opponent *The London Magazine* intended to tackle. John Scott told Baldwin:

> I need scarcely, I suppose, mention, that as Editor I would expect to be left perfectly free as to opinions Literary, & Political. This of course would not prevent *Communications* of sentiments differing probably from those expressed by the Conductor. Everything that can fairly be called *personality* should certainly be avoided. I have seen two Nos. of Blackwood's Magazine—& from them can sufficiently judge of the whole. I sent to England for them, because some one had said (I was told) that *I* had written the scandalous articles on Mr Hunt! Articles which I read with disgust and abhorrence.

In writing to the publisher from Rome in April about the general financial policy of the magazine, he protested the fee suggested for outside contributions of ten guineas per sheet of sixteen pages was too low:

> I find the quantity of matter stipulated for from my pen to be rather heavy, for in the mode of arranging the page of a Magazine provision is made for almost double the quantity of the words contained in the Page of a Review. But in such an undertaking, I am sensible that all concerned must do their utmost, to ensure its success.—With reference however to the remuneration paid to Contributors the circumstance I have just mentioned is one of some importance. The Sum of £10.10 a sheet for original communications to such a Magazine as yours will be, cannot be considered as more than £5.5 a sheet for the British Review, because in an article for a Review there are almost always extracts from the work reviewed. Now, for this sum I do not think you can expect any writer of distinguished Talent.

On 14 August 1819 he wrote to Baldwin from 89 Piccadilly, saying he thought: 'a *Variety*, more judiciously & widely distributed, and above all more *punctually maintained*, than it is in any of the Periodical Works with which I am acquainted' was desirable in the new work. Scott continued:

> The contents of your Magazine should, I think, take the most general range, make the most complete circuit, and above all, as I have said, be most exact in regularly keeping up this allotted course. The Readers of your work ought to acquire confidence, from experience, in opening the pages of each new No. that something will be found within, on every subject of interest, foreign or domestic, properly belonging to the month. It ought to be looked to as affording the best panoramic view of all that is going forward in Literature, Art, Science, & Politics, throughout Europe.

This letter displayed some wishful thinking. He visualised regular articles on a wide range, almost certainly too wide a range, of topics, in spite of past experience of the difficulty in providing a steady stream of copy from his own pen, let alone from contributors.

His role was formidable. Scott wrote:

> The part of the Magazine that would devolve on the Editor, to be regularly filled up, with or without assistance as it might happen, may perhaps be divided under the following stated heads, to be continued from one month to another:
>
> Review of Politics.
> The Drama.
> Selected Extracts from Foreign Literature.
> Notices of New Books.
> Newspapers, Magazines, Reviews &c. (monthly criticism of home periodicals)
> Foreign Journals, Periodical Works, &c. (ditto)
> Literary & Scientific Intelligence.
> Works preparing for Publication.
> Monthly Chronicle of Events, foreign & Domestic.
>
> After which, would follow the usual Tables and Notices of Deaths, Markets, Promotions, Bankruptcies, Agriculture, the Weather, &c.

Scott wanted to make the *London* noted for its coverage of Continental as well as English literature, and he told the publisher: 'I hope soon to be in case to read German, for I have no doubt that Germany is now the richest mine of materials fitted for your purpose.'

Scott took time off from his labours to renew acquaintance with his painter friends. On 3 October he dined at Haydon's studio in Lisson Grove with David Wilkie and William Young Ottley, artist and writer. Haydon said in his diary:

> After dinner we insisted that Wilkie, the tory, the cautious tory Wilkie, should drink success to Reform! He resisted a long time, kept putting the

glass up to his mouth, & begging for mercy. We then affected great candour, appealed to his gentlemanlike feelings, and I asked him with affected concern if it was kind to disturb the harmony of the evening so. This hit told. His simplicity of mind believed me sincere, and, with a face like Pistol when he was forced to swallow the leek, he said . . . 'Success to Re-re-form (but very moderate, remember)'. We roared at our triumph.

Haydon wrote of Scott:

> It gave me infinite pleasure to see that misfortune had moderated and deepened his feelings, hard reading and perpetual solitude stored his mind; his understanding had taken a larger scope and altogether he was advanced in the scale of intellect.

John had established his home with Caroline and their two surviving children in Sheen Lane, Mortlake, near the Thames. It was from there he wrote to Baldwin two weeks after his evening with Haydon, evidently replying to a suggestion Charles Lamb should be approached as a possible *London* contributor: 'I should be very glad to have Mr Lamb as an auxiliary,—but I have no very ready means of procuring him: and indeed I believe he is what is called a very idle man,—who hates trouble, & above all a regular occupation.' This seems hard on the man who considered himself the slave of the East India Company, but Scott was probably thinking of the time when Lamb appeared so fleetingly in *The Champion* as an essayist.

He was working on the prospectus which would announce *The London Magazine* to the world, and on 9 November he returned a proof to Baldwin, taking the opportunity to proclaim his moderate political views:

> I quite agree with you as to the principle of stating little or nothing to alarm any party in our Prospectus. The reason for avoiding this seems to be, that the *statement* only can go into a Prospectus; the *arguments*, which ought to gain and convince cannot be given. This does not however apply to the Magazine; &, reflecting on our Conversation of this morning, I feel anxious to mention to you without any loss of time, that I shall be inclined to take at once fully and fairly my ground in Politics,—& that in the 1st No. I have long been convinced that the general idea of its being unsafe to speak out, when what one says may be of a nature to displease all the more violent parties, is a much mistaken one.

It sounds as if Baldwin, or possibly his partners Cradock and Joy, would have preferred the magazine to be all things to all men.

The prospectus promised rather more than any product of human ingenuity was likely to achieve. It proposed mixing sound philosophy with entertainment and miscellaneous information, reflecting the life of London, 'that mighty heart whose vast pulsations circulated life, strength, and spirits, throughout this great Empire'.

Engaging contributors with a popular following had become urgent.

Scott told his employer: 'I am sorry to find you telling me that Coleridge gave nothing like a *promise* to us, I would again impress upon *you the necessity of securing him*, if it were only to keep him out of Blackwood's Tent. You can suggest in a neat way, that your Editor is an admirer of his,—has been long a determined stickler for Wordsworth,—& one of his personal friends.'

But although Coleridge had been attacked in *Blackwood's Magazine*, he agreed to accept what he described as handsome terms to write for it. Nor was he likely to be influenced by the reference to Wordsworth, since there was a coolness between the two poets.

Modern readers, who know Coleridge principally as the author of brilliant but uneven poems, and of philosophical jottings clouded by opium, have little conception of the way he dominated those who knew him. It was an age of good talkers, and he was the best of soliloquists. He had written much as a journalist, and was regarded with awe by fellow practitioners.

Scott also failed to secure the services of Thomas Moore, who had gone abroad, but other friends rallied to his support. Octavius Gilchrist wrote from Stamford agreeing to contribute. Horace Smith replied to a request for help:

> I shall have much pleasure in assisting your magazine, not only by procuring subscriptions but by contributing some original nonsense . . .
>
> I am very intimate with Reynolds and do not recollect ever to have heard him make the complaint to which you allude—with every allowance for the poetical temperament he must surely have forgotten any such trivial offence by this time, & if his professional occupations will allow him I have no doubt he will cheerfully become a contributor.

Since his *Champion* days John Hamilton Reynolds had become a partner with James Rice, another member of Keats' circle, in a firm of solicitors. Whatever their past difference was, Reynolds did write some lively articles for his old editor in the *London*.

Scott also canvassed Sir James Mackintosh and his wife for support. On 22 November 1819 Lady Mackintosh wrote from Mardocks to say she would commend his letter and prospectus to Sir James, and would also ask a friend of hers who was Consul General in Egypt to contribute.

Charles Eastlake, in addition to promising his own articles, recommended an artist friend, Edward Gandy, as a possible author. Scott wrote to Gandy: 'So multifarious are the subjects which a Magazine may take up, & so diversified the manner in which it permits them to be handled, that I should think in one shape or other we might be enabled to profit by your favourite pursuits, however small the time you are enabled to devote to literary composition.'

Gandy wrote poetry and plays, but he does not seem to have contributed to the magazine. It is a pity Scott was apparently unaware that in the autumn of 1819 John Keats spoke of engaging in journalism to eke out his decreasing capital. He had written some theatrical criticism for *The Champion* after Scott sold it.

Other duties took up the editor's time. He had to honour his agreement to cooperate with Frederick Nash in a kind of coffee table book produced in parts. The *Annals of the Fine Arts,* edited by James Elmes, an architect friend of Haydon, announced:

> Mr Nash's beautiful drawings of Views in the City of Paris, and of the Scenery in its Environs, have been put into the hands of the first engravers in the country, and a superb work is announced to make its appearance on the first of February next, and to be continued by quarterly numbers. The proprietors, ambitious that it should combine every species of interest which such a publication can fairly include, have engaged Mr John Scott, the traveller in France and Italy, to conduct the literary department.

Controversy attended the birth of *The London Magazine* on New Year's Day, 1820. Another London Magazine appeared at the same time, and the publishers, Gold & Northhouse, claimed they had announced their work before Scott's prospectus was circulated. This brought a dignified rebuff from Robert Baldwin, pointing out his old-established firm had published a *London Magazine* in the eighteenth century, and plans for its revival had been settled early in 1819.

Gold's London Magazine, as it came to be known to distinguish it from Baldwin's, was a poor publication, but the affair did nothing to ease the establishment of Scott's own production. This proclaimed its attachment to the capital by appearing in a cover showing the Thames and St Paul's Cathedral. Apart from the editor's own writings, the first issue contained major articles from Octavius Gilchrist, who introduced the peasant poet John Clare, Bryan Waller Procter, a young barrister who wrote under the name Barry Cornwall, and Charles Eastlake, who sent two pieces from Rome. There was poetry from Quaker bank clerk Bernard Barton, and verse by Horace Smith. In spite of Scott's intention to handle play-going himself, Hazlitt wrote on the drama, and continued to do so for most of the first year of the *London.*

In a reversal of roles between the old colleagues, Hazlitt's dramatic notices were followed by an account of the fine arts from Scott; the editor appeared throughout the magazine in many roles, including poet, although articles were anonymous, or at most pseudonymous.

First item was 'General Reflections suggested by Italy, seen in the years 1818 and 1819'. A footnote said 'the author of this article wishes it to be considered as introductory to a work on Italy, which will soon be published'. Scott's conscience must have reminded him of the still unfinished account of his travels in France, Switzerland, and Italy, which he owed to Longmans.

His other main contribution to the January number was entitled 'The Author of the Scotch Novels', the first in a series on Living Authors. It was a piece of which he was particularly proud, combining as it did his love of literature and of his native land. But as always, John was balanced in his enthusiasm:

> Without taking upon us directly to affirm, that their author is the greatest writer of the present day, we may be permitted to say for ourselves, that there is no living author whom we would so much wish to be. . . . More than any other writer, except Shakespeare, and not less than Shakespeare himself, he renders the reading of his works encouraging to human nature, by putting us in good humour with whatever he offers to our attention . . . he is not studiously moody, like Lord Byron, nor involuntarily mystical, like Wordsworth, nor laboriously gay, like Thomas Moore.

Scott went on to express 'gratitude to the author, for having fixed and delineated the remarkable features of a national character, such as no other people can parallel, at the very moment before it was too late. A little longer, and the lively remembrance would have faded.' Like most readers of his time, John overestimated the durability of the novelist's attraction, saying it was 'certain that his honours will perpetuate themselves, that his popularity will not pass by, that the numerous volumes which have streamed, as it were, from his pen, will give as much pleasure to readers hereafter as they give to us today'.

He concluded: 'We fancy we hear a cry of "name! name!" . . . from all we have heard of the personal character and accomplishments,—the talents, worth, and patriotism of the most popular Scottish poet of the present day, we should be very much mortified were it afterwards to turn out, that these fine works have been improperly attributed by the public voice to Walter Scott.' The novelist became a baronet in March of this year.

In another review, of *A Sicilian Story*, by Barry Cornwall, Scott made some play with the author's name, saying 'we suspect such a person is not to be found between this and the Land's-end'. He included an unfortunate gibe at Leigh Hunt:

> We can decide more readily who he is not, than who he is. Mr Cornwall is certainly not Mr Leigh Hunt, because there are no vulgar affectations, nor cold indecencies in his compositions; because he has a more correct sense of Beauty, and never causes us to revolt from his images;—but, also, because his hand hath not yet that distinct, certain, masterly touch, with which Mr Hunt calls into play our sensibilities, when he happens by good luck to feel his subject more strongly than himself. Nor is Mr Cornwall, unless we much mistake, Mr Southey, because such little cant as he may have (and we are

afraid he has a *lee*-tle—just the least in the world)—is of the joyous and pastoral kind,—not of the moody and devotional. Nor is Mr Cornwall Mr Lamb. We have heard it said he is. If so we are blockheads. It appears to us that he has much of Mr Lamb's feeling, and love of simplicity and pathos, and familiarity with the gentle and sorrowful things of the world;—but he has not Mr Lamb's imagination, or depth, nor has he quite so extensive a sympathy with humanity. He wants the *"something far more deeply interfused"*, which we find in Mr Lamb's pieces. We shall be surprised if it turns out that Mr Cornwall is Mr Shelley, or that Mr Cornwall is Lord Byron. We are sure he is not ourselves—and we are sorry for it. We have read his poems with great pleasure, and should have been happy to have written them;—but we cannot do everything. We have been fully occupied lately in correcting proofs, and arranging the prices of cow-hides and molasses.

John's principal poem in the issue was entitled *Vevey*. It was on the theme that haunted him, the loss of Paul in Paris in 1816, but as poetry showed considerable advance on *The House of Mourning*. His grief had grown more refined, or perhaps it was impossible to write really bad verse in sight of the moon shining on Lake Geneva. The poem ended:

> All but my withered soul was bright;—
> It lay in shadow of the tomb;
> Yet shrunk not from the splendid sight,
> But gazed from its abode of gloom:
>
> 'Tis grand 'mongst grandest things to feel,
> The powerful hand by which we're tried;
> 'Gainst nature's wonders in my zeal,
> Myself I measured—and had pride.
>
> Though high in air those mountains shine,—
> *Mind* far above their tops can go;
> Yon silent gulf defies the line—
> But deeper still is human *woe*.

Scott revealed something of the bustle that went into launching *The London Magazine* in his notes to readers:

> We are at once astonished, gratified and puzzled by the number of our Contributors:—all firing at our first number as if it were a target. . . . We heartily thank our friend who has sent us the *Epitaph* instead of the promised *Epigram*. The least we can do, in return for the favour, is to keep it unprofaned for his tombstone. . . . We have received an excellent, and most amusing article *On the Art of Loading Stage-Waggons*, signed *Corydon*. The esteemed author, however, wishes us to promise that it shall be placed first in the number where it appears. To which we reply, that we must positively sit at the head of our own table; we have magnanimity enough to bear a brother *next* our throne, but not exactly *upon* it.

There was a sad item in this January *London*. The Colonial news contained extracts from a letter written by Scott's old friend of Aberdeen and Brussels days, Lieutenant George Logan, from Jamaica and dated 2 September 1819. Headed 'Ravages of the Yellow Fever', it said:

> I believe I mentioned in a former letter, the general opinion of the impropriety of sending troops to the West Indies, at such an advanced period of the year. . . . This opinion, I am sorry to say, has been most awfully verified; a fever having broken out in the 50th regiment six weeks ago, which very soon after attacked the 92nd. . . . The 92nd has lost Lieut-Colonel Blaney, Adjutant Mackie, Lieut. Rich. McDonnell and 130 men!

A footnote to the letter read:

> We have just received the afflicting news that the excellent and amiable writer of this letter has himself fallen a victim to the dreadful disorder.

Among minor contributors to the opening number was Thomas Griffiths Wainewright, later unmasked as a forger and poisoner, but at that time cutting a figure in artistic circles as a dilettante and collector. He was a customer at Paul Colnaghi's printshop, and known to Hazlitt and Haydon. Wainewright had suffered a severe illness, followed by depression, and been recommended varied amusement as a tonic. Scott suggested he should put on paper some of his opinions about painting.

Although he did write on art for the *London* later, his first effort was several stanzas of doggerel under the name Egomet Bonmot. He indicated in the introduction to his rhymes this pseudonym would be subject to change: 'To distinguish contributions by the signature of my name will henceforth be useless, except on particular occasions. Suffice it, that in your richest numbers whatever is wisest, virtuousest, discreetest, best, may safely be attributed to the pen of Bonmot.'

His verses were a joyous dig at people who prided themselves on their ancestry, and began:

> Three thousands years, if I count right,
> Have heard the critics Homer cite,
>   (His poem's good 'tis true;)
> But what can hide the Poet's shame,—
> No one can tell from whence he came—
>   The son of Lord-knows-who!

Among the better lines were

> Milton, for all his epic fire,
> Claims but a scriv'ner for his sire—

and

> A mere upholsterer got Molière.

Judging from the freedom with which his friends poked fun at upholsterers and tailors, Scott was either not sensitive about his father's trade, or managed to keep it a secret. The latter seems unlikely when Alexander Scott, during his lifetime, was a regular visitor to London, and John's young brother, Alexander Dick, was learning the business in the capital at the time the magazine was launched.

After the January issue Baldwin and his partners announced: 'The demand for this work so greatly surpassed the expectations of the publishers, as to exhaust the whole of a considerable impression on the first day.'

A letter from Scott to Robert Baldwin, dated 18 January 1820, explained Hazlitt had been persuaded to write on the Drama to put him off other topics, presumably political views unacceptable to the editor and publisher:

> I am sorry to say that I cannot honestly tell you that Mr Hazlitt's MS. is likely to suit us in the Mag. It falls into all these errors which I know are his besetting ones,—but which I hope to keep him clear of when he is directed to particular topics, such as the Drama, &c. His talent is undoubted,—& his wish to serve us I believe at present very sincere. . . . If I could have told you that the Essays, of which a specimen has been forwarded, would surely suit us, the difficulty probably would be small: but altho' very anxious to find it so, I would not act fairly by you were I to give this as my opinion. At the same time I will engage for the gentleman, from what I know of his character, that he would be most ready to listen to suggestions & to strain every nerve for us, in return for a service. He is naturally grateful, & though an original is an honest one. I have not spoken to him for several years until Sunday last, but I see that in a very short time I shall be able to influence him to proper subjects & to a proper manner of handling them.—I mean *proper* in regard to the Magazine:—generally speaking I should have little claim to be his judge or guide.

With this coaxing Hazlitt embarked a few months later on the *Table Talk* essays, perhaps the most popular of his works.

Scott underlined his business and other worries in a letter from Mortlake to his mother on the last day of January:

> I could never have urged, with so much reason, the excuse of want of time for not writing to you, as at present. For the last three months I have been occupied every day, every hour of the day, and several of the night. I now, however, begin to get a little before my work, as far as the Magazine is concerned; which you will be glad to hear seems to promise well. Independently of this, and my Italy, which is a good way behind, I am writing short descriptions of Paris, for a work of Engravings, which pays me very well for the trouble it gives—but this, though not much of itself, is still an addition to my other labours.

I was much obliged by your kind New Year's day Letter. It however made me very anxious about the state of the business, the burthen of which is so heavy a one for you to sustain, and on the tolerable success of which so much depends. I have had long conversations with Alexr. about you; and the result seems to be, as far as his opinion goes, that you are not in serious danger, though in a good deal of difficulty. I think you will find yourselves more comfortable when he is again with you, for he seems to me steady and attentive, and to have very judicious notions on business matters.... I cannot bear to contemplate the possibility of your getting into any embarrassments of this nature, at your time of life, and after so indefatigable a course of exertion, and discharge of duty.

Caroline sends you her kindest love: she hopes you got her letter, indeed she does not doubt you did,—thought it has not been particularly mentioned. She is still poorly—indeed very much so.... I cannot continue to live in the country, but at the same time am loath to move her and the children, with whom it agrees. At present I have a lodging in town, where I live during the latter half of the month. This however is unpleasant; but what I shall do in the way of change I have not yet determined. When two or three Nos. of the Magazine shall have proved to us what its fate is likely to be, I shall be enabled to decide on better grounds. The income I derive from it, at all events for a year, is ample, and will enable me to keep my engagements with my Creditors which are however heavy....

We are all here very quiet hum-drum people. Poor Peter is incurably blind,—and his health is far from good. Mrs Colnaghi is fast getting old, Caroline is always in bad Health,—and I am always busy.

The February issue of the *London* opened ominously, with the announcement, 'Living Authors No II will appear in our next Number.' Various other articles were also promised for March. It had not taken long for Scott to miss his avowed aim of keeping up the various items punctually. He again opened the proceedings, this time with a book review which included some comments on Byron. He ended by expressing pleasure that 'England can boast of a Wellington to gain such battles as that of Waterloo, and of a Byron to decry them with such poetry as that of Childe Harold'.

The editor contributed a long article on 'The Spirit of French Criticism', and another from his pen was again critical. It was an assessment of Hazlitt which became justly famous, and seemed to have had its genesis in the letter to Haydon from Paris three years before, when John likened his unpredictable colleague to a guard dog. Discussing the publication of Hazlitt's *Lectures on the Literature of the Age of Elizabeth*, Scott wrote:

> Whatever faults Mr Hazlitt may have, as a writer, want of meaning is not one of them. He has always something particular, and, in his view, important to say; when he attempts to say anything . . . the whole force of his intellect

seems always fairly put into play to elicit his sentiments, whatever the topic may be; so that we have nothing at second-hand from his pen.

He went on:

> What we should decline robbing Mr Hazlitt of, are his *politics*. We do not think that we need have any scruple to mention these latter, though our present business is with a literary work, for the author himself does not scruple to introduce them everywhere, and on all occasions,—they come, like a mastiff, by his side, into all the companies he frequents,—whether of old poets, or modern players; and 'love me, love my *dog*,' is his maxim. To this he sturdily adheres, in spite of any symptoms of confusion or alarm amongst silk stockings, and muslin petticoats. As we happen to have neither ourselves, we are very well inclined, so far as our own tastes go, to put up with the creature, that we may enjoy the pleasure which the talents of its master are calculated to afford.

After this teasing, probably a hint to his friend to avoid politics in writing for the magazine, Scott paid high compliments to Hazlitt's talents:

> With a comprehension of innate character, absolutely unequalled by any of his contemporaries,—with a finer and more philosophical taste than any other critic on poetry and art whose name we can cite,—with an intense feeling of the pathetic, the pure, the sublime, in quality, action, and form,— he is not, we think, by any means done full justice to by people at large . . .
>
> He catches the mantles of those, whose celestial flights he regards with devout, but undazzled eye. . . . Nothing that is common-place or unmeaning—none of the expletives of criticism—enter into his discourses.

While *The London Magazine* was aimed at a cultured, comfortable readership, it did not ignore the social stresses at lower levels of Regency England.

> Perhaps the most interesting incident of the last month, is the lively awakening of public charity in the metropolis, and over the country generally in favour of the poor classes of society, exposed to more than common hardships, from the late very extraordinary inclemency of the weather [Scott wrote]. The streets of London are heart-rending, to the compassionate passenger,—when the inclemency of the weather adds to the evils which poverty always suffers under, and renders them more obvious to the eye. Do not let us refine too much on this subject: the question of mendicity loudly calls for the sober and cool inquiries of the political economist, and statesman; but prominent and palpable misery demands relief. Have the poor an interest in being naked, and houseless, and hungry? It would almost seem so, from the tenor of certain late representations on the danger of charitable donations.

Scott was handicapped by ill-health during the preparation of this second number, and some of it showed hasty work to fill space. Gilchrist helped with a review of Spence's *Anecdotes*, mostly extracts from the book. But, as had happened in Scott's days on *Drakard's Stamford News*, Gilchrist took the chance to start a literary war. This time his foe was the Reverend William Lisle Bowles, who had edited Alexander Pope in a manner not sufficiently laudatory of the poet's works or life to suit his admirers, who included Lord Byron and Thomas Campbell. Gilchrist accused Bowles of gross insinuations, flippant sarcasm, and pruriency.

By the time he wrote his introductory notes to the March issue of the *London* Scott was in top form:

> We were musing very seriously the other evening on the duties of our office, and its various trials. Before us lay a pile of papers, to which our regards were fascinated, it having a power over us similar to that of the rattlesnake over its prey. Contributions, Remonstrances, and Compliments formed the mighty mass:—contributions too poor for insertion, and too good for rejection; remonstrances meeting the compliments full in the teeth, on the same point, and thus dashing themselves to pieces, and wounding us with the splinters of both. One writer accuses us of a want of spirit; and another says we have the spirit of a fiend,—as witness our last article on Kean. We have been severely handled for presuming to think that personal figure enters for something among the qualifications of an actor:—and above a hundred 'Sprigs of Shelalah', as they all sign themselves, write unpaid letters to demand satisfaction for personal insults, offered to each in hinting that Miss O'Neill owed but little of the excellence of her acting to her beauty.

In the March number Eastlake wrote from Rome, reminding Scott of happy hours spent together the previous year and of his admiration for Thomas Moore: 'I know you are one of his zealous admirers, both as a man and an author. You remember the day of our party to the Gardens of the Borghese Villa; you remember the Irish Melodies sung under the shade of Italian pines and the canopy of an Italian sky; and we all remember your encomiums of these national hymns,—for so you termed them,—and the zealous panegyric you passed on their author.'

Scott himself was in reminiscent mood when he began the second of his Living Authors series, on Wordsworth:

> The little island of Ischia is one of those fragments of a land of volcanoes which have been flung into the sea, and now freckle the light face of the bay of Naples. The three days we spent there last year, in the house of a priest, with little of his company, and none of anyone else's, will for ever remain hoarded in the *museum* of our memory, as one of the rarest and fairest specimens of existence; a thing 'to dream of, not to tell'.
>
> We were seated in the shade, on the priest's balcony, one beautiful Sunday morning. A woman, with the high and fanciful white head-dress of the island, was moving below amongst the green leaves of the vines, and loudly singing a religious ballad of her native place. The sun was shining, bright and hot, on the mainland, where were the Elysian fields, their tombs, and the

promontory of Misena, full in front; the lake of Acheron and the Stygian river, grey and steaming, a little on the left; the ruins of Cumea, and the Sybil's cave, were just visible in the distance; and a path of silver lay across from these objects, undulating over the small swellings of the summer water, up to the deep blue of the basin of Lacco, close at our feet. At this moment a stirring breeze suddenly sprang up, and caused all the features of this beautiful sight to quiver like arrows:—it also brought a brigantine in full sail round the headland of the island, and placed the stately vessel in the very midst of the picture, with its canvas hanging like clouds round its lofty masts, and its topmost streamer spreading quietly over them, like the sceptre of an unquestioned monarch. Very common poetry, we think, would not be apt to intrude itself on so regal a scene; yet we confess that we felt it but a glorious visual realization of Wordsworth's lines—

> Or, like a ship, some gentle day,
> In sunshine sailing far away,
> A glittering ship, that hath the plain
> Of ocean for her vast domain

Perhaps this may not be exactly the fit introduction to an article of a critical nature; but the circumstance suggested itself so forcibly to our minds in writing the name of Wordsworth at the head of the page, that we could not resist the temptation of going into the description.

Scott went on to bestow high praise on the poet, but not without discrimination. He wrote:

> The Waggoner we think one of the finest, if not the very finest, of Mr Wordsworth's professed sketches from common life. . . . His poetical characters are all marked with the impress of his own personal one; and therefore we think it, on the whole, a pity, that he should attempt anything but pieces where this impress would be the best of recommendations. In spite of his familiarity of phrase, and long drawn-out minuteness of description, his hedge-menders and ditch-cutters would be shyly looked at by the set at the Swan or the Red Lion, we fear. They would be set down for Methodists, or fellows that could not take their own parts. Even his old women, though they gossip tediously, do not gossip heartily, and would be slightly estimated at the village conclave of a summer evening. The reason of this is, that they are one and all of the Wordsworth fashion, and that is not by any means the true style of pothouses and gossiping-matches.

Some pages later, Scott praised the work of a man who knew at first hand what it meant to be a poor countryman. He quoted from *Poems Descriptive of Rural Life and Scenery,* by John Clare:

> Oh, sad sons of Poverty!
> Victims doomed to misery;
> Who can paint what pain prevails
> O'er that heart which want assails?
> Modest shame the pain conceals:
> No one knows but he who feels!

The London Magazine: Introducing Table Talk and Elia

Scott wrote: 'In the reality of wretchedness, when "the iron enters into the soul", there is a tone which cannot be imitated. Clare has here an unhappy advantage over other poets.'

The reader turning the pages of *The London Magazine* is struck by some minor pieces written by men whose identity is still a matter of speculation. In the early numbers a series of medical hints appeared, probably by Dr Darling. His theme was preventive medicine, and he was particularly severe on female folly in risking sudden changes of temperature in flimsy frocks:

> Dress is completely under the influence of caprice or accident, that is to say of fashion; and it too often happens that fashion forgets that dress should also be clothing. How shocking the absurdity, ordered by fashion, of muffling one's self up in woollens during the morning, and warm part of the day: and when the chilling and damp evening comes, all these are thrown off to make way for the silks, gauzes, laces and the other flimsy textures, which mischievous ingenuity has contrived for female attire. . . . But worse than all this, fashion orders that the chest and arms, with the skin of which the delicate lungs so readily sympathise, shall be completely uncovered!
>
> The power of the human constitution to resist the causes of disease, and to accommodate itself to circumstances, is such, that even considerable degrees of exposure to cold, when uniformly submitted to, and gradually brought about, cease in a great measure to be harmful. Witness the bare legs of the Scotch Highlander wading among his winter torrents, and the driving snows of his hills. . . . Witness the comparative safety with which some of our fashionable belles spend seven nights in the week, in a state of semi-nudity, after being warmly clad all the morning.

Notes on music were refreshingly candid. They have been attributed to R M Bacon, editor of *The Quarterly Musical Magazine and Review*, which would account for the fulsome praise of that publication in his first article. At times the comments are reminiscent of Bernard Shaw's views on opera:

> Signor Albert . . . is certainly not of the first rank. He is a bass, completely realizing the idea of mediocrity in vocal science, in power, compass, and execution, while his unfortunate bulk and obesity unfit him almost for motion.
>
> The story of *Gastone e Bayardo*, like all the operas since the days of Metastasio, is light and perplexed; the incidents meagre and dialogue insipid to the last degree of insipidity.

Recording George III's death, Scott called him 'an honest man and a perfect gentleman', and added a personal recollection:

> When we were last at Windsor, which is some years ago, we saw in the entrance to St. George's Chapel, a neat marble slab fixed in the wall, with an inscription, couched in few and simple words, but very nervously expressed, stating that it was put there as a monument to the worth and fidelity of a

humble female *domestic*, by her *grateful* master and Sovereign George the Third.

John played very little part in the next issue on 1 April. This carried an introductory note: 'There is a deficiency in this Number in our Notices of New Books: also an omission of the usual Political Article, and of the News of the month; these have been occasioned by the severe illness of the Conductor of the Magazine.'

Scott's chronic bilious ill-health can hardly have been improved by a jocular note he received in his London lodgings at 9 Little Argyle Street from Horace Smith: 'You are well off not to be quite off, to be laid up with fever and bile when you might have been nailed up with shroud and sheet, for this weather is most killing. Let us all look forward to a jump into Summer without taking a spring (for this you know is leap year).'

Although Scott could not fill his quota of pages in the April *London*, he made a guest appearance in an article by Wainewright. Lacking the editor's restraining hand, 'Sentimentalities of the Fine Arts, by Janus Weathercock, Esq', was an extravagant piece of fine writing. Nevertheless it reflected the strange friendship between the man who had been called 'Propriety John' and his foppish columnist.

Wainewright, like Scott, was living in Mortlake in 1820, and this was the setting for his article: '*I was aware* (as the old romances have it) of coming feet over the slippery oil-cloth; and, issuing from the glass door, was seen the long-desired face of my respected friend Hippolito.'

For the sake of baffled readers Wainewright referred them in a footnote to a contemporary book which said of Hippolito 'Few men draw their arrows more closely to a head, and few men send them forth with a more deadly precision of aim . . . you may rely generally upon his taste and judgment', and then continued his article:

> About half a dozen hearty hand-shakings, excited concussions all over our respective bodies sufficient to have ruptured the stays of a dozen dandies, being performed, we reentered the library; where, finding my visitor had journeyed twelve miles on foot since a very early breakfast, I proposed to him to take *something*, as it is emphatically called. His assent being given in a remarkably sweet and ready manner, I forthwith caused the contents of the larder to be paraded upon a stout table by the side of a roaring fire, in due form; and, in the twinkling of a lady's eye, a pair of knives and forks were imbrued up to the hilts in the partridge-flavoured gravy of a vast veal and ham pye, baked in an unfathomable *red* dish (a whimsey of ours) guarded on the one side by a peck loaf *home-baked,* on the other by a fine ripe *Stilton,* and the whole amiably harmonized by a running accompaniment of home-brewed ale,—pale, amber-coloured, foaming—contained in a capacious brown stone-jug, silver-tipped. Soon was the fair smug face of the luncheon-tray changed—the lily lavender-smelling cloth was covered with splinters of

the Pate's stout outworks—upper and under crusts were cut sheer away from their parent loaf by the 'griding' blade—quicksands of salt, and quagmires of mustard obscured the radiant colours of Spode's loveliest plates. . . .

Hippolito, letting fall his weapons with iron clash, and pushing away from him in disdain, his empty glass, turned round with cordial smile to the deserted fire; when, having comfortably arranged one leg over the other, and, with elbows leaning on the arms of the chair, carefully brought the fingers' ends of his right hand into exact juxtaposition with the corresponding ones of his left, thus he spoke: 'What illustrious obscure shall now be illuminated by the piercing beams of thy discrimination? What gems of price shall now be drawn up from the stifling depths of the dull lake of neglect, and brandished by thy tantalizing hand before the lounging eyes of the pleased, yet bewildered readers of Baldwin's Magazine?'

In spite of Wainewright's fantastic over-writing—he said Scott claimed he had to delete every other sentence of one article—he had a real feeling for words and put some glitter into the pages of the *London*. He was also a genuine connoisseur of art, an early admirer of Blake and Constable. Scott perhaps appreciated Wainewright's slyness in putting into his copy some outrageous plugs for prints sold by Colnaghi and J H Bohte, which it would have been indelicate for John to write himself. He had moved his lodgings to rooms at the premises of Bohte at 4 York Street, Covent Garden, now part of Tavistock Street.

Wainewright was, inevitably, irregular in providing his copy, and the following month Scott reproved him with a Lamb-like jest, referring to 'our esteemed friend Mr Weathercock (who we are much afraid is dead)', adding in a footnote, 'We have since instituted particular inquiries, and find, with pleasure, that Mr W. only made *an attempt on his life,* which luckily proved abortive.' Wainewright responded by referring to Scott as 'Jonas Wagtail, our Mr Fine Arts', and picking an imaginary quarrel with him over an exhibition of paintings—'Mr Weathercock' was in fact a more discerning critic of contemporary art than his editor.

In the May *London* Scott indicated he hoped to visit Edinburgh on holiday: 'We purpose visiting Auld Reekie sometime soon, when the elegant new smack, the *Walter Scott,*—(why not the Sir Walter?) in regard to whose preparing accommodations Rumour is now busily employing all her hundred tongues,—shall be afloat. The truth is, we are much in need of a holiday to recruit our health, at present seriously hurt by damp proofs and dry manuscripts.'

John probably intended to accompany his brother Alexander, who returned to Aberdeen the same month. Alexander announced in *The Aberdeen Journal* he would carry on his late father's business of upholsterer and cabinet-maker, having learned the business in London. There is no evidence John got his proposed holiday, and it seems clear from his contributions to the magazine he remained in London and Mortlake during May.

Scott demonstrated his ability to admire talent while deploring its application when he reviewed *The Cenci,* Shelley's drama of incest and violence:

> It is no more than fair towards Mr Shelley to state that the *style* of his writings betrays but little affectation, and their matter evinces much real power of intellect, great vivacity of fancy, and a quick, deep, serious feeling, responding readily, and harmoniously, to every call made on the sensibility by the imagery and incidents of this variegated world . . . the most beautiful images, the most delicate and finished ornaments of sentiment and description, the most touching tenderness, graceful sorrow, and solemn appalling misery, constitute the very genius of poesy, present and powerful in these pages, but, strange and lamentable to say, closely connected with the signs of a depraved, nay mawkish, or rather emasculated moral taste, craving after trash, filth, and poison, and sickening at wholesome nutrient.

He attributed this to weakness of character—'which is a different thing from what is called weakness of talent'—and concluded: 'This tragedy is the production of a man of great genius, and of a most unhappy constitution.'

The candour of Scott's pen was about to cost him the friendship of a very old acquaintance, Benjamin Robert Haydon, who had at last completed the enormous canvas *Christ's Triumphal Entry into Jerusalem.* There were many setbacks during its painting, the work often interrupted while he turned to less important but more remunerative commissions, or to pacifying creditors. Haydon laid himself open to ridicule by depicting his friends Wordsworth and Keats in the painting as onlookers, and by putting in the head of Voltaire.

Haydon hoped the unveiling of his masterpiece would set the seal on his career, so it was unfortunate Scott was light-hearted in some of his comments:

> We are carefully informed in his advertisement, that his picture has been 'six years on the easel'. What is meant by this? Does he mean to say that he cannot paint such a picture in less time than six years? . . . The public we think, have nothing to do with the time employed in productions of talent to which their attention is called. Suppose we were to advertise 'a criticism on Mr Haydon's picture which has been six hours on the author's writing desk!' . . .
>
> In the same light we regard the introduction of Voltaire's head into this fine work. There is something so grossly, so obviously, improper in this, that we are compelled at once to trace it to a desire to increase the interest of the exhibition with those least able to do justice to the merits of the picture.

After this, it was no consolation to Haydon that Scott went on to call the work 'certainly the finest historical picture which England has ever produced'. Even Wordsworth, complimented by inclusion in the painting, is said to have told the artist his nickname should be Teniers 'for you have been ten years about this work'. Wordsworth had enquired after Scott in writing to Haydon, but although the poet visited London in 1820, he and Scott do not seem to have renewed their brief acquaintance of 1815.

It was in the June 1820 number of the *London* that Hazlitt's first Table Talk *On the Qualifications necessary to Succeed in Life* was published. Although Hazlitt continued to write dramatic criticism, his monthly 'talk' became a leading feature of the magazine, eclipsed only by Lamb's *Essays of Elia*, which began two months later with *Recollections of the South Sea House*. Robert Baldwin secured Lamb's services, and his contributions were paid for at double the basic rate.

Scott quickly seized on the reemergence of the essayist he had welcomed to *The Champion* six years before. According to his biographer, Sir Thomas Noon Talfourd, Lamb signed himself Elia because it was the name of a clerk he had worked with thirty years before: 'The editor afterwards used it to distinguish Lamb's essays, and he finally adopted it.' In the October number Elia was given the place of honour, usually reserved for Scott himself, his *Oxford in the Vacation* occupying first place in the magazine after the introductory notes.

Much as he admired his two essayists, Scott did not leave them entirely to their own devices. It was not his practice to alter such contributions, but he sometimes indicated disapproval. Hazlitt, in the same number that carried Elia's second essay, wrote Table Talk No IV *On the Present State of Parliamentary Eloquence,* and accused Scott's old friend, Henry Brougham, of being a trimmer between all parties. A footnote ran: 'We must not be understood as at all participating in these sentiments; this may indeed be owing to our infirmity of judgment; and certainly, the general ability of the article tells against any difference of opinion.—Ed.'

The following month there was no Table Talk, and when No. V appeared in December, Hazlitt chose a safer topic, *On the Pleasures of Painting.*

Scott also adopted a more direct method than the footnote for addressing contributors and correspondents, turning the introductory notes into a feature called 'The Lion's Head'. Taking as his motto Shakespeare's description of Owen Glendower, 'Valiant as a lion, and wondrous affable', Scott declared his purpose in the July magazine:

> This article,—or rather this string of short affable roars, from the Lion's Head of the London Magazine,—will, for the future, occupy the first pages of each number; and Correspondents, and others who may be in expectation of any particular announcement, will do well to look amongst these for what may concern them. Any one, too, who may have committed a particularly good action, or a particularly bad one,—or said or written anything very

clever, or very stupid, during the month,—ought not, by any means, to neglect interrogating the Lion's Head.

An example followed of how he meant to proceed: 'Where did our Friendly Correspondent, who has dropped into our mouth some savoury morsels of Mr Maturin's Sermons (which we are digesting into an article) learn that we *"dislike* his Lordship"—Lord Byron to whit? . . . whose talents are not more certain to conquer admiration, than his manners are to excite attachment.'

Scott closed this new feature by saying: 'We are happy to be able to inform inquirers, that our "Living Authors" are not extinct: No. 3 of the series will appear next month.'

His choice of title for these notes to correspondents had a double significance. Scott used the clan badge of a heraldic lion's head as a bookplate and seal for letters. When Venice was an independent state the open-mouthed figures of two lions were used as post-boxes outside the Doge's Palace; anonymous accusers could drop into them charges of treason against their enemies.

In August 1820 John published another doleful poem. Completed two years before, it was prefaced: 'Lines written at a village amongst the mountains near Grenoble, after there reading the accounts given in the English newspapers of the Death of the Princess Charlotte of Wales, and of the Manifestations of the Public Feeling at that Event.' It occupied nearly three pages of the magazine, and cannot have done much to raise the spirits of readers, or circulation, since it contained many lines in the vein of

> The soul droops watching o'er the lingering grains
> That show how draggingly its sand-glass drains.

The London Magazine took the side of Charlotte's mother, Queen Caroline, when she returned from abroad and faced proceedings by the Government intended to convict her of adultery and enable her husband, now King George IV, to discard her and remarry. But Scott discussed the case with some distaste, and his views, while hostile to the King and ministers, were not likely to appeal to those radicals, and the London mob, who made a heroine of the indiscreet consort.

The third in the series of Living Authors, William Godwin, was not perhaps worthy of full-length treatment. But Godwin, a man who preached anarchy and practised middle-class virtues, had an important influence on young men at the time, and his novels were highly praised. Scott summed up:

> Mr Godwin . . . regards the passions as divided and determinate powers, and he puts them in action, as they try the ordnance at Woolwich, not from a desire to forward any certain plan of general operations, but to assay and

strain their own strength, the energy of their resistance, and of their violence. ... His instinct is that of the bloodhound; he will follow on one track with wonderful vigour, and a perseverance that might be termed remorseless; but except for the single scent which has excited him to the chase, he has neither observation nor sensibility.

One of Scott's happiest articles was a review of poems by Bernard Barton. It is not surprising one commentator tried to credit these remarks to Lamb:

> His muse may be said to possess a lovely Quaker countenance,—such as we have sometimes had the good fortune to see in stage coaches, and have invariably fallen in love with, whenever we have seen it. The eye sparkling, but quiet in self-possession and modesty; the delicate complexion reflecting health of body and mind; the regular features, ever undisturbed by wayward or lawless feelings;—such is a Quaker beauty; graceful in reserve,—holy as a nun, yet performing, or ready to perform her proper part in society; a Venus in a poke-bonnet, whose presence causes strangers to feel the authority and power of virtue, and to discipline their discourse, so as to pay homage to purity.

The editor gave his writers full play, even at his own expense. In the September issue Wainewright, as Janus Weathercock, wrote a piece addressed to 'Dear, respected, and respectable Editor!' saying an illustrated book on Paris and other French scenes by Captain Robert Batty 'though worse drawn and worse engraved than Nash's ... is nevertheless, I am afraid, a prettier book. Why this is I cannot tell—but so it is.'

Weathercock was not seen in the *London* for several months after this dismissal of the book on which Scott had collaborated with Frederick Nash. But his contributions had been intermittent for some time before. It must be admitted his artistic judgment was, as usual, correct. Batty's drawings were alive with people, whereas Nash's partook too much of architectural exercises, and Scott's accompanying text showed little of his descriptive power.

In the same issue Scott reviewed Keats' last book, *Lamia, Isabella, the Eve of Saint Agnes and other Poems*. The critic took exception to some stanzas of Keats which derided two brothers in *Isabella* because they were merchants. It was not often Scott showed any kinship with the class from which he came, but on this occasion he leapt to its defence. Probably his attitude was coloured by the knowledge his brother Alexander had returned to Aberdeen to grapple with the problems of the business on which his mother and sisters depended. Scott told Keats:

> A face cast up towards the moon does not more certainly infer an amiable or susceptible disposition, than a contracted brow cast down over a ledger of bad debts ... fainting away over a fair bosom does not, unless accompanied

by other symptoms, prove much more in favour of the refinement of the transported person than clasping a moneybag, or ogling a haunch of venison.

Scott complained of verses which sneered at ledgermen:

They are no better than extravagant school-boy vituperation of trade and traders; just as if lovers did not trade—and that, often in stolen goods—or had in general any higher object than a barter of enjoyment!... That most beautiful Paper (by a correspondent of course) in our last number, on the 'ledger-men' of the South Sea House, is an elegant reproof of such short-sighted views of character; such idle hostilities against the realities of life.

Scott went on to praise the poet's work, drawing special attention to *Ode to a Nightingale* which he called distinct, noble, pathetic and true.

In the last issue of 1820 Scott told his readers 'we have been lucky enough to make some most valuable acquisitions of Contributors'. Among them were Charles Macfarlane, who wrote from Naples, Reynolds, and Allan Cunningham. The latter's articles on alleged Traditional Literature surely owed their length to the editor's fondness for his native land. A contemporary justly described Cunningham as 'this very clever writer, whose grand sin is that he never knows when to have done'.

One of the new recruits provided a solution to John's biggest problem, the conflict between the amount of writing he was expected to do and the task of overseeing the contributions of others and checking proofs. Peter George Patmore offered to act as sub-editor and look after routine work. Patmore was friendly with Hazlitt, and rapidly became on intimate terms with Scott and his wife. He lent his mare to Caroline, and Scott wrote to his new coadjutor from his Covent Garden lodgings:

Fly is a little lame we think, but is not less a favourite with her mistress on that account. Will you breakfast with me ($\frac{1}{2}$ past 9) on Monday. I am only here for five minutes today.

I hope you wont come angry about Croly's article: I can now show you lots of communications from him—all tolerably good—& if you are to be sub-editor or acting editor—you will find him useful.

Patmore reviewed the Reverend George Croly's poem *Angel of the World* in the November *London*, and Scott apparently toned down his comments. 'What a passion some people have for *striking out*', Patmore had written to Scott.

A cryptic note from Patmore to John probably refers to some verses addressed to Caroline Scott: 'If on reading the accompanying lines you find them applicable to anyone whom you know, you will—if you think proper—give them to that person, from me:—If not, throw them in the fire—as they are not intended for the magazine.'

With Patmore taking on much of the hackwork, Scott promised to provide a series of monthly articles in the coming year under the title 'The

Travels and Opinions of Edgeworth Benson, Gentleman'. Drawing on material collected for his long deferred travel book, John said he would write about Venice, Naples, and other places he had visited.

In a letter dated 29 December, Scott renewed his correspondence with his eldest sister, Margaret, living as a widow at Kinross with two young daughters:

> My dear Margaret,
>   It is now a long time since I have written to you—so long that perhaps you will be more startled than pleased at the first glimpse of this Letter—It will be perhaps like a face, once familiar, but for years estranged, which when it first appears again excites surprise & painful memory, before the other more genial feelings can have got into exercise. However, by degrees you must relapse into all your old disposition relative to my epistles—& think of them with nothing but kindness, & as proofs of an affection that neither time nor worldly collision can efface. I cannot write you a long letter even now, when at length I have set about it,—for I wish you to receive it on the New Year's Day, that I may have some benefit from the association of season with my hand-writing.

Margaret had continued to write to John's wife, and he had heard 'your young ladies . . . thrive in worldly wisdom'. Scott went on:

> All anecdotes of yourself, and little promising charges, which are suffered to transpire from certain mysterious letters which Caroline from time to time receives, I hear with the greatest interest. I hope you have made them aware that the Editor of a Magazine, has neither horn nor tail, nor anything to distinguish him unfavourably from other men, or to hinder him from claiming a share in their good graces, as an Uncle. Remember me most affectionately to them. I am alone in town, having just closed my month's work—so have no loves to send from anybody—which is lucky as my sheet will hold no more.

Margaret's young ladies grew into a pair of pert belles, to judge from a highly coloured portrait of them that survives.

Chapter 8

COCKNEYS *VERSUS* BLACKWOODSMEN

The London Magazine and its editor plunged into 1821 with renewed vigour. When Horace Smith encountered Scott he told him: 'How healthy and how happy you looked when I met you yesterday, riding with your wife.' He received the reply: 'And well I might, for I consider a man, when mounted on a good horse, and riding with such a wife as mine, to be as near to Heaven as the conditions of humanity will allow.'

A note from Smith to York Street about the magazine said: 'Hill tells me you have risen 5,000 this month, which with the usual division by 50 & deduction from the product for oriental exaggeration still leaves a very satisfactory increase.'

The Lion's Head had bantering words for correspondents and readers in the January issue. Replying to *Medicus*, Scott wrote: 'We have taken a vast deal of physic in our time. . . . We have been active and passive—objects and subjects—in medicine. The result is, that we profess, what we really entertain, much esteem for Doctors, and an earnest wish to be kept out of their hands.'

With a touch of Wainewright coxcombry, he gave a glimpse of himself at work, contemplating a review of *Melmoth the Wanderer*, by Charles Robert Maturin:

> We have this extraordinary and striking novel, of which we might say much, now before us:—the time evening; the scene our study, the lamp well-trimmed, and the fire comfortable. A quire of long paper, and a bundle of mended pens, tempt us with a look of preparation:—Nothing to interrupt us between this and two hours past midnight—up to which time we know we can rely on our eye-lids retaining their rigidity. . . . It is just such a subject as we want for a good article: and a good article we shall certainly write upon it—but as the devil's in it—(we mean the novel; he is the chief agent) we cannot do it *now*: it would take six pages, and our remaining space will scarcely suffice—(so says a note just received from the printing office) for

articles that must appear *'to keep the symmetry of the number—'* The symmetry of the Number! there is no resisting that phrase. There are papers just before which we would willingly take out,—but that would be losing time, says the printer: and the printer is despotic in the Magazine. The editor is only his prime minister; the publishers his secretaries of state.

But there were other articles from his pen in the issue. They included a continuation of the 'Living Authors', in which he turned to the man who both attracted and repelled him as the city of Paris did. Scott's article began:

> Lord Byron's compositions do not entitle him to be called the best of our present poets; but his personal character and the history of his life have clearly rendered him the most interesting and remarkable of the persons who now write poetry. If he is not, as we have said of another, 'the author we would most wish to be', he is certainly the living author who is chiefly 'the marvel and the show' of our day and generation.

He went on to poke fun at Byron's love of tragic posing. Quoting the lines

> Seared in heart, and, lone, and blighted—
> More than this, *I scarce can die*

Scott commented:

> Thus concludes Lord Byron's Farewell, on the occasion of his leaving England, and we have had good reason since to admire the strength of the vivacious principle in his breast. His subsequent productions have seemed to intimate that dying was as far from his own thoughts, as his death is far from the wishes of book-sellers and book-readers, and the admirers of genius.

In view of his own role in leading press attacks on the poet over the separation from his wife, Scott showed disingenuousness in continuing:

> It was a foolish and very wrong thing to write the Farewell; and not a well-judged thing to write the Sketch from private life: but it was also foolish, and wrong in the public to raise such an outcry in a matter that would not at all have concerned them, but for those unlucky publications, and which they made much more of than even these publications warranted.—To say the truth, then, we long to see Lord Byron once more amongst us. . . . That he is beloved as a friend we know; that he is generous, or rather magnificent, in his temper; hospitable and kind when occasion serves; frank to forgive causes of offence,—we also know.

In discussing Byron's attitude to his heroines, Scott put a finger on why the poet's marriage ended in disaster, while his own, in spite of setbacks and tragedy, endured:

> His females are fair and pellucid formations, without distinct features or definite properties. The female character is reduced in them to a certain

intense power of communicating delight to man, and awakening enthusiasm in his breast:—they love, dazzle, and die. . . .

But we do not look in Lord Byron's poetry for traces of that tenderness of soul, which has its depth in reason and will; that concession of self, which has its value in worth and weight of character; that full companionship, and closely and entirely associated sympathy, which give importance and solemnity to the union of the sexes, at the same time increasing its zest.

There was lyrical power in the way Scott summed up Byron's place among his contemporaries:

We have living poets—several—whose contemplation is more intense,—whose passion is more exclusively poetical,—whose language is more pure, and expedients more select; but none whose spirit is so active, or range of sensitivity so wide. He spreads himself out over nature, and history, like a bird of prey; the storm does not beat down his wings, and he sails in the calm sunshine without fainting.

Giving a new twist to the expression the Lake School, used to describe Wordsworth and his friends, John continued: 'The best specimens of poetry which the present day has produced, lie deep and clear like lakes: Byron's verse rushes like a mountain river through many realms . . . often shallow, sometimes showing dry bald spots; but usually rushing forward with vehement impetuosity.'

Not many fellow-critics saw Byron plain as Scott did.

Charles Lamb opened the January number with an Elia essay, *New Year's Eve*, but he was quick to acknowledge the main feature in the issue was the first in the promised series on *The Travels and Opinions of Edgeworth Benson*. Writing to Baldwin to thank him for payment for 'my little labours', Lamb said: 'Our last No. was strong. Edgeworth Benson is a great accession.'

This article was principally about Venice, and the choice of pen-name perhaps reflected John's admiration for the Irish authoress Maria Edgeworth, and for the Countess Bensone, whom he met while visiting Byron. Scott referred to her as: 'A lady at whose palace is held the most agreeable and respectable conversaziones of that city, and whose person, though she is now between sixty and seventy, still justifies the sweet and well-known Venetian ballad,

La Biondina in gondoletta, etc

which was, we understand, suggested by her charms and written by one of her admirers.'

In the second instalment of his Benson series in February, Scott described a very different woman, whom he met while travelling by mailboat from Venice to Ferrara:

Not the least talkative, nor the least agreeable member of our society, which had eight-and-forty hours' existence, was a corpulent and itinerant *prima donna,* whose husband held a poor place in the police at Bologna, while she travelled Italy over, making much money at its theatres, attended by a hump-backed maid servant, whose Bolognese jargon drew almost constant peals of laughter from the other Italians. The years of the mistress only numbered twenty-seven; but she had flesh for forty, and experience enough for any age. ... I never saw such examples of full animal spirits, overpowering health, enjoyment of the air of life,—which they respired, with a zest, as if it tickled their nerves and circulated cordially round their hearts. Nothing did, or could, come amiss to them,—for they meant no evil, and saw none . . . if there was one thing more remarkable than another, in the singer, it was the warmth and volubility of her domestic affections. She talked vehemently, of the approaching meeting with her *poor* husband, as she called him, while tears of joy and eagerness stood in her eyes, and her face was suffused with the genuine glow of her spirit. No secret was made, either by her, or her servant, of the latitude, as to fidelity, which she deemed warranted to travellers like herself; but she always had been, and always would be, she said, scrupulously punctual to visit her *povero,* at least once a year!

In the same issue John returned, after several years, to dramatic criticism, having attended the first night at Covent Garden of *Mirandola,* by Bryan Procter. The evening led to reconciliation with Haydon after the break over the artist's *Jerusalem* painting. Haydon recorded the scene: 'We both came into the orchestra box and were alone the whole evening: we shook hands distantly.' Perhaps Procter, who was the friend of both men, engineered this meeting.

In his review Scott praised the author highly, but pointed out he owed much to the acting of young William Macready and veteran Charles Kemble. 'The writer of this notice is not in the frequent habit of going to the theatre—his department in the Magazine being that of the essays and fracas,' he said.

It was clear from Scott's burst of original contributions to the *London* he was taking full advantage of Patmore's assistance. Patmore, son of a successful Ludgate Hill jeweller, is best known for becoming the father of poet Coventry Patmore. At this time he was young, and foolish to judge from his letters and his articles. Being an only child he was spoilt, and had the reputation of being a dandy.

Thomas Noon Talfourd had also been recruited. A law student about to be called to the bar, Talfourd eventually became a judge and was knighted. As a schoolboy he had contributed to *The Statesman,* after Scott ceased to be editor, and later wrote for *The Champion* while John was abroad. Talfourd got to know Charles Lamb, and late in 1820 the essayist asked Scott to consider him as a contributor.

On 9 December 1820 Scott wrote to Talfourd from what was then Kew

Lane, Mortlake, where he and his family had moved to a house called Brickstables. It has since been renamed West Lodge, and the lane Kew Meadow Path. Evidently the editor's distaste for political controversy had reached the stage where he wished someone else to take on that department of the magazine, for he told the young lawyer:

> We shall be very happy to commence with the Political Summary on the terms of fifteen Guineas,—the article to be understood as not exceeding beyond eight pages per month—You will not, however, I hope, think me wrong in just mentioning that, as the plan is altogether a new one, the political summary being in general regarded as distinct from the original Papers of a Magazine—we should wish to have the engagement considered in the first instance as an *experiment*.

Early the next year Talfourd called on Scott at breakfast in his York Street lodgings. The lawyer later wrote of Scott that he was 'a perfect model of an editor', and said he found him 'amidst the luxurious confusion of newspapers, reviews and uncut novels, laying in fascinating litter . . . as the editor carelessly enunciated schemes for bright successions of essays, he seemed destined for many years of that happy excitement in which thought perpetually glows in unruffled but energetic language'.

In spite of Talfourd's respectful approach, he did not take over the political column. His first appearance in the magazine was an article on 'Pulpit Oratory' in February 1821. Scott himself wrote on politics in the number, setting out to defend his moderate views against the radicals. They cannot have been pleased by such cautious remarks as 'we dare not affirm that we know exactly what we ought to recommend', and 'Politics, at the best, are but a necessary evil; absolutely necessary, but still an evil'.

As when he edited *The Champion*, Scott found literary success was not matched by financial reward; circulation was well below 2000 a month, far less than *Blackwood's*. There was the nagging presence of the other *London*, published by Gold in Covent Garden close to Scott's lodgings. This poked fun at its rival with an account of a dinner party said to have been given by Baldwin, Cradock, and Joy for Scott and contributors to their magazine on 3 February. Among more heavy-handed thrusts this commented, 'Glass circulates—thousand pities the Magazine does not circulate as well.' It was no consolation to Baldwin's men to know Gold's magazine sold even fewer copies than their own.

A more formidable contender appeared when publisher Henry Colburn, owner of the *New Monthly Magazine* relaunched it in 1821 with poet Thomas Campbell as editor, assisted by an experienced journalist, Cyrus Redding. But it was the defects of *The London* itself, rather than competition, which depressed sales. In spite of the Elia essays—Lamb's February contribution was *Mrs Battle's Opinions on Whist*,—there was truth in Horace Smith's remark to the editor: 'People say you are too serious—or rather (for there is a great deal of difference in the meaning of the phrase), they say *you are not sufficiently merry.*' Unfortunately his solution was to provide a comic poem entitled *Miller Redivivus* of unrelieved insipidity. But Smith indicated a deeper problem in writing to Scott: 'When I look at the Mag I pity you for what you have to write, but in looking at this long scrawl & its enclosures I pity you for what you must have to *read* every month.'

Until Patmore came to his assistance, Scott had been overworked and inevitably his own articles in the first year were uneven in quality. His attempt to reflect the best in European literature often degenerated into translations of dull stories. Commuting between Caroline and the children at Mortlake and his duties in London was a drain on his strength and temper.

Scott reacted to the situation as he had in the past when faced with sluggish circulation and too much space to fill: he fired off attacks on his rivals. From the early days of the *London* he continued his unpleasant sneers at Leigh Hunt. Later he derided Byron's friend, Hobhouse (he may have heard of the latter's attempt to influence John Murray against him while he was touring Italy). Scott also delivered a stinging rebuke to J W Croker, accusing him of cold-blooded dishonesty in writing on Keats in *The Quarterly Review*. This was a little ironical since Scott himself handled the young poet roughly on more than one occasion. But he always stressed the great beauty of much of his work and the glorious future for Keats if freed from the unfortunate influence of Leigh Hunt. Keats himself came to think harshly of his early mentor. It is possible both Keats and Scott had their opinion of Hunt coloured by Haydon, who turned against his old friend as he at times turned against Keats and Scott.

But the wrath of the *London* editor was directed mainly at *Blackwood's Magazine* and the men he believed to be its editors, John Gibson Lockhart and John Wilson. In addition he attacked Sir Walter Scott for his equivocal attitude to the excesses of the Edinburgh publication and his failure to dissociate himself from it publicly when his connection with Lockhart and Wilson, the men he had described as its conductors, was well known. Lockhart married Sir Walter's elder daughter early in 1820.

There were many strands to what became the most notorious literary squabble of a quarrelsome age. It was complicated by the custom of writers using a pseudonym, or several pseudonyms, while discreetly letting their friends know they were responsible for the witty, brilliant articles in such-and-such a magazine.

In *Blackwood's* Lockhart appeared variously as Baron von Lauerwinkel, William Wastle, Z, and Dr Peter Morris, whose articles were later enlarged into a book about Edinburgh, Glasgow and their leading citizens called

Peter's Letters to his Kinsfolk. Wilson masqueraded as Christopher North, the mythical editor of the magazine, and wrote articles both in praise and abuse of Wordsworth. He also ridiculed Samuel Taylor Coleridge, later welcomed as a contributor. In times of trouble all the paper tigers sheltered behind the proprietor, William Blackwood, who apologised and paid damages if the victims could not be pacified in any other way.

Occasionally Blackwood's writers were themselves victims of mistaken identity. William Maginn assailed the essays of Elia, calling him a Cockney scribbler, but wrote later, 'I have since learned, with unaffected pain, that they were written by Mr Lamb, a gentleman whose avowed writings I have always perused with the utmost pleasure.' He concluded lamely that the author had been contaminated by appearing in *The London Magazine* with Hazlitt and other deplorable men.

It could be argued Hazlitt and Coleridge laid themselves open to attack through their own outbursts against former associates, although calling the essayist 'pimpled Hazlitt', as Lockhart did, and describing Coleridge as a 'child blubbing for the moon', in Wilson's words, plumbed new depths. Even less excusable were the scorn poured on Keats and Wordsworth, and attempts to question the scholarship of eminent Edinburgh academics.

Such articles formed only a small part of the contents of *Blackwood's*. Others were serious in tone and some, especially those by Wilson, were broadly humorous and described feats of eating and drinking by himself and his friends. Wainewright summed these up neatly in the *London* as 'slang and whisky'. But it was the sensational contributions that made *Maga* notorious and prosperous.

Sir Walter Scott remonstrated with both Blackwood and Lockhart in private. But his letters make it plain his principal worries were that Lockhart might be drawn into a duel by his writings, and that some items were offensive to his own friends and people he met in society. Nor did Blackwood hesitate to point out Sir Walter was a contributor to his magazine when its integrity was questioned. There is no indication the baronet felt any sympathy for writers he regarded as radicals who became targets for *Maga*'s scurrility. That it was scurrilous can be judged from the fact that Baldwin, Cradock and Joy, who had been its London agents, withdrew after receiving complaints about its contents. John Murray did the same, after briefly joining Blackwood as publisher of the magazine, although he himself owned *The Quarterly Review,* an outspoken Tory publication.

The worst vendetta, and one which involved John Scott indirectly, was that conducted by Lockhart, writing as Z, against Leigh Hunt. Ostensibly discussing the poem *Rimini*, Lockhart deplored Hunt's ignorance of Greek and German, which he himself had studied. He followed up by calling him a man of low birth and low habits, the chief doctor and professor of the

Cockney School of Poetry: 'With him indecency is a disease and he speaks unclean things in perfect inanition. The very concubine of so impure a wretch as Leigh Hunt would be to be pitied, but alas! for the wife of such a husband!' It is clear that in the eyes of *Blackwood's* Leigh Hunt's real crime, apart from his radical views, was that *Rimini* was popular; Lockhart complained of the 'success with which his influence seems to be extending itself among a pretty numerous, though certainly a very paltry and pitiful set of readers'. Both Lockhart and Wilson were minor poets—minor even in comparison with Leigh Hunt.

When he read this and a second attack John Hunt, without consulting his brother, published a paragraph in their newspaper inviting Z 'to send his address to the Printer of the *Examiner*, in order that justice may be executed on the proper person'. Leigh Hunt later claimed the intention was to challenge the writer to a duel. But the reference to justice sounded more like an action for libel. Lockhart and Blackwood decided to lay down a smokescreen. Blackwood wrote to his London agents at the time, Robert Baldwin and partners, claiming he was unable to control his editor, who had received the objectionable article from a London writer.

The affair was allowed to rest with Leigh Hunt in *The Examiner* calling Z a liar and a coward, while Lockhart in *Blackwood's* threatened uneasily to come forward, but in fact turned his pen against Keats. How the rumour arose that John Scott, who was abroad at the time, had been responsible for Z's attacks is not clear. Keats told his brother, Tom, that Hunt believed it was almost certain Scott had written the articles on the so-called Cockney School. Hunt had good reason to distrust John after his attacks on himself at the time of the Byron affair, but there may have been some genuine confusion, for he also suspected Sir Walter Scott of being involved.

Suggestions John was the hidden libeller presumably led Keats to write to his friend Benjamin Bailey: 'I dont mind the thing much—but if he should go to such lengths with me as he has done with Hunt I must infallibly call him to an account—if he be a human being and appears in Squares and Theatres where we might possibly meet.' The idea of Keats fighting a duel with a critic seems absurd, but when he died his books were found to include *Fencing Familiarized*.

John Scott had other reasons for disliking *Blackwood's*. It attacked many of his friends, including Haydon, Moore, Brougham, and Sir James Mackintosh. One article sneered:

> Sir James has really lived quite long enough upon the remembered sweet sayings of Madame de Staël and the eternal advertisement of that eternal work, his history of Great Britain.

This was a projected book Mackintosh never completed. The offensive nature of the piece can be judged from a couplet running:

> His gait is a shuffle, his smile is a lear,
> His converse is quaint, his civility queer.

The author of this squib was believed to be John Wilson, who in 1820 became Professor of Moral Philosophy at the University of Edinburgh. It was a post Sir James would have liked himself, but most people assumed it would go to Sir William Hamilton, eminently qualified to take the vacant chair. Wilson was chosen by the city council, and his largely political campaign was handled by that skilful lobbyist, Sir Walter Scott, who thought the responsibility of office would wean his friend from reckless writing in *Blackwood's*. However, Wilson remained the mainstay of the magazine, although he also became a popular professor.

Another target for running gags by Wilson in his role of Christopher North was John Scott's new colleague, Patmore, referred to as Cockney Tims, 'he of Ludgate Hill'. Patmore had been a contributor to *Blackwood's*, and on one occasion received a letter signed 'The Editor of Blackwood's Edin. Magazine' which hinted he might like to pass on information about some of his London friends. He ignored this suggestion, but wrote on the drama for the magazine, and gave an account of a series of lectures by Hazlitt. When he wrote for the *London* he was dropped by the Blackwoodsmen.

Scott himself had been mildly satirised in a piece of doggerel written by Lockhart as William Wastle. Entitled *The Mad Banker of Amsterdam* it contained a description of a canal journey reminiscent of Scott's own voyage through the Low Countries on his way to Brussels, and his complaints of poor service at his hotel there. Wastle described him as

> A lean Scots scribe, the type of craft and care,
> Very much sneezed at everywhere by waiters,
> A native of the town of Aberdeen
> With two light goggling eyes 'twixt grey and green.

Lockhart may have been ruffled by unfavourable comparisons drawn between Walter Scott's book on his visit to France and those written by John.

During the early months of *The London Magazine* both Scott and Hazlitt exchanged some barbed banter with *Blackwood's*. Scott referred to its 'merry ruffianism' in attacking Keats, and to the 'comfortable chair' of the new professor of moral philosophy.

The response from Edinburgh was mild, but well-calculated to irritate Scott. Christopher North assured his rival editor, 'We are absolutely coining money . . . we find that as editor and contributor, we nett about £6,000 per annum.' He went on to claim *Blackwood's* circulation was 17,000 copies a month, and the *London's* only 1100. Comparing various magazines to coaches plying for hire, Wilson wrote: 'Gold and

Northhouse, we hear, are making money, and they deserve it—their vehicle is a little too jaunty, and panels too highly varnished—but it trundles along very easy—the cattle show more blood, and the drivers are quiet, civil, and obliging. Of Baldwin's new bang-up concern, we, at present, just civilly ask the Jehu, John Scott, to keep his own side of the road—not to be so fond of running races—and not to abuse passengers who prefer going by another conveyance.'

Wilson was always careful to see his name was not brought before the public, however he might revel in private in his reputation as Christopher North. It was bad manners on his part to name John Scott as occupying the driving seat on *The London*. Scott made little secret in literary circles of his connection with the magazine, but it was a different matter to be identified in print, and thus made the target for anyone who might seek him with a cudgel or a writ.

In the November issue of the *London* he hit back in a twelve-page article headed 'Blackwood's Magazine: They do but jest—poison in jest—no offence i' the world!' Its length, and perhaps part of its content, owed something to Hazlitt. He did not contribute a Table Talk to the issue, and failed to deliver his expected drama review. This left Scott with much space to fill in a number already short of articles of real weight—his own leading contribution was a nostalgic piece on books for children.

In attacking the Edinburgh publication he took a high tone, while sometimes descending to the kind of language the nameless Blackwoodsmen used themselves:

> Here we have two men, whose habits of life are notoriously free—not to use a stronger word—and whose real opinions are known to be loose and sceptical,—starting a publication, in which, systematically and of aforethought, the most licentious personal abuse was to be the lure for one class of readers, and the veriest hypocritical whine, on matters of religion and politics, the bait for another;—in which the violation of decency was to render it *piquant*, and the affectation of piety render it persuasive, and servility to power render it profitable;—which should be made to circulate amongst the spiteful and ill-tempered with its venom; amongst the interested by its baseness; amongst the simple by its cant and quackery! It is in furtherance of this honourable obsequy that they have assumed the externals of harlequinade and buffoonery; that false names have been taken; false recommendations and characters forged.

Having dealt severely with the pseudonymous Peter Morris and Christopher North, Scott went on to involve his namesake:

> Sir Walter Scott, during his last visit to London, had spoken freely of the improprieties of the magazine in question—coupling his disapprobation with something very like an assurance that its cause would for the future be removed—we very gladly and frankly accepted his testimony as valid,

knowing that his opportunities of acquiring information on this subject were as excellent as, in our view at least, his interest in ascertaining the fact was strong....

Amongst the many sterling claims to public attention, and legitimate means of exciting public interest, which Sir Walter Scott possesses, he is pleased (supposing him to be the author of the Scotch Novels) to employ one of a less valid kind—namely *mystery as to the authorship*. The question remains a perpetual puzzle; and in some respects it may be said to become more puzzling in proportion as it seems more certain who the writer really is.

He went on to suggest that Sir Walter's cloak of mystery led to imitation by less worthy pens, citing the novelist's account of his Continental travels *Paul's Letters to his Kinsfolk* having formed the model for *Peter's Letters to his Kinsfolk*. This book, published in 1819 and purporting to be impressions of Scotland and its residents by a visiting Welshman, was written principally by Lockhart as Peter Morris. John Scott described it as prying into private life and 'the most notorious and profligate example of this felon conspiracy against the dignity of literature, and the order and peace of society', adding it was a work which mingled fabrication with facts.

Much of the book was only mildly malicious, and part of it contained disingenuous apologies for *Blackwood's* sins; Dr Morris spoke of repentance for gross outrages, dwelling particularly on articles written by Wilson and Maginn. When it came to his own vulgar abuse of Leigh Hunt, and to the slighting references to Hazlitt, he gloried in them, calling 'The Cockney School' a 'conceited knot of superficial coxcombs' and boasted these criticisms had succeeded in 'entirely silencing their penny trumpets of sedition and blasphemy—to say nothing of their worthless poetry . . . they cannot possibly last twenty years in the recollection even of the Cockneys'. Once again it was clear that what raised Lockhart's almost hysterical rage was the Cockneys' success as well as their politics.

In his book Lockhart passed comments on religion, suggesting the Secession church had dissented from the established Presbyterians on very trivial grounds. He pointed out not only had the Seceders split into Burghers and Anti-Burghers, but the latter had then divided into Old Light Anti-Burghers and New Light Anti-Burghers. In Edinburgh the Old Light were led by Dr Thomas McCrie, and the New Light by the now elderly Dr Jamieson, the minister who reproved John Scott as a youth for not visiting Scone. Lockhart wrote: 'Nothing surely can be more absurd than that two such clergymen should be lending support to two such pitiable sets of schismatics,' and spoke of 'these little Lilliputian controversies about burgess oaths'.

However merited such comments were, they must have grated on Scott with his memories of the pious faith of his parents, and the clergymen who married his sisters. Dr Jamieson and Jane Scott's husband, Dr Robert

Balmer, were instrumental in reuniting the Burghers and Anti-Burghers in 1820.

In his *London* article John passed on to question Sir Walter's role in helping John Wilson obtain his professorship:

> It would scarcely be too much to say, that Sir Walter has, to a certain extent identified himself with these men, and their scandalous publication, by the excessive zeal of his late endeavours to secure for one of them an appointment of momentous trust and honourable name. . . . The election of a Professor to the Metropolitan University of Scotland, was an affair in which the interference of Sir Walter Scott could not but be highly important, both to himself and the public. He is not a common man, and, the occasion was not a common one. That it was not so esteemed, may be inferred from the fact, that the vacant chair was respectfully tendered to Sir James Mackintosh. . . . But the University of Edinburgh has not been so lucky;—instead of the late Chief Justice at Bombay, at present a member of the British Parliament, it has added to its Academical strength—Whom?—one of Blackwood's Men—a co-editor of a slanderous periodical work!

John pursued the quarrel in the December issue, attacking 'The Mohock Magazine', and naming John Gibson Lockhart (Scott spelt the name Lockart) the Emperor of the Mohocks. Scott declared:

> We do most seriously and sincerely declare, that we have been induced to write these articles solely by the indignation rising and swelling in our minds at the still-renewed spectacle of outrage, hypocrisy, and fraud, which the succeeding numbers of Mr Blackwood's Publication present. Long impunity, or, at least, insufficient exposure, from whatever cause proceeding, has at length converted what was at first but a system of provocation into a downright *system of terror*. We know for a fact, and dare contradiction, that Blackwood has openly vaunted of holding to grateful behaviour an individual who has been first *abused*, and then *defended* by the *same writer* in his Magazine: *If he is not duly respectful, we have more for him from the same hand!*

In this broadside Scott referred to Dr Morris as the principal editor of Blackwood's assuming wrongly that Wilson had withdrawn on becoming a professor. This was one of the traps set by the multiplicity of aliases used by the Edinburgh writers. Scott may have relied too much on information from Patmore on his dealings with William Blackwood, and on gossip from booksellers who regarded the magazine with distaste. Perhaps he also discussed matters with Allan Cunningham who had been a *Blackwood's* contributor before joining the *London*, and met Sir Walter in London in 1820.

John Scott made another attempt to get his namesake to disown publicly the excesses of his son-in-law, contrasting his reticence with John Murray's decision to give up partnership in the magazine in 1819:

Mr Murray acted on this occasion with the promptitude of one who sets store by his character, and sees it endangered;—yet, while we cannot but congratulate him on his decision, we own we shall be mortified by it, if it turn out that Sir Walter Scott has no such sensibility on the subject! This eminent individual is *known* to have written some things for the Magazine in question; he is *suspected* to have written others: It is certain that several offensive articles have been composed under his own roof; and the nuisance has now become too deadly to allow of any delicacy towards its aiders or abettors. Mr Murray, as we have seen, thought it due to his character to *extricate* himself from all connection with Blackwood's Magazine: we shall be happy to have the Baronet's *disavowal* of any such connection.

John Wilson was attacked by name as the man who ridiculed Wordsworth. Scott pointed out he had then had the effrontery to apply to the poet for a reference in his canvass to become a professor.

But the *London* editor was particularly severe in his remarks on the treatment of Coleridge, prompted by regret at the philosopher's decision to contribute to *Blackwood's* rather than his own magazine. In fact Coleridge, then living in seclusion in Highgate in an attempt to give up opium, produced very little of substance. Lockhart was cynical about the value of this work, writing to Blackwood: 'Coleridge is evidently mad and unintelligible, but I venture to say you will never repent giving him sixteen pages a month. There will always be thoughts and expressions of the most inimitable beauty—quite enough to interest all men of literature.'

In September 1820 *Blackwood's* published an article by Coleridge headed 'Letter to Peter Morris, M.D. on the Sorts and Uses of Literary Praise'. Lockhart, in his role of mysterious Welshman, wrote a flippant introduction which hinted it was a private letter to himself. This play-acting rebounded, for he was pained to discover John Scott had taken him at his word and accused him of abusing a confidence.

Scott wrote: 'This letter, contrary to the usage of gentlemen, he has published in his Magazine, without the writer's consent, and, as we have reason to know, *very much to the writer's displeasure.*' Scott described it as the unauthorised publication of a private letter and went on: 'No man who reads that letter can avoid perceiving that it is as unfit to be given to the public eye as any letter can be. We can take upon ourselves to state that he disclaims having ever authorized or contemplated its publication.'

Coleridge's friends and relatives were upset because the letter contained a thinly-disguised attack on Wordsworth. Professor David V Erdman, who has made a close study of Coleridge as a journalist, has pointed out an unwitting Charles Lamb probably misled Scott over this affair. When Lockhart wrote Coleridge a letter signed as coming from the Editor of *Blackwood's Magazine* and demanding an explanation of his apparent repudiation of the contribution, the reply was of such a nature that it is kind to remember Coleridge was then in decline, struggling to support himself and his scattered family.

Coleridge wrote:

> Some weeks after appearance of my Letter to you, I heard that both my Sons had been vexed and distressed at the circumstances, on the ground that so many persons would know that it alluded in part to Wordsworth—that it would widen the breach or rather convert a coolness into a break—but chiefly that it was distressing to them & still more their Mother and Sister at Keswick.—I was vexed myself at the circumstance, sorely vexed; but *only with myself*. Not you—how could I? but myself I did blame inwardly for sending off a letter in the first sketch, written in the first warmth of feeling. I recollect *some* visitor, I think it must have been Lamb, but I cannot distinctly recollect, spoke of it with strong expressions of regret, adding—You could never have meant it for the Public Eye, I am sure—or to that purpose. I answered, or muttered rather, impatiently—a foolish vexatious business. . . . But as to telling anyone that it was a *confidential Letter to a Friend*—What nonsense a man may choose to *infer*, I cannot say—but that it should have been said by me, or fairly inferable from my words, is out of the Question.

Even if Coleridge was entirely honest in recollecting what he said, Lamb would have been justified in indicating to his editor the poet denied writing the attack on Wordsworth for publication.

It was unfortunate the issue of *The London* which contained Scott's indignant defence of Coleridge also carried sneering remarks on the same man by Hazlitt. He wrote that Coleridge 'is the man of all others to swim on empty bladders in a sea, without shore or soundings: to drive an empty stage-coach without passengers or lading, and arrive behind his time; to write marginal notes without a text'. He concluded with a spoof account of Coleridge talking away at the theatre till players and audience had gone. It was doubly unfortunate that Coleridge noticed this piece of satire when Lamb showed him the magazine.

John had particular reason to be sensitive at that time about the use of private letters in public controversy; he himself was the victim of the quarrel over Pope between his contributor, Octavius Gilchrist, and the Reverend William Lisle Bowles, who was an honorary canon of Salisbury Cathedral, as well as a country parson.

Wordy pamphlets were published by Bowles, in which he sneered at his opponent as a tradesman, and by Gilchrist, who wrote to his friend at Mortlake commiserating on his misfortune in 'being wedged between the Prebend of Sarum and the Grocer of Stamford in their controversy'. Scott became involved after he was introduced to the clergyman by Thomas Moore. When Bowles complained of the attack on himself in *The London Magazine* early in 1820 written anonymously by Gilchrist, John told him such an unsigned article would not have been admitted had he not been dangerously ill at the time, and unable to attend to his editorial duties. Bowles referred to this admission in one of his pamphlets, and then apologised for the use of Scott's name, promising to be more circumspect in his next pamphlet.

This drew from Scott on 3 January 1821 a letter telling him:

> I am obliged to you for the expression of your readiness to word your contemplated rejoinder to Mr Gilchrist '*as nearly as possible in conformity to my wishes*'.—My wish originally would have been that my name should not have appeared before the public in consequence of my private letters to you;—or as editor of the London Magazine, which I have never publicly acknowledged myself to be:—but that wish being no longer of any avail, I must beg to leave it entirely to yourself what further use you may be pleased to make of my letters, conceiving it would be indecorous in me to attempt interfering with your sense of propriety, and responsibility as a gentleman, in regard to private, and I may say, *confidential* correspondence.

Scott's accusation that 'Dr Morris' had acted 'contrary to the usage of gentlemen' and even stronger terms scattered through his December article amounted to fighting talk in an age of hasty duels. In a note to Patmore, which was undated but apparently written at this time, Scott asked: '*If Lockhart & I go out, will you accompany me?*' Young Patmore was not a good choice as a second but Scott, unlike Byron, did not mix with men skilled in resolving such delicate affairs. However, there was no immediate challenge from Edinburgh.

The *London* attacks had come at an embarrassing time for Blackwood and his men. Lockhart's wife was expecting their first child, and was seriously ill. Wilson was in the early months of his duties as professor of moral philosophy. Sir Walter Scott could not have relished being drawn into the kind of trouble against which he had warned Lockhart. The expenses of his new honour as a baronet, and of launching his elder son on an army career, in addition to expanding his house and estate at Abbotsford led him to write too many novels too fast. *The London Magazine*, while still praising his talents, noted a falling off in standards; Sir Walter's affairs were already showing signs of the ruin which overtook him six years later.

John Scott concluded he had silenced his northern rivals, and in the first issue of his magazine in 1821 boasted, in terms worthy of G K Chesterton, of his victory over those 'who made a common joke of common honesty'. He also derided their use of 'Cockney' to abuse writers they did not like. Pointing out that, in spite of his birthplace, he had himself been called an unfortunate Cockney, Scott wrote:

> Our ELIA too—the pride of *our* Magazine, and *the object of praise of theirs under his real name*—he is set down as a 'Cockney scribbler!' This gentleman, in his capacity of acknowledged author, they have never mentioned but to

eulogize; as, indeed, who does not eulogize his writings for displaying a spirit of deep and warm humanity, enlivened by a vein of poignant wit,—not caustic, yet searching,—and recommending a shrewdness of judgment on men, books, and things.

Scott gave his own sly definition of the term:

Cockneys in general, are little men; but they are smart, clever, and active; quick observers, and wonderfully occupied with whatever is going on about them. They observe every thing, however, with an immediate and exclusive reference to themselves: being born and bred up in the metropolis renders each, in his own estimation, a member of a privileged class, and all novelties and varieties from their habits, are set down by them as singular exceptions, remarkable occurrences, things to be entered in their journals. They themselves constitute a standard, in their own estimation; and hence they are always measuring other people by themselves. If taller, they are giants; if shorter, dwarfs. Cockneys are thus unpleasantly pert in their manner, without meaning to be offensive.

The onslaught on Lockhart and Wilson, and the implication of Sir Walter Scott, reflected genuine indignation at their activities and attempts to talk down to the Londoners. But John also hoped to cripple a successful rival and bring his own magazine into public notice. His finances were, as ever, parlous, and a draft letter among his correspondence shows he was having to ask creditors to be patient a little longer.

He received encouragement from his friends in the course he was pursuing. A note from Hazlitt urged: 'Dont hold out your hand to the Blackwood's yet, after having knocked those blackguards down.' Gilchrist wrote from Stamford on 11 January saying: 'I did expect to have something from you here on yesterday's coach relating to kill or to be killed,—for the world cannot tolerate a quarter of a dozen such fierce fellows as Baldwin's and Blackwood's men at once on her surface.'

Keats' friend Charles Brown wrote to the poet, dying of consumption in Rome: 'I know you dont like John Scott, but he is doing a thing that tickles me to the heart's core, and you will like to hear of it, if you have any revenge in your composition. By some means (crooked enough I daresay) he has got possession of one of Blackwood's gang, who has turned King's evidence, and month after month he belabours them with the most damning facts that can be conceived;—if they are indeed facts, I know not how the rogues can stand up against them.'

Unhappily for Scott they were not all facts. He had assumed Christopher North was one of Lockhart's many disguises when in fact the name was used by Wilson. Nor was he aware some of the worst excesses were committed by William Maginn. Scott voiced his suspicion Sir Walter Scott had a hand in a series of articles actually written by John Galt. He also failed to exercise discrimination in his criticism of the use of multiple pseudonyms, lashing his opponents for harmless sallies with the same vehemence he applied to disgraceful libels. There was truth in the remark of Mary Russell Mitford that *Blackwood's* was 'a very libellous, naughty, wicked, scandalous, story-telling, entertaining work'.

All might have been well if Scott had not in his January issue taunted the man he spelt Lockart once more. He referred to an action for libel in which Professor John Leslie, accepting common report in Edinburgh, named Lockhart as editor of *Blackwood's Magazine*. The offending article, ridiculing Leslie's standing as a scholar, was by Maginn. Scott wrote:

> We have been told that Mr John Gibson Lockart, having been originally included in the action now pending, has given it under his hand, that *he is not the Editor of the Magazine*. The people of Edinburgh are not surprised at this denial: it is well known there that *Doctor Morris,* under the assumed name of Christopher North, is the Editor of the work, and the author of the most malignant articles! Would the Doctor have the baseness to make a similar denial? We believe he would; for all the professions of a merry careless temper, by which it has been attempted to characterize the publication he conducts, have evidently been intended to cover an organized plan of fraud, calumny, and cupidity. The cowardice which denies a perpetrated wrong, is the natural associate of such qualities. Doctor Morris would deny just as firmly as Mr Lockart.

Such a direct charge could hardly go unanswered, particularly as the *Blackwood's* camp was becoming uneasy. Thomas De Quincey, a contributor, wrote to his friend John Wilson in high indignation. 'My chief subject of anxiety at the moment is that infamous attack upon you in the London Mag. by John Scott,' he wrote. 'I am burning for vengeance. . . . I do so loathe the vile whining canting hypocrisy of the fellow.'

De Quincey urged 'Christopher North' to reply in kind, but Wilson was still playing the role of a respectable professor, and on 8 January 1821 De Quincey wrote to William Blackwood, complaining about the consequent mildness of the magazine: 'This horrible dulness, which is enough to afflict apoplexy, happens to coincide with these infernal articles from London. And to these it seems we are to knock under!'

Three days later Maginn wrote to the publisher from the capital: 'The London Magazine is very insolent. You must put them down in some strong way.' Another contributor who urged retaliation was John Galt, whose articles on the Ayrshire Legatees endeavoured to treat London Society in much the same way Dr Morris wrote of Edinburgh, and had been strongly criticised in the *London* by Scott. But Blackwood told him: 'We are not quite determined in what way we shall notice these Cockneys, or indeed if we shall notice them at all.'

Lockhart received a letter from a London friend Jonathan Henry Christie at the turn of the year, expressing anger at Scott's attacks.

Christie, a young lawyer, said cryptically: 'I think you must do more with him than kill the zinc-eating spider.'

Lockhart replied early in January:

> I was in the country when the first of Master Baldwin's philippics was published, and, being entirely concerned with running down hares and sticking salmon, did not hear of it for many weeks. The second distressed me very much, not on account of myself, but of Scott, of whose hitherto unprofaned name such base use was made in it—although, if any insult could move a man's rage, without doubt the allusions to my marriage, wife etc, were well entitled to do so.
>
> Now, however,—I mean in the January number, which has been sent me this morning,—I find myself charged with distinctness in a sort which neither present engagement, or any thought for the future, can induce me, or could induce any man, to overlook.

This sensitivity over his marriage and relationship with Sir Walter—the *London* had referred to 'the fortunate youth of Abbotsford'—contrasted oddly with Lockhart's own record in such matters. In the early days of *Blackwood's* he urged the publisher to take advantage of Sir Walter's association with it to ward off critics, and he dragged Leigh Hunt's wife into his slurs on that man's character. Lockhart suggested Christie should enlist the help of another lawyer friend, James Traill, in forcing either an apology or a duel over the *London* articles:

> Talk over the whole affair with Traill, and one or both of you go to this Mr Scott (or whoever the editor may be) ... you will dictate according to your own discretion, which I can trust better than my own, an apology to be inserted in the front pages of his next magazine, and wherever else I please. If there is any difficulty about this, it remains only that you fix a day for the man to meet me at York or any other place halfway between Edinburgh and London.

Lockhart added he would probably have written a month earlier but for the illness of his wife. A nineteenth-century biographer of Sir Walter Scott, the Reverend G R Gleig, said Lockhart told the baronet he intended to seek redress in a duel, and Sir Walter replied: 'I am sorry for it, John, but you cannot do otherwise, you must fight him.' The novelist himself said the affair had gone too far for him to intervene when he learned of it. In any case it is unlikely Sir Walter, with his strong sense of personal honour, would have tried to restrain Lockhart, and even less likely his son-in-law would have paid any attention if he had.

On 10 January Christie called on Scott at his Covent Garden lodgings and asked whether he acknowledged responsibility for the articles in *The London Magazine* which Lockhart regarded as injurious to his honour. On learning Lockhart was still in Scotland, Scott declined to discuss his own editorship unless the complainant was at hand and would declare his relationship with *Blackwood's*. Lockhart hurried to London, and on the 18th Christie delivered a letter from his friend demanding an apology.

Scott then acknowledged he was editor of *The London,* but said Lockhart could not expect to enjoy the privileges of a gentleman unless he would disavow having been concerned with *Blackwood's Magazine,* 'whose scandals, calumnies, and falsehoods, have placed it without the pale of honourable literature'. Christie argued no statement was necessary. Later in the negotiations, which were spread over two days, Scott modified his demand, saying all he required was 'that Mr Lockhart should declare upon his honour, in explicit terms, that he has never derived *money* from any connection, direct or indirect, with the *management* of that work; and that he has never stood in a situation giving him directly, or indirectly, a *pecuniary* interest in its sale'.

It is as difficult for us, in the twentieth century, to judge the niceties of the Georgian code of duelling as it would be for us to dance a quadrille. Although Scott muddled the issue by modifying his request for a preliminary explanation from Lockhart, it seemed reasonable to expect some statement from him. On Lockhart's own admission he did not decide to take up the cudgels until Scott accused him of lying when he denied being editor of *Blackwood's*.

Christie shuttled between the belligerents, delivering messages. Horace Smith was brought into the negotiations, Caroline Scott having persuaded her husband to ask their old friend to handle the matter rather than Patmore.

Horace Smith, in his reminiscences about the affair written twenty-six years later, said he told Scott he did not believe in duelling and was ignorant of how such encounters were conducted, adding, 'I would not be a party, under any circumstances to a hostile meeting, though I would eagerly render him my best services as a mediator with a view to an amicable adjustment of the affair.'

It is hard to reconcile this declaration with his notes to Scott at the time. On the day Christie announced Lockhart was in London, Smith sent his friend a message with a reminder of Lockhart's reticence when Leigh Hunt and his brother asked for the name of the scurrilous Z in *Blackwood's*. Smith wrote:

> It occurred to me just after you went that good use in the way of argument might be made of L's refusal to answer Hunt's call, not that I suppose any similarity in the cases, but that without any reference to the quality of the attack, no one who has declined as an aggressor can insist on satisfaction of that nature when he happens to be the aggrieved.
>
> It never rains but it pours. — I forgot to tell you of a new complaint against you contained in a letter which I received this morning from Shelley at

Pisa—It seems he ordered all the reviews of his Cenci to be sent out to him, & against one of the most bitter & virulent character someone has written 'John Scott'—whereat Shelley naturally asks How can I have injured John Scott? Now I am pretty certain that you have written *no* review of the Cenci except that in the London, & I rather think he alludes to one in the Literary Gazette.

The following day, Friday, Smith wrote to Scott in the evening from his Fulham home:

> Mr Christie called upon me before I left the City, and showed me the whole correspondence—between you, Mr Lockhart, and himself. After perusing it, I asked him whether Mr Lockhart had complied with the preliminary upon which my interference was conditional, as stipulated in your last memorandum; and, upon finding that he had not, I said I conceived Mr Christie's call was irregular; and that I was not bound, as matters then stood, to listen to any propositions, or make them.—If Mr Lockhart could make the avowal required, I *repeatedly* told Mr Christie that I was authorized by you *to offer him satisfaction*, and I expressed *my entire concurrence in the sentiments of your last communication.*
>
> Mr Christie admitted, that as my interference was made dependent upon a condition not performed, it was irregular to call on me.

The Smith of 1821 clearly knew more about affairs of honour, and played a more active role in this one, than the Smith of 1847 recollected. But it is true he acted as peace-maker, as was right for a second or prospective second. In 1827 he told a correspondent, that because of his stand in the exchanges, Lockhart 'had some idea, I was told, of calling me out!'

Lockhart, meanwhile, was receiving advice from a very different quarter, John Wilson Croker, a friend of Sir Walter's and the victim of some of John Scott's sharp comments over his writings in *The Quarterly Review*.

Croker suggested Lockhart should 'post' Scott, a device whereby a man who considered himself insulted, and was refused satisfaction, turned the tables by insulting his opponent, in the hope he would then issue a challenge. It was apparently in response to this suggestion that Lockhart left a note for Croker at the Admiralty saying:

> The moment I have it in my power to let you know how this shuffling Dog is to conclude the affair you shall probably hear from me in a couple of hours—or if possible I shall call on you. Believe me with the deepest sense of my obligation to you. . . .

The 'posting' was in the following note:

> Mr Lockhart, in consequence of Mr Scott's having refused to act towards him according to the rules by which gentlemen are accustomed to regulate their conduct, thinks it necessary to inform Mr Scott, that he, Mr Lockhart, considers him as a liar and a scoundrel.

> Mr Lockhart also thinks proper to inform Mr Scott that it is his intention to set off for Scotland on Tuesday morning, bearing with him no other feeling in regard to Mr Scott, except that supreme contempt with which every gentleman must contemplate the utmost united baseness of falsehood and poltroonery.

Scott declined to be drawn. In two hours he replied, saying that he considered this note 'as coming from the editor of Blackwood's Magazine'. He had no intention of granting Lockhart a meeting on equal terms without first wringing from him some admission which would be damaging either to the Edinburgh writer or to the magazine with which he was associated.

Both men were acting like bar room brawlers, loud in their threats to set about each other, if only their friends were not holding them back. Lockhart was anxious to fight, but refused to make the concession he was assured would grant his wish; Scott was anxious to accommodate him, provided Lockhart would make the concession he persisted in refusing.

This insistence on points of punctilio then took an extraordinary turn. Lockhart made the required avowal of his connection with *Blackwood's*, but in a manner which increased the confusion. Instead of leaving London as he had announced, he lingered and composed a statement running to nearly 3000 words, retailing what had passed between himself, Christie, Scott and Smith. Towards the end he repeated his 'posting' of Scott as a liar and scoundrel, and Scott's rejoinder he regarded this as coming from the editor of *Blackwood's*. Lockhart added:

> This last new miserable subterfuge is as false in assertion, (Mr Lockhart not being the Editor of Blackwood's Magazine,) as its motive is despicable; and Mr Lockhart has now only to regret, that his ignorance of the manners and character of Mr John Scott, should have involved him in any discussion with a person alike incapable of giving, or of receiving, the explanation of a gentleman.

When Scott read this lengthy document, he consulted Patmore and Smith and decided to take no action. Lockhart went with his statement to Dr John Stoddart who, after being dismissed as editor of *The Times* had started the rival *New Times*. When Lockhart told Stoddart he intended to publish it, the doctor, as he later stated 'took the liberty to observe, that if he did so, it would be advisable to satisfy the public by a more explicit declaration than was contained in that paper, that he was not the Editor of *Blackwood's Magazine*. I added, that for the sake of clearness and intelligibility, I thought such declaration ought to precede the narrative. This remark appeared to strike Mr Lockhart very forcibly, and Mr Christie acquiescing in it, Mr Lockhart immediately sat down, and wrote the paragraph which now stands at the head of his narrative.'

This paragraph and the rest of the article were published in the paper on 31 January. Although couched in careful language, it went a great deal farther than a terse denial of editorship. It read:

> Mr Lockhart thinks it proper to introduce the following narrative with a distinct statement (which he would never have hesitated about granting to any one who had the smallest right to demand it), concerning the nature of his connection with Blackwood's Edinburgh Magazine. Mr Lockhart has occasionally contributed articles to that publication; but he is in no sense of the word, editor or conductor of it, and neither does, nor ever did derive, any emolument whatever from any management of it.

What Lockhart and Christie apparently forgot in inserting this disavowal was that a footnote had been added to the long apologia: 'N.B.— The first copy of this Statement was sent to Mr Scott, with a notification, that Mr Lockhart intended leaving London within twenty-four hours after the time of his receiving it.'

But the version sent to Scott did not contain the introduction written at Stoddart's suggestion. Scott, who had already issued one statement on his side of the affair, seized on this discrepancy in another even longer than Lockhart's. He said if Lockhart had made the avowal about his connection with *Blackwood's* to him that he now made to the public, there would have been no difficulty about taking the field in a duel. He also underlined the fact that by the time this avowal was published Lockhart was on his way to Scotland, and charged him with lying in saying a copy of the statement had been sent to Scott.

Both men circulated their accounts of the affair widely, and their respective camps each decided their own man had won the war of words. Sir Walter Scott assured his elder son: 'Lockhart has had a foolish scrape with a blackguard who abused him in a London Magazine by name blustered when at a distance and when Lockhart applied to him seriously shirked most pitifully and sate down under the handsome apellatives of scoundrel and liar.'

Charles Lamb, in a note acknowledging receipt of John Scott's statements, said, 'I have read both carefully and most heartily acquiesce in the whole conduct of the affair on OUR PART.' Even in such a potentially serious matter, the essayist could not resist a joke, suggesting their rivals were such a nest of impostors, the man who travelled from Edinburgh might have been James Hogg, the Ettrick Shepherd, impersonating Lockhart and 'come to impose upon you and take pot luck—or shot luck— for his friend', closing his note, 'Vivat Lond. Mag cum Editore Scriptoribusque.'

Backing came also from John Ramsay McCulloch, a leading member of the staff of *The Scotsman,* in Edinburgh, itself engaged in controversy with

Blackwood's. He wrote: 'I believe the great majority of the public of this city, are quite of opinion that you have treated Lockhart just as he deserved to be treated and that you have done a very great service by assisting in exposing the atrocious system of literary assassins. . . . You are right in thinking that Lockhart was to all intents and purposes the editor of Blackwood's Magazine. . . . He was in truth the real manager of the work—wrote the great part of it himself, and solicited contributions from all his friends.' McCulloch added the magazine's printing had been taken over by Ballantyne & Co: 'This is a most important fact—Sir W. Scott is a partner of Mr Ballantyne; so that *in future the libels* of the son-in-law will be printed by the father-in-law.'

Charles Maclaren, editor of *The Scotsman* added his congratulations to Scott in a letter dated 27 January 1821, praising his firmness in refusing to accept Lockhart's challenge. He said Lockhart had forfeited his character as a man of honour by his connection with *Blackwood's*, and added: 'Had you gone out with him, you would have set yourself up as a mark for a man drenched in disgrace to clear his reputation on. It would be a very easy way of recovering a man's character were the mere fact of exchanging shots with another person to cancel a long train of infamous acts.'

As so often in the past, family sickness added to Scott's worries. On 26 January he wrote to his sister Margaret: 'Kate's Letters from Aberdeen have thrown us into sad anxiety about my dear Mother: her last, recd. yesterday, speaks of some amendment, but still leaves the chances of her recovery very doubtful. If she were lost at this moment to her family it would be very dreadful—& to me particularly painful, as I entertained a peculiar wish to see her again once more.' But Mrs Scott lived another sixteen years.

The battle of the magazines seemed to have ended well. Nobody had been shot, and the exchange of abusive articles had been halted. But there was an undercurrent of uneasiness. Society had been robbed of the duel it expected. John Scott, as he distributed his statement, began to have second thoughts, to fancy people thought he should have agreed to fight a man he considered a liar and a scoundrel. Caroline Scott told Haydon her husband could not sleep at nights. The atmosphere was tense when Sir Walter Scott arrived in London.

Chapter 9

MYSTERY AT CHALK FARM

Sir Walter was in London on business, but he soon became involved in the Lockhart affair. Jonathan Christie grew alarmed at the use John Scott was making of Lockhart's blunder in revealing to the public, belatedly, what he had refused to reveal to the man he was pressing to fight. Christie was a popular young man who disapproved of his friend's magazine, but he shared John Scott's own stubbornness, for he was himself from Aberdeenshire, and had studied at Marischal College, some years after John left it. He took it upon himself, as Lockhart's second, to reopen negotiations.

On 6 February 1821 Horace Smith found the following letter at his city office in Throgmorton Street:

> Sir,—I have this moment seen a copy of Mr Scott's second statement. It does not appear to me to be necessary, on the present occasion, to explain the reasons which induced Mr Lockhart to insert the more explicit disavowal contained in the introductory paragraph of his statement, after having sent a copy to Mr Scott of the statement as he at first intended that it should appear.
>
> If Mr Scott means it to be understood that if that disavowal had been contained in the copy sent to him by Mr Lockhart, it would have made any difference to his (Mr Scott's) conduct, then there is no reason why the disavowal should not now have the same effect. In order to obviate all apprehensions of disappointment I pledge my word of honour that (however little Mr Lockhart may be called upon to make such a concession), if Mr Scott will take the same journey to find Mr Lockhart that Mr Lockhart took to find Mr Scott, Mr Lockhart will give him a meeting instantly.

Smith forwarded this new challenge to Scott with a note:

> Dr Scott
>   I find the enclosed in my box & have just written to Christie desiring any future communications may be made to you direct as I decline further interference,
>   yours in haste
>   H. Smith

Fortunately for his second, Lockhart approved of this belligerence, perhaps comforted by Christie's assurance in his letter explaining his action that Scott 'most assuredly never will fight'. On 8 February Christie, with the collaboration of Dr Stoddart of *The New Times*, printed a statement of his own. This contained a detailed account of how Lockhart's published explanation came to differ from that sent to Scott. Christie concluded by saying:

> If after this statement, Mr Scott can find any persons who believe that there was any thing more atrocious than an oversight in the circumstances of the two statements, Mr Scott is perfectly welcome to the whole weight of their good opinion.

It was left to Sir Walter Scott to inject a note of caution into the business. In a note from his hotel, the Waterloo in Jermyn Street, on Tuesday evening, 13 February, apparently addressed to Christie in reply to a query about the letter to Smith, Sir Walter said: 'I greatly doubt the propriety of publishing the letter.... I would give Mr Scott full time to digest it. The rascal wants only to sell his book and will make replies to the end of time keeping Mr Lockhart... on the tenterhooks.'

The baronet also invited Christie to breakfast the next day. At this meeting his advice was less fortunate, for on his suggestion Christie sent a copy of his statement to Patmore, who had emerged as John Scott's second following Smith's decision to withdraw.

Sir Walter reported by letter to Lockhart, whose wife had just presented him with a son: 'I saw Mr Christie yesterday. You will see the friendly and ready zeal with which he met Scott's impudence both in his letter to Smith of which I highly approve and in his printed statement.' He urged his son-in-law to 'keep clear of magazine-mongers and scandal-jobbers in future,' adding: 'The fellow will live on this affair for half a year which I dare say is all he wanted for as for fighting he thought as much of flying.'

But John Scott, on reading Christie's statement, decided the last paragraph was a provocation he could not ignore. It has been suggested that 'busy friends' urged him on, but there is no reason to suppose his natural irascibility, increased by the desire to demonstrate his courage, needed such stimulation. Patmore was dispatched to Christie's home to demand a public explanation that his words were not meant to reflect on Scott's character. When Christie refused, Patmore presented him with a challenge from Scott. At the lawyer's suggestion it was agreed the meeting should take place with as little delay as possible at Chalk Farm, then on the outskirts of London. Speed was advisable, for judges were more lenient when duellists acted in anger rather than after deliberation, or at any rate when that interpretation could be put on their actions.

Patmore borrowed a pair of pistols from his father, the Ludgate Hill jeweller, and arranged for a surgeon, Thomas Joseph Pettigrew, to be on hand. Scott wrote a letter to his wife, and another to her brother Dominic Colnaghi, and left them with John Hamilton Reynolds to be delivered if he were killed.

In duels, as in war, truth is the first casualty; sometimes it is the only casualty. But accounts of what happened on the night of Friday, 16 February 1821, while varying in detail, give a broadly consistent picture.

At seven John left Caroline at her father's house in Cockspur Street, saying he was dining with a friend in the Temple. Instead he joined Patmore and they travelled by postchaise to Chalk Farm Tavern, near Primrose Hill. The tavern, rebuilt in the middle of the last century, was then in open fields, the scene of many duels.

There the two men ordered a bottle of wine. After a while they left, telling the waiter they would return to finish it. The moon was up, but the night was foggy. Scott was soberly dressed, and wore a cloak; Patmore was in a white great-coat, perhaps to ensure neither of the principals shot him by mistake. They walked up rising ground to a spot some 300 or 400 yards away, where a hedge and trees sheltered them from observation from the inn.

They were followed shortly afterwards by Christie, with his second, James Traill. Before long two more men appeared at the tavern, surgeon Pettigrew with a pupil, William Morris. They enquired where the others had gone, and hurried to join them. It was about 9.30.

Pettigrew said later: 'I reached the top of the hill, and saw four gentlemen in the neighbouring field, two of them were walking backwards, and the two others were by the side of the hedge, between the hill and the field. I heard the knocking of pistols, the priming of pistols, and the shutting of the pan—soon afterwards shots were exchanged.... I heard the sound, and saw the flash; I then heard an exclamation from one of the gentlemen on the ground, as if wounded. I got over the hedge, and found Mr Scott on his knees, on the ground—he pointed out to me that he was wounded on the right side—the other gentlemen were supporting him.... I partly undressed him, and examined the wound.'

What the surgeon witnessed was the second fire. Christie had arranged with Traill that on his first shot he would fire in the air. Scott also missed. Urged by his second to defend himself Christie took careful aim the second time at the classic duelling mask of a man standing side-on to his opponent, the gut. The ball from his pistol tore a hole an inch across in Scott's right side, between the ribs and the hipbone, and penetrated ten inches to lodge on the other side of his abdomen.

Scott fainted as the surgeon examined him, but quickly revived. Christie took him by the hand and said: 'I would rather that I was in your situation and that you were in mine.' The wounded man replied: 'Whatever may be the issue of this case, I beg you all to bear in remembrance that every thing has been fair and honourable.'

Christie asked Pettigrew what he thought of the wound, and when told if the ball had perforated the intestines he feared it was mortal, the duellist, wringing his hands in agony exclaimed: 'Good God, why was I permitted to fire a second time, I fired down the field before, and could do no more, I was compelled to fire in my own defence.' In the meantime the seconds had withdrawn some distance from the contestants and were quarrelling over the first fire; Patmore could be heard saying, 'Then why was it not communicated to me—I knew nothing of it.'

Scott told the surgeon he wished to be taken to his Covent Garden lodgings, and Pettigrew went to arrange for his reception there, leaving his assistant, Morris, to care for the wounded man. Criticised later for this, Pettigrew maintained his services as a surgeon were not required. It was not the first time he had left things to an assistant. Two years before £800 damages were awarded against him because he sent one to treat a workman who dislocated an arm; the task was bungled, the man losing the use of his arm.

Morris realised Scott was too badly hurt to be moved to Covent Garden, and Traill ran to the Chalk Farm Tavern for help. The ostler, James Ryan, and another man took a shutter to the spot and Scott was carried back. He was in pain, and cried out several times on the journey. At the tavern he was found to be very cold, and was lifted upstairs and put to bed, attended by Morris and Patmore. The landlord, Hugh Watson, with a practised eye for such scenes, sent for a doctor and a Bow Street officer. Christie thought it time to leave, and Traill followed him when Scott's relatives arrived.

Whatever differences there had been between the hot-tempered editor and his in-laws, they rallied to him. His wife was accompanied by her father and brothers, Dominic and Martin, when she hurried to Chalk Farm. Caroline immediately sent for the man who saved her life five years before, Dr Darling, and he arrived soon after midnight. Caroline nursed John throughout the night.

'From what my husband said to me, when first I reached him,' she wrote later, 'I soon perceived that he had not the power to recollect correctly what had taken place on the field, and I forebore to press him on the subject.' However, Scott did tell his wife there had been mismanagement, and he ought not to have been in the state she saw him in. Meanwhile John Davis arrived from Bow Street and arrested Patmore, but the second gave him the slip and joined the others in flight.

The morning after the duel a surgeon, John James Guthrie, examined Scott with Dr Darling and decided he was not fit to have the ball extracted straight away. The wounded man lifted his head from his pillow and said: 'I have only one question to ask, is my wound necessarily mortal?' When the surgeon replied it was a case of the greatest danger, but he had seen recovery from similar wounds, Scott said 'I am satisfied', and sank back. But Darling saw John Taylor later the same day and told the publisher, 'It is very likely the poor fellow will not live 24 hours.'

Although he had lost much blood when Scott became feverish he was, in the medical language of the time, copiously bled. On Sunday afternoon Guthrie extracted the ball and the doctors—some half a dozen medical men were called in at various times—became optimistic. *The Observer* reported on Tuesday, 20 February: 'Mr Scott submitted to the painful operation with great fortitude, and passed the night with comparative tranquillity. Yesterday morning he was restless, but still his medical attendants entertain the most cheering hopes of his ultimate recovery'.

Caroline continued to nurse her husband, but did not relax her care in other matters. On Sunday morning she told the landlord, Watson, that John's gold watch and seals had disappeared. The watch was returned a few days later.

The sick-room at Chalk Farm was the centre of anxious inquiries, not least by those who had played a part in events leading to the duel and on the field itself. Sir Walter Scott wrote to Lockhart from London on 24 February that Christie was 'lying quiet with the purpose of starting in the evening for Calais and waiting the event on the other side of the Channel'. He went on: 'I am truly glad to report Scott's amended state. For two days there was little hope, the inflammation and fever having been very high and I who care little about anybody living or dying in such cases was anxious for Christie as there must have been a trial.'

Patmore wrote to his mother explaining it was necessary for him to be out of London for the time being, and telling her, if Scott died, 'I lose the dearest friend I ever had, among men.' He, Christie and Traill were all liable to arrest for their part in the duel. On 23 February Christie wrote to Sir Walter from France: 'I could only have avoided this thing at the expense of my own life, or by submitting to a personal degradation which must have followed from my making any concession on the *demand* of Mr S., and more particularly from my recognizing his title to respect in any manner, however indirect. As I doubled the chance against myself by forbearing to defend myself till I was sure that my life was sought, my conscience acquits me of having left anything undone which I could do.'

The duel, coming in the middle of the month, when Scott would normally be working on the next issue, threw *The London Magazine* into confusion. Robert Baldwin, seeking extra articles from Talfourd, wrote 'increasing hopes of Mr Scott's safety add greatly to the stimulus not to suffer the Magazine to deteriorate during his unfortunate inability to support it'.

Nine days after the duel it seemed Scott had survived the worst that bullet, surgeon, and doctors' bleeding could do, but on the night of Monday, 26 February, there was a change for the worse. Caroline realised she was at the bedside of a dying man. Her father and brothers joined her. John remained in a languid state and, as *The Morning Chronicle* recorded, at 9.30 on Tuesday night 'the unfortunate gentleman expired, with apparent ease, and without a groan'.

Many friends, including Horace Smith, had journeyed to the Chalk Farm Tavern during Scott's battle for life. But it was Wainewright who described in *The London Magazine* 'his painful end at a wretched inn on a squalid bed'. This was a fanciful picture, but there was real emotion in the words: 'Poor fellow! at this moment I feel, fresh as yesterday, round my neck the heart-breaking, feeble, kindly clasp of his fever-wasted arm—his faint whisper of entire trust in my friendship (though but short)—the voice dropping back again—the look—one stronger clasp! May the peace which rested over his last moments remain with him for ever!'

Sir Walter Scott wrote to Lockhart: 'It would be great hypocrisy in me to say I am sorry for John Scott. He has got exactly what he was long fishing for.' Perhaps Sir Walter was feeling uneasy about his own role as adviser to Christie when he wrote to his brother Thomas in Canada, saying that after Lockhart challenged Scott 'the fellow being absolute *dunghill* would do nothing but shuffle . . . when Lockhart had returned to Edinburgh Scott began again to clap his wings & finding that he was scouted in society he fastened a sleeveless quarrel upon Christie a young man who had carried him Lockhart's message. A more absurd pretext of a supposed offence was never made out but Scott was that dangerous animal a coward made desperate. . . . Scott is dead of his wound which is vexatious but men must die and the worms eat them.'

Sir Walter did express sympathy for the widow and children, but his letters at this time give ample justification for Joanna Richardson's remark: 'One contrasts his public conduct, his courtly manners, with his private comments, one feels that affection and self-interest, civility and vulgarity went hand in hand.'

Among those who followed the wavering fortunes of John Scott's last days was Fanny Brawne, fiancée of Keats. She discussed the affair with her neighbour, Charles Brown, who wrote to the poet's companion in Rome, Joseph Severn: 'You refer to Keats' enemies, cursing them as his friend,—I suppose you mean the villains of the "Quarterly" and "Blackwood". I understand (as indeed Keats told me) how he intended to treat Lockhart. Now Lockhart was violently attacked in the "London" by John Scott for his atrocious libels on Keats and others . . . Scott is killed. Keats never liked Scott, but in such a case how hard that he should die. I tell you this, as it is in a degree part of Keats' history.' Keats himself was dead before this letter left England.

The inquest on Scott opened at the tavern two days after his death. Dr George Darling gave the most startling evidence when he referred to a memorandum of a conversation he had with his friend the morning after the duel. Dr Darling told the court Scott said to him: 'This ought not to have taken place, I suspect some great mismanagement—there was no occasion for a second fire. All I required from Mr Christie was, a declaration that he meant no reflection on my character; this he refused, and the meeting became inevitable; on the field, Mr Christie behaved well, and always ready; for the first fire he called out, Mr. Scott, you must not stand there; I see your head above the horizon; you give me an advantage; I believe he could have hit me then if he liked. After the pistols were reloaded and everything was ready for a second fire, Mr Traill called out, "now Mr Christie, take your aim, and do not throw away your advantage as you did last time" I called out immediately, what! did not Mr Christie fire at me? I was answered by Mr Patmore, "you must not speak; it is now of no use to talk; you have nothing now for it but firing". The signal was immediately given, we fired, and I fell.'

Dr Darling added Scott expressed himself satisfied with Christie's conduct, and described his opponent as very kind to him after he was wounded. The inquest was spread over two days, and on the second evening surgeon Pettigrew said Patmore stated to him that if Christie and his friend had agreed he should not return Scott's fire, Traill was bound, after the first fire, to have communicated to him the conduct pursued by Christie, of which Patmore was entirely ignorant.

The effect of the evidence was to throw the blame for the fatal outcome on Patmore or Traill or both. It was customary, when the challenger had not been shot at, for him to declare honour was satisfied, thus ending the encounter.

However, the jury could return only one verdict on the evidence: that, in legal terms, Christie, Patmore and Traill 'not having the fear of God before their eyes, but being moved and seduced by the instigation of the Devil . . . feloniously wilfully and of their malice aforethought . . . did kill and murder' John Scott. Warrants were issued for their arrest.

In view of Dr Darling's evidence, Patmore was particularly alarmed. In his agitation he thought Scott had deliberately thrown the blame on him. His legal advisers were Reynolds and his partner James Rice, and on 6 March, the day after the inquest Reynolds wrote to tell their client 'the feeling of the jury and of the public, is certainly strong against you'. However, he said Dr Darling believed Scott, in making his statement, did not mean it to be used against the seconds, but to indicate his anxiety to clear Christie of blame.

Reynolds went on to tell Patmore:

Yesterday I had an interview with Mr Baldwin, who the Evening before had seen Mrs Scott and conversed with her for a considerable time. She had written a letter to you, going towards affording you some consolation for the dreadful loss of Mr Scott, and quoting a few words from the letter written by him to her (which I had delivered to Mr Dom Colnaghi, together with his own, *previous* to the arrival of your letter,—and which has safely reached Mrs Scott's hands) stating that 'you had done all you could to prevent a meeting'. This letter of Mrs Scott threw the blame on Traill, whose name occurred twice in it, on reading which Mr Baldwin hinted at the propriety of forwarding a written Document of this nature, which you might be compelled to produce as evidence. To this observation, Mrs Scott made the following important reply—'As to producing any letter of mine—there will not be occasion for such a measure, as I shall hold myself quite ready to come forward, if necessary, to give evidence of what I know. And I shall then speak of Mr Traill as I now write.'

Caroline Scott wrote to Patmore in the same terms. Reproving him for 'the tone of reproach in which you have written to me', she told him:

> If that moment of agony had been impressed upon your mind as it was upon mine, (I mean when I left you to return to my dying husband) I should not, I think, have now to tell you that you may command me in any way that can be of service to you. Nothing will give me greater satisfaction than that all the world should think of you as I do ... but I must not forget *that* which I ought to have most at heart. Do all you can to clear yourself—but at the same time be careful of our poor John's memory—for I am certain he never—never meant to hurt you. He was too sincere a man to have received you, had he been conscious that he was acting a double part. He could not have done it—did you not know enough of him to feel convinced of this? ...
> God bless you my poor friend
> Believe me most anxiously yours
> Caroline Scott

It was an astonishingly calm letter, balancing her friendship for Patmore against overriding loyalty to the husband who was buried two days later. On Friday 9 March a hearse and four carried his body from the lodgings at Mr Bohte's shop in York Street to St Martin-in-the-Fields through crowded streets. The hearse was followed by sixteen coaches filled with mourners, and seven private carriages, it being the custom for wealthy people to send carriages to a funeral as a mark of respect, even if they did not attend. Haydon was in the church and recorded the scene in his diary:

> As I squeezed by the coffin that contained the body of my former Friend, with the long pall and black plumes trembling as the wind blew in the aisle, I shivered. All our conversations on Death and Christianity and another world, crowded into my mind, and when the four men took up the coffin, two at the head, and two at the foot and staggered and reeled beneath its weight,

my mind darted through the lid, & saw inwardly the pale corpse, still! stretched silent! and cold!

As the coffin was taken down to the vault, the plumes were taken off, and when they nodded to the followers against the light window, I thought them endowed with human features, as fates that bowed, as we walked in submission to their power!

I descended steps into a dark chamber, & saw at a distance doors open & piles of black coffins to the ceiling, inside, each having a trembling light fixed to its side. The mourners crowded forward; I felt too much to move, & was hustled about, without one effort to resist before the room was half obscured by heads; I listened and heard the dry scraping of the cords, & then a dead jerk as if the body had settled to its place. Immediately after a mellow voice rose up inside like steam, reading the funeral service. Poor Scott! I took a last look at the coffin and walked away.

A public subscription was opened for the dead man's family, although Reynolds suggested this should be delayed for fear of increasing resentment against those accused of murdering him. Several close friends joined the appeal committee, Sir James Mackintosh, Dr Darling, Horace Smith, and Robert Baldwin. Other members included John Murray, and the Reverend Dr Alexander Waugh, great-great-grandfather of Evelyn and Alec. Dr Waugh, who had studied at Marischal College, was Secession minister at Wells Street chapel in the West End, and his congregation were mostly immigrant Scots. In addition to the committee themselves, contributors to the fund, which raised several hundred pounds, included David Wilkie, the Reverend W L Bowles, Taylor and Hessey, surgeon Guthrie, Earl Spencer, Francis Jeffrey, Lord Holland, Charles Lamb, and Haydon, who could surely ill afford the five guineas he promised.

Byron sent £30 anonymously for the family of the school-fellow of whom he said, 'He died like a brave man, and he lived an able one.' The more cautious Wordsworth made inquiries about Caroline's circumstances and did not subscribe; he may have felt the Colnaghi family should support her.

Meanwhile Christie and Traill remained abroad, awaiting their trial with hope and fear. On 19 March Christie wrote to Lockhart: 'Our counsel think our case good—that is they think that the verdict will be manslaughter . . . we can scarcely expect anything less than three months.' They returned to London secretly early in April.

Traill also corresponded with Lockhart saying that when he urged Christie not to fire away from Scott again, he prefaced the words with a request to be heard by all parties. He did not hear Scott call out, 'What, did Mr Christie not fire at me?.

Traill wrote:

The fact was Mr Scott said nothing louder than could have been heard by his second who stood about three or four feet from him and indeed there did appear to be some conversation between Mr Patmore & Mr Scott after my words were uttered. Mr Patmore then came to where I stood and without saying anything gave the signal. . . . I had no reason whatever to suppose that Christie's fire had passed without observation. Our arrangement had been that he should fire in the air, and at the time I was not aware that he had fired with his pistol levelled away from Mr Scott. My eyes at the time of the fire being fixed on Mr Scott . . . & could have told with absolute certainty whether he had fired designedly away from Mr Christie had he done so.

Patmore had also been in France, and returned to London. But when the trial opened on 13 April at the Old Bailey he did not appear, on legal advice; if he and Traill had been called to testify their evidence would have conflicted and inevitably prejudiced the court against at least one of them.

So only Christie and Traill were in the dock when the proceedings opened before Lord Chief Justice Abbott. Dr Darling gave evidence, but the Chief Justice conferred with two fellow judges on whether the statement made by Scott to the doctor could be included. The evidence of a dead man was only admitted if he knew himself to be dying at the time, on the grounds that someone on the edge of eternity would tell the truth in the same way as under oath. They ruled Scott's statement was inadmissible, as it was uncertain he considered himself at the point of death. So the judges, who failed to silence Scott in life, managed to do so after death.

Prosecuting counsel assured the jury that although the proceedings were instituted by the relatives of the deceased, they disclaimed vindictive feeling, and were anxious only that the facts should be examined. Witnesses avoided identifying the men seen at Chalk Farm on the night of the duel.

Traill and Christie did not give evidence, merely calling clergymen and others eminent in the law and in public life who testified to their general good and peaceful characters. Chief Justice Abbott summed up with some severity, particularly on the absent Patmore. He told the jury they must consider: first, if the prisoners were present when Scott was shot; next if this was occasioned from 'heat of blood and irritation which might lessen the offence', or if it was coolly and deliberately determined upon.

The judge said Patmore engaging a surgeon to attend made it, as far as he was concerned, a deliberate murder; but this did not affect the prisoners at the bar, who might have been ignorant of such an arrangement. After twenty-five minutes deliberation the jury found Christie and Traill not guilty.

The Guardian, a weekly newspaper, reported:

> When the verdict was announced a death-like silence prevailed throughout the court. Mr Traill immediately caught Mr Christie by the hand, and he remained for some seconds as if in a mixed mood of profound reflection and inexpressible gratitude; his hand uplifted to his mouth, and his eye bent

rather towards the ground than to the Jury. After a few seconds more he turned towards the Jury, and bowed most respectfully to them. Mr Christie and Mr Traill immediately left the dock, and on their passage throughout the Court received the hearty congratulations of their mutual friends.

Christie described their release in a letter to Lockhart the following day: 'It seems that we were not the men that fought the duel at all, they ran away as soon as the man was shot, & we good creatures happening to be walking by moonlight were attracted to the spot . . . we are the luckiest men in the world . . . the prosecution was conducted in the mildest manner. In fact, I have no doubt but they could have proved our identity if they had been so disposed. The summing up was clearly for a verdict of manslaughter.'

Proceedings at the Old Bailey had made Patmore's position even more uncomfortable, if not dangerous. He prepared a statement to vindicate his part in the duel. Referring to the earlier dispute, Patmore said it was by his advice Scott finally declined a meeting with Lockhart, and added he repeatedly urged his friend to ignore Christie's statement and actions after that affair.

Of events on the field, Patmore's statement said:

> With respect to the nature of the *first fire,* the pistols of both parties were levelled, and both fired immediately on the signal being given and nearly at the same instant of time; and not a word passed from either party as to the nature of this fire, until they were on the point of firing again; at which time the friend of Mr Christie addressed some words to that gentleman *by name,* and which Mr Patmore therefore considered himself as not entitled, much less called upon, to attend to; though he did hear them, and they were perfectly unintelligible to him. Mr Scott also appeared to hear them; and the effect of them was to irritate him in the highest degree—for the impression he (evidently) received from them was that Mr Christie's friend meant to insinuate something against his (Mr Scott's) conduct, in having fired *too quickly.* Mr Patmore was fearful, from the irritation of Mr Scott's words and manner at this time, that he might say something offensive, which would place the probability of an adjustment still farther off; he therefore urged Mr Scott to be silent.

Patmore included in his account of the duel a brief statement which, he said, had been taken down by Mrs Scott while her husband lay wounded at Chalk Farm Tavern. This said: 'Mr Scott was not made aware till *after* his second fire that Mr Christie had said that he had discharged his pistol in the air, no communication to that effect having been made by Mr Traill to Mr Patmore. Such a statement, had it been understood, would have been deemed by Mr Scott and his friend completely satisfactory, and would necessarily have prevented any further proceedings.

'The proposal to meet at night, Mr Scott states to have originated with Mr Christie, but Mr Scott willingly acceded to it in order that the affair might be terminated as quickly as possible.'

Patmore's statement was not published, but he clearly regarded it as of great importance, for even late in life he contemplated using it in defence of his actions.

The differing accounts of what happened between the first and second fires seem irreconcilable, but one modern commentator has suggested a solution so logical and simple it must surely be right. Patmore was the only Englishman among the quartet; he heard but did not understand the words of Traill, who came from Caithness, in the far north of Scotland. It is also possible that Scott, at such a tense moment, reverted to the accent of his boyhood.

Another element of mystery is added by some manuscript notes on Colnaghi family history, said to have been compiled by a great-niece of Caroline Scott. They include the statement: 'The quarrel that led to the duel was forced upon Mr Scott most unfairly. His death was practically a murder as true to his principles he fired in the air.'

This may be no more than a muddled recollection of an oft told tale. Traill maintained he observed Scott taking aim at Christie on the first fire. But there is no account of the second fire. It is at least possible, in the strange chivalry of the duelling code, that having been informed Christie had not aimed at him the first time, Scott threw away his second fire.

Caroline did not waver in her belief Patmore was blameless, while showing exasperation with his recriminations over Scott's statement to Dr Darling. Patmore apparently felt John harboured suspicions about his friend's feelings for Caroline, perhaps thinking of the verses he had asked to be passed on, and about the loan of the mare. On 26 April Caroline sent Patmore a letter revealing something of the complexity of her partner's nature:

> I will endeavour to set you right with regard to the opinion you entertain of my poor husband's character. I do not think *distrust* was in his nature; on the contrary he was in my opinion too confiding—where he loved; he *distrusted* himself, and his talents, I grant; the feeling most prevalent in his mind against others was *disgust*, but not *distrust*. He used often to say of myself that with all my faults I never disgusted him; that he never saw any woman but myself who would have managed to do this. This was his common way of expressing himself—and I often saw that he took *disgusts* at persons—but I never knew him to be suspicious.

Scott seems to have used the word disgust in its original sense of distaste rather than full-blooded modern meaning. Evidently Patmore remained unconvinced, for two days later Caroline wrote:

> It is a melancholy circumstance for us both that there should have arisen anything of this kind to disturb the sacred devotion to his memory on your part. I should have had a melancholy satisfaction in recounting to you under

different circumstances what he had said and what he had written in the cause of truth and justice—in proving to you that he had never written a word that 'dying he would have wished to efface'. But this will be denied to me now—for you think him *untrue* and *unjust*—and you would hear anything in his favour with suspicion. This is one of the bitterest drops in my cup of wretchedness.

The 'Memoir' will be done carefully—at least with as much care as I have power to bestow upon it— and not hastily. I propose printing it with what letters I have of my poor John's which may be thought worthy of publication.

Patmore finally appeared at the Old Bailey on 9 June. Any apprehension he would be endangered by evidence he arranged for Pettigrew to attend the duel was quickly allayed. In the words of the official record:

> Mr Pettigrew (surgeon) and Mr W. B. Morris, his assistant, on being called, were informed by the Court that if they had attended on the field, knowing a duel was going to take place, for the purpose of giving surgical assistance, should it be necessary, they were liable to criminal prosecution themselves and that they were therefore at liberty to refuse being examined in this case.

Both men took the hint and declined to give evidence. Finally Mr Justice Bayley summed up, telling the jury blandly there was nothing to show the prisoner had a hand in Scott's death, and they found him not guilty.

From the legal point of view the defence in both trials was masterly. In the absence of testimony from Patmore, and the discounting of Scott's own statement to Dr Darling, Christie and Traill had only to keep their mouths shut to be safe. Once they were acquitted, not even the contortions of Regency justice could have secured the conviction of Patmore.

But the proceedings failed to establish what really happened that night at Chalk Farm. Patmore was dissatisfied because his name had not been cleared. Caroline was unhappy because she felt Christie and Traill should not have gone unscathed. Two days after the trial she wrote to Patmore, saying it had been her intention to express her displeasure to the solicitor who handled the case for the family, complaining he had not followed instructions. But she went on to say her father had forbidden her to do so:

> He seems to think that by writing or making any particular bustle as to what has been done, now that you are free, will only give reason to doubt the propriety of my motives in protecting you. He says that if you are a reasonable man you will be satisfied, and that you will not wish me to expose myself—when there is no necessity for it—in short he said many things on the subject which I did not like to hear, nor would you.

Two months after Scott's death his long-awaited book of travel was published. Entitled *Sketches of Manners, Scenery etc in the French Provinces, Switzerland and Italy*, the second half had been put together by Horace Smith from John's notes. The book contained the dead man's best descriptive writing, some of which had already appeared in his articles and letters. We could wish Smith had been less discreet in his editing, for he assured readers he had 'taken all possible care to exclude every thing which might wound the feelings of Mr Scott's friends', adding 'essays and papers, found among the Author's manuscripts, have been withheld from publication for reasons with which it is unnecessary to trouble the reader'.

These literary remains seem to have caused controversy, for Messrs Longman complained about Caroline's action in passing some of them to Robert Baldwin. Presumably Longman's, who had waited so patiently for Scott to complete the book for which he was paid several years before, felt they had first claim on them. Perhaps this was the reason Caroline never wrote the promised memoir of her husband. According to Haydon, she burned Scott's journal, and apparently other personal papers as well, for nothing belonging to him except two portraits and his bookplate seems to have been preserved by her own family.

Another possible reason for abandoning the biography was that his enemies were still alert. On 10 April 1821 William Maginn wrote to Blackwood: 'I have just this moment heard of poor Keats's death. We are unlucky in our butts. . . . If the threatened life of Scott comes forth, then indeed, if anything impertinent appears we may draw the sword again.'

A long hymn of praise to Christopher North in the April *Maga* included the words 'Gruff-looking Z is there, wet with the blood of the Cockneys. . . . Hail to thee, pride of the North! Hail, Christopher of Edina! Many a man has been slain by thy trenchant and truculent falchion.' This must surely have been written before the duel.

Lockhart himself withdrew, at least temporarily, from such raffishness. The consequent letter of complaint from William Blackwood hardly sounds like that of a publisher to the 'occasional contributor' Lockhart claimed to be:

> Either by yourself or your friends it has been given out that you had dropped all connection with it . . . they were not friends of yours who circulated reports of your having abandoned the Magazine: for were this true it would be an acknowledgment that the personal attacks upon you were well founded, and you were therefore forced to give way to public opinion . . . if you knew a thousand part of the miseries I have endured—and much of them on your account.

Blackwood's continued to attack Patmore, calling him a 'little Cockney chatterer', and worst of all in 1844 referred back to its rough handling of Keats in a disgusting article on the poems of Patmore's son Coventry. Lockhart had no hand in this, for he became editor of *The Quarterly Review* in 1825. It is amusing to find by that time Sir Walter Scott was referring to his son-in-law's involvement with *Blackwood's* as 'his very slight connection', and his being 'engaged in some light satires'.

Caroline Scott worked in her father's business, and her son John Anthony eventually became a partner. Her daughter Caroline died before reaching maturity; in 1839 the widow became Mrs Ellis, marrying a wealthy Lloyd's underwriter older than herself, a widower with several children. It is tempting to suspect he may have been the 'gentleman in a very extensive line' who had lost the bewitching Caroline to John Scott thirty years before.

Tragedy continued to pursue her. Her only grandchild died as a baby, and John Anthony, who never enjoyed good health, died in 1864. His portrait shows a delicate humorous face strongly resembling his father's. His mother lived another ten years, and was still corresponding with Scott's favourite sister, Margaret, a few years before her death.

Alexander Dick Scott did not continue the family upholstery business in Aberdeen for long, taking a post in a merchant's counting house. It was suggested to Alexander he should supply particulars of his brother's life for Chambers Scottish Biographical Dictionary, but he refused, and always appeared distressed at any mention of John's death. Their mother, Catherine Scott, remained alert late in life, judging from the firm, kindly face gazing serenely from her portrait by the young John Phillip, who started his career in Aberdeen.

After a life of hard work, sorrows and anxieties, her cause of death in 1837 was recorded as 'old age'. She lies in the Aberdeen churchyard of St Nicholas, with her husband, their infant son, several of their daughters, and many grandchildren.

The London Magazine was sold to Taylor and Hessey for £500 soon after the duel. Late in 1821 Thomas De Quincey contributed to it *Confessions of an English Opium Eater,* written in Scott's Covent Garden lodgings, which still stand. Thomas Carlyle also became a *London* author, and Thomas Hood joined it as sub-editor. But even with the continued support of Elia, the magazine failed to prosper under the editorship of John Taylor.

Lamb felt the loss of the first editor acutely. It was presumably to him 'The Lion's Head' was speaking in the April 1821 number when, after announcing Scott's death it added: 'We respect, and sympathize in the feelings of C.L. on the melancholy subject he has chosen for his Muse; but he must be aware, that circumstances of a very delicate nature must restrain us at present.' Years later, lamenting the decline of the magazine, Lamb asked, 'Why did poor Scott die?'

The simple answer is, because Christie shot him; the complicated answer also points to Christie. Other men shared his guilt. The reckless way Blackwood, Lockhart and Wilson conducted *Maga* was fated to end in bloodshed. It would have happened sooner if their victims had not been, in the main, distant poets or peaceful philosophers. Sir Walter Scott cannot escape some responsibility; his attitude to *Blackwood's* was at best ambivalent, and he did little to restrain the warlike Lockhart and Christie.

John Scott's attack on Lockhart was merited, but it was also intemperate and in part ill-founded; more resolution in sticking to his chosen second and in his grounds for refusing Lockhart's challenge would have preserved his reputation if not his life. At Chalk Farm the principals behaved well, but Patmore and Traill did not. Pettigrew vanished when he was needed most.

Yet no one was more culpable than Christie, a man admired by all who knew him, who lived his long life firm in the conviction he was the innocent victim of circumstances. It was Christie who urged Lockhart to the challenge. In the negotiations he got into arguments with Scott and Smith which sowed the seed for the final conflict. He allowed Lockhart to alter for publication the statement already sent to Scott, an astonishing blunder for two lawyers to make.

He tried to provoke Scott into renewing hostilities with Lockhart. The paragraph that concluded his own statement was an open sneer and he sent it to Patmore to ensure it could not be overlooked. In the duel, having told his second he would fire in the air, Christie fired down the field, which was difficult for Patmore and Scott to observe. If he had chosen to fight by day rather than night, his action would have been unmistakable and there would have been no second fire. When he did fire again his pistol, whether by accident or design, pointed at the mark which would kill rather than disable.

So ended, at thirty-six, the brilliant erratic career of John Scott just when he had found a role which might have brought him, if not fame and fortune, respect and solvency. We do not know what he might have become, but we can judge what he was. Many modern commentators have praised him, sometimes immoderately, as editor of *The London Magazine*. Yet we are closest to him in the words of Haydon, who knew him better than anyone except his wife and mother:

> Scott was a man of singular acuteness of understanding and power of mind, but he was not what might be called a man of genius. His power of conversation was very great, his knowledge considerable. . . . He was very entertaining and had a good heart at bottom, but it was so buried in passions that its natural goodness had seldom power to force its way. He had a strong taste for character, and in my opinion the soundest political views.

John Scott was a powerful writer—'Every one of your words tells', Wordsworth assured him—without being a great one. But he was a great journalist, one of the many hot-tempered, improvident, talented Scotsmen who have left their mark on Fleet Street.

As an editor he has been compared with Jeffrey and Gifford. But his skill was of a different kind from theirs. They moulded their reviews and contributors in their own image. He gave his leading writers their heads, encouraging and guiding Lamb, Hazlitt, Barnes to give of their best. He had also an eye for the lesser talents of Wainewright, Reynolds, Eastlake, Procter and others.

His critical assessments of Wordsworth, Byron, Keats, and Shelley, taken in the round, were more perceptive than those of his contemporaries, and superior to most written since. While alive to the charm of minor poets like Clare, Barton, and Hogg, he rarely confused the second rate with the best.

His dramatic reviews suffer in comparison with such giants of the art as Hazlitt, Lamb, Barnes and Leigh Hunt. But his account of Kean's first London season was discriminating as well as laudatory. Fond as he was of the fine arts, he was not as quick to appreciate contemporary painters as Wainewright was; but his championing of David Wilkie was surely just, as well as patriotic.

Although sensitive and quick-tempered, Scott's personality attracted the lasting friendship of diverse characters. One of them, Horace Smith, said of him: 'In the wide circle of my literary friends, I know not that I could mention one whose society I found more uniformly welcome. He did not set himself up for a wag or jester, or a pleasant fellow, but he was something much better—he was invariably pleasing. In manner, appearance, deportment, mind, he was a perfect gentleman.' It sounds as if one of the reasons for Scott's popularity was that he was a good listener. It was certainly a feat to retain the friendship of the touchy Hazlitt over several years, in spite of political differences. This makes it all the stranger that the gregarious Leigh Hunt should have become anathema to his fellow editor.

John Scott's political writings often showed balance and common sense ahead of his time. His crusading articles on military flogging, electoral reform, press freedom, legal humbug, and penal savagery, sometimes Dickensian in their fervour, helped to create the climate for the social changes which lay ahead. But he was at his best when he was most the journalist, describing what passed before his eyes: a royal procession in London, Brussels after Waterloo, a canal barge full of Dutchmen, Byron at a Venetian ball, the death of a favourite son, the street scenes of Paris, a trial for libel.

In these pieces he came to life, as he did in his letters. The tenderness of those to his mother and sisters make us wish Caroline had not destroyed his notes to her. But these may be matters into which we should not pry. John Scott, who proclaimed proudly he was a public writer, remained a very private man. As Professor Willard B Pope has said, John and Caroline Scott were two tragic and attractive people.

Chronological Outline

As John Scott appears on nearly every page of the biography he is not included in the index. These are the principal dates in his career:

1784 Born in Aberdeen
1792 Enters Grammar School
1796 Visits Windsor. Admitted to Marischal College
1799 Leaves College
1801 Bank clerk in Glasgow
1803 War Office clerk in Whitehall
1807 Editor of *The Statesman*. Marriage to Caroline Colnaghi
1808 Son Paul born. Attack on Duke of York. Scott becomes editor/proprietor of *The Censor*
1809 Debts cause row with Caroline's parents. The young couple settle in Stamford
1810 Daughter born
1811 Trial for libel over 'One Thousand Lashes'
1812 Maiden speech at a Boston dinner
1813 Back in London. Scott becomes friendly with Haydon and visits Leigh Hunt in gaol
1814 Thomas Barnes, Hazlitt and Lamb write for Scott's *Champion*
     First visit to Paris
1815 Waterloo and Paris again
1816 Second son born. Friendship with Wordsworth. Attack on Byron. Scott follows him into exile. Death of Paul Scott
1818 Scott's father dies
1819 Reconciliation with Byron in Venice
1820 *The London Magazine* launched. Attack on Lockhart
1821 Death

Selected Bibliography

PUBLISHED WORKS OF JOHN SCOTT

The Necessity of Reform by the Editor of the *Stamford News* (pamphlet, 1810)
Remarks Suggested by the Proceedings of the late Meeting at Lincoln held for the purpose of initiating a system of National Education by the Editor of the Stamford News (pamphlet, 1812)
A Visit to Paris in 1814
Paris Revisited in 1815
The House of Mourning, A Poem: With Some Smaller Pieces (1817)
Statement, Etc and *Mr Scott's Second Statement* (pamphlet concerning the dispute with John Gibson Lockhart. 1821)
Sketches of Manners, Scenery etc in the French Provinces, Switzerland and Italy (1821)
Picturesque Views of the City of Paris and its Environs:
  The Original Drawings by Mr Frederick Nash
  The Literary Department by Mr John Scott (1820–3)

PUBLICATIONS EDITED BY JOHN SCOTT

The Statesman 1807–8
The Censor 1808–9
Drakard's Stamford News 1809–12
Drakard's Paper 1813
The Champion 1814–16
The London Magazine 1820–1
He also contributed to *The British Review* between 1816 and 1819

MANUSCRIPT SOURCES

There are collections of letters from and to John Scott or his wife at the Houghton Library, Harvard; the British Library in London; the National Library of Scotland in Edinburgh; the Wordsworth Library at Grasmere; Princeton University Library (the P G Patmore collection); and in the Longman archives at the University of Reading. Individual letters from John Scott are contained in the John Murray archives, Edinburgh University Library, and the Samuel Whitbread Collection deposited at Bedfordshire County Record Office. The text of a letter from Scott to Talfourd is given in a typescript work by Robert S Newdick entitled 'Sir Thomas Noon Talfourd, D.C.L.' lodged at Reading Central Library, and another from Scott to the Reverend William Lisle Bowles is transcribed in Octavius Graham Gilchrist's *Third Letter* to the clergyman about the Pope controversy.

DOCTORAL THESES

A Biographical and Critical Study of John Scott by Donald A Low. University of Cambridge 1966. It was this work which revealed the family letters available to researchers. Dr Low also suggested the reason for the fatal failure of communication between Patmore and Traill as seconds at the duel.

John Scott's Champion by Josephine Bauer. Birkbeck College, University of London 1953. Professor Bauer traces the course of the quarrel between John Scott and James Henry Leigh Hunt.

The London Magazine (1820–1829) by T Rowland Hughes. Oxford University 1931

Studies in the London Magazine by Elmer Leroy Brooks. Harvard University 1954

Information about John Scott and his family can be found in:
Aberdeen Parochial Registers (General Register Office, Edinburgh); Burgess Book of Aberdeen, Grammar School Record Book, and Minute Book of the Decisions of the Magistrates (all Aberdeen Town House Archives); Dispositions and Deed of Settlement and Inventory of the Personal Estate of Alexander Scott (Scottish Record Office); Burse Book of Marischal College (Aberdeen University Library); St Mary le Bone Marriage Register; St Martin-in-the-Fields Baptism Register and Burial Register (Westminster Public Library Archives); and Middlesex Session Rolls (for inquest verdict: Greater London Council Record Office)

BOOKS (Classified by subject rather than author)

WORKS OF REFERENCE

Aberdeen Grammar School Roll of Pupils 1795–1919 by Theodore Watt (1923)
Fasti Academiae Mariscallanae Aberdonensis (New Spalding Club 1889–98)
The New Cambridge Bibliography of English Literature
The Oxford History of English Literature Vol X 1815–1832 by Ian Jack (1963)

Selected Bibliography 175

British Literary Magazines ed. Alvin Sullivan (to be published by Greenwood Press, Westport, Connecticut). Judging from one item I have been allowed to study in manuscript, this will be a valuable work.

Index to the London Magazine by Frank P Riga and Claude A Prance (Garland Publishing, New York, 1978)

A Bibliography of Articles in Blackwood's Magazine 1817–1825 by Alan Lang Strout (1959)

A Directory of Printers: London and Vicinity 1800–1840 by William B Todd (Printing History Society 1972)

The Dictionary of National Biography

The Political History of England Vol XI by George C Brodrick and J K Fotheringham (1906)

The Waterloo Roll Call by Charles Dalton (1890)

The Book of Family Crests by Henry Washbourne (1875 edition)

BACKGROUND INFORMATION ON CONTEMPORARY JOURNALISTIC AND SOCIAL LIFE

An Account of the London Daily Newspapers and the Manner in which they are conducted by James Savage (1811)

Biographical and Critical History of the British Literature of the Last Fifty Years by Allan Cunningham (1834)

Cyrus Redding's *Literary Reminiscences and Memoirs of Thomas Campbell* (1860), *Fifty years Recollections Literary and Personal* (1858), *Past Celebrities Whom I have Known* (1866), *Personal Reminiscences of Eminent Men* (1867), and *Yesterday and Today* (1863)

The Newspaper Press by James Grant (3 vols 1871–2)

Literary London 1779–1853 by Dr Thomas Rees with extensive additions by John Britton (1896)

Henry Crabb Robinson on Books and Their Writers ed. Edith J Morley (1938)

Politics and the Press c.1780–1850 by A Aspinall (1949)

The Rise and Fall of the Man of Letters by John Gross (1969)

The Romantic Reviewers by John O Hayden (1969)

That Sunny Dome by Donald A Low (Dent 1977)

Newspaper History ed. George Boyce, James Curran, and Pauline Wingate (Acton Society, Constable, 1978)

GENERAL BIBLIOGRAPHY

Aberdeen Awa' by George Walker (1897)

A Thousand Years of Aberdeen by Alexander Keith (Aberdeen University Press 1972)

Aberdeen Historical Walkabout (Department of Information and Tourism)

The History of Aberdeen by Walter Thom (1811)

Bon Record: Records and Reminiscences of Aberdeen Grammar School ed. H F Morland Simpson (1906)

A History of the University of Aberdeen by John Malcolm Bulloch (1895)

The Churches of Aberdeen by Alexander Gammie (1909)

History of the Secession Church by Revd John McKerrow (1841)

Merchant and Craft Guilds: A History of the Aberdeen Incorporated Trades by Ebenezer Bain (1887)

Thomas Barnes of The Times by Derek Hudson (1943)

Annals of a Publishing House: William Blackwood and his Sons by Margaret Oliphant (1897)

Lord Brougham and the Whig Party by Arthur Aspinall (1927)

The Life and Times of Henry Lord Brougham written by Himself (1871)

Works of Henry Lord Brougham (Vol IX, 1872)

Recollections of a Long Life by Lord Broughton (John Cam Hobhouse) ed. by his daughter Lady Dorchester (1909–11)

The Letters of Charles Armitage Brown by Jack Stillinger (1966)

Byron's Letters and Journals ed. Leslie A Marchand (John Murray, Vol IV, 1975)

The Works of Lord Byron, with his Letters and Journals, and his Life, by Thomas Moore (1832–3)

Byron: A Biography by Leslie A Marchand (1957)

Lord Byron's Wife by Malcolm Elwin (1962)

The Collected Works of Samuel Taylor Coleridge Vol 3: Essays on his Times in *The Morning Post* and *The Courier* Part I ed. David V Erdman (Routledge and Kegan Paul, 1978)

Collected Letters of Samuel Taylor Coleridge ed. Earl Leslie Griggs (Vol IV, 1959)

Colnaghi's 1760–1960. The introduction by Mrs E Manning gives an outline of the family's history

Archibald Constable and his Literary Correspondents by his son Thomas Constable (1873)

The East India House by Sir William Foster (1924)

Sir Charles Eastlake and the Victorian Art World by David Robertson (Princeton University Press 1978)

The Diary of Benjamin Robert Haydon ed. Willard Bissell Pope (5 vols 1960–3)

The Life and Death of Benjamin Robert Haydon by Eric George with additions by Dorothy George (1967)

Benjamin Robert Haydon Correspondence and Table Talk by Frederic Wordsworth Haydon (1876)

The Letters of William Hazlitt ed. Herschel Moreland Sikes assisted by Willard Hallam Bonner and Gerald Lahey (Macmillan 1979)

Notes of a Journey through France and Italy by William Hazlitt (1826)

Selected Bibliography

Hazlitt by Ralph M Wardle (1971)
William Hazlitt by Herschel Baker (1962)
The Life of William Hazlitt by P P Howe (1947 edition)
Four Generations of a Literary Family by W C Hazlitt (1897)
Keats and His Circle by Joanna Richardson (Cassell 1980) This contains portraits of several friends of John Scott
A Life of John Keats by Dorothy Hewlett (third edition 1970)
The Poems of John Keats ed. Jack Stillinger (Harvard University Press 1978)
The Letters of John Keats ed. Hyder Edward Rollins (1958)
The Keats Circle: Letters and Papers 1816–1878 ed. Hyder Edward Rollins (1948)
The Life of Reginald Heber by his Widow (1830)
The Correspondence of Leigh Hunt ed. by his eldest son Thornton Hunt (1862)
The Autobiography of Leigh Hunt (1878 edition)
The Autobiography of William Jerdan (Vol I, 1852)
Fanny Kelly of Drury Lane by Basil Francis (1950)
The Letters of Charles and Mary Anne Lamb ed. Edwin W Marrs (Cornell University Press, several vols, 1975–)
The Letters of Charles Lamb ed. E V Lucas (1935)
The Life of Charles Lamb by E V Lucas (fourth edition, 1907)
Memoirs of Charles Lamb by Thomas Noon Talfourd ed. Percy Fitzgerald (1894)
Sidelights on Charles Lamb by Bertram Dobell (1903)
Charles Lamb: A Memoir (1866) and *An Autobiographical Fragment and Biographical Notes* (1877) by Barry Cornwall (Bryan Waller Procter)
The Life and Letters of John Gibson Lockhart by Andrew Lang (1897)
John Gibson Lockhart by Marion Lochhead (1954)
Peter's Letters to his Kinsfolk by John Gibson Lockhart ed. William Ruddick (Scottish Academic Press 1977)
The London Magazine by Josephine Bauer (1953)
Peppercorn Papers by Claude A Prance (1964) Contains two chapters about *The London Magazine* and its editor, including a letter from John Scott to Edward Gandy
Mary Russell Mitford by Vera Watson (1949)
The Letters of Thomas Moore ed. Wilfred S Dowden (1964)
Memoirs, Journals and Correspondence of Thomas Moore ed. Lord John Russell (1853–6)
A Publisher and his Friends: Memoir and Correspondence of the late John Murray by Samuel Smiles (1891)
My Friends and Acquaintances by P G Patmore (1854)
The Life and Times of Coventry Patmore by Derek Patmore (1949)
Memoirs and Correspondence of Coventry Patmore by Basil Champneys (1900). The appendix includes Caroline Scott's letters to Peter George Patmore

Thomas Love Peacock: Letters to Edward Hookham and Percy B Shelley ed. Richard Garnett (1910)

Selected Prose of John Hamilton Reynolds ed. Leonidas M Jones (1966)

The Letters of John Hamilton Reynolds ed. Leonidas M Jones (University of Nebraska Press 1973)

The Letters of Sir Walter Scott ed. H J C Grierson (1932–7)

Memoirs of the Life of Sir Walter Scott, Bart by John Gibson Lockhart (1837–8)

Sir Walter Scott: The Great Unknown by Edgar Johnson (1970)

Scottish Banking: A History by S G Checkland (Collins 1975)

History of the Royal Bank of Scotland by Neil Munro (1928)

James and Horace Smith by Arthur H Beavan (1899)

Stamford Guide (Town Development Committee)

The Making of Stamford ed. Alan Roger (1965)

The History of Stamford published by John Drakard, probably written by Octavius Graham Gilchrist (1822)

The Town of Stamford A report by the Royal Commission on Historical Monuments (HMSO 1977)

A Publisher and his Circle: The Life and Work of John Taylor by Tim Chilcott (Routledge and Kegan Paul 1972)

Essays and Criticisms by Thomas Griffiths Wainewright ed. W Carew Hazlitt (1880)

Janus Weathercock by Jonathan Curling (1938)

The War Office by Hampden Gordon (1935)

William Wordsworth: The Later Years by Mary Moorman (1965)

The Letters of William and Dorothy Wordsworth: The Middle Years Part II ed. Ernest de Selincourt revised by Mary Moorman and Alan G Hill (1970)

By Royal Appointment by Paul Berry (1970) Describes the Duke of York–Mrs Clarke scandal

ARTICLES AND MISCELLANEOUS PUBLICATIONS

The Aberdeen Journal Its advertising columns contain much information about Alexander Scott's business. The University of Aberdeen Library has a valuable typescript guide to the editorial matter, 'Index and Notes Aberdeen Journal 1747–1847', by Thomas A Henderson

Hypocrisy Unveiled and Calumny detected in a Review of Blackwood's Magazine anonymous pamphlet (1818)

Byron's *Second Letter . . . on Pope* and appendix to *Marino Faliero, Doge of Venice* The poet's comments on his attitude to people who visited him in Venice and his views on John Scott

Old Chalk Farm Tavern by Anthony Cooper in *Camden History Review* No 6 (1978)

Coleridge and the Review Business by David V Erdman in *The Wordsworth Circle* (Winter 1975)

Selected Bibliography

George IV: Patron of Literature by Joanna Richardson in *Essays by Divers Hands* Vol XXXV

Reply to Mr Octavius Gilchrist's Statement pamphlet printed by Newcomb and Son (1812)

Notes on the Reverend Lawrance Glass by R Murdoch Lawrance (1907)

Benjamin Robert Haydon on Byron and Others by Duncan Gray and Violet W Walker in Keats–Shelley Memorial Bulletin (Rome 1956)

The Conversation of Authors by William Hazlitt

Charles Lamb and 'The Champion' by Josephine Bauer in the January 1955 issue of *The C.L.S. Bulletin* (now *The Charles Lamb Bulletin*)

Some Unpublished Letters of John Gibson Lockhart and John Wilson Croker by Alan Lang Strout in *Notes and Queries* (25 September 1943)

John Scott: Editor, Author and Critic by T Rowland Hughes in *The London Mercury Magazine* (April 1930)

The Editor of the London Magazine by Jacob Zeitlin in *The Journal of English and Germanic Philology* Vol XX (January 1921)

The Old London Magazine and Some of its Contributors by Major S Butterworth in *The Bookman* (October 1922)

The Scott–Christie Duel by Leonidas M Jones in *Texas Studies in Literature and Language* Vol 12 No 4 (1971). Gives a very clear analysis of a muddled affair

Trial for the Murder of John Scott by W M Parker in *Blackwood's Magazine* (April 1939)

A Literary Duel by Derek Patmore in *The Princeton University Library Chronicle* Vol XVI (1954–5)

Two Duels by J G Lockhart in *Blackwood's Magazine* (May, 1958)

Story of a Libel, with Thoughts on Duelling by Thomas De Quincey in *Tait's Magazine* (February 1841)

The Death of John Scott by J F George in *The Aberdeen Weekly Journal* (9 December 1903)

Central Criminal Court (Old Bailey) *Sessions Papers* contain accounts of the trials of Lockhart and Traill, and of Patmore. Newspapers at the time also carried reports of the duel and subsequent events, notably *The Morning Chronicle* (19 February, 1 March and 10 March 1821), *John Bull* (11 June), *Bell's Weekly Messenger* (4 March), and *The Guardian* (4 March)

The Aberdeen Herald for 10 and 17 December 1870 printed a long obituary account of Alexander Dick Scott and his family

A Graybeard's Gossip about his Literary Acquaintance A series of articles by Horace Smith in *The New Monthly Magazine* (1847)

Report of Commissioners for Military Enquiry WO 46/151 (1807)   Contains details of Scott's employment at War Office

The Whig Party and the Press in the early Nineteenth Century by Ivon Asquith in *Bulletin of the Institute of Historical Research* Vol XLIX (1976)

Wordsworth to John Scott by W M Parker in *The Times Literary Supplement* (27 December 1941)

Index

Abbotsford 76, 146, 149
Abbott, Lord Chief Justice 164
Abercrombie, Revd George 2
Abercrombie, Provost John 3
Aberdeen 1-29 (*passim*), 33, 57, 67, 101, 102, 117, 125, 129, 140, 154, 169
Aberdeen, Earl of 13
Aberdeen Grammar School 3, 4, 9, 50, 104
Aberdeen Herald, The 15-16
Aberdeen Journal, The 1, 2, 4, 7, 9, 102, 125
Addington, Henry (later Viscount Sidmouth) 13
America 32, 42-3, 77
Amiens, Treaty of 13
Andrews, William Eusebius 72
Angers 87, 88
Annals of the Fine Arts 114
Anti-Jacobin, The 23
Arden, Lord 44
Ashford Heath 7
Auber, Peter 107
Austen, Jane 77
Ayton, William C 45

Back of the Narrow Wynd 2
Bacon, R M 123
Bailey, Benjamin 139
Baldwin, Cradock & Joy 100, 112, 118, 136, 138, 139
Baldwin, Robert 100, 101, 104, 108-14, 118, 127, 134, 159, 162, 163, 168
Ballantyne & Co 154

Ballantyne, John 33
Balmer, Dr Robert 16, 142-3
Barnes, Thomas 25, 52-3, 62, 68, 171
Barnett, George 73
Bartlett, George 3
Barton, Bernard 114, 129, 171
Batty, Captain Robert 129
Bayley, Mr Justice 167
Beckford, William 77
Ben Lomond 12
Belsches, Williamina 5
Bensone, Countess 134
Bewick, William 100
Birthday Ode, A 20
Blackwood's Magazine 109, 110, 113, 136-54, 160, 168-170
Blackwood, William 109, 110, 138, 139, 143, 144, 146, 148, 149, 168, 169
Blake, William 125
Blore, Thomas 33, 34
Boaden, John 54, 64
Bohte, J H 125, 162
Bombay 25
Bonmot, Egomet—see Wainewright
Boston 46, 75
Bowles, Revd William Lisle 121, 145, 146, 163
Brawne, Fanny 160
Brickstables 136
Brighton 71
British Review, The 100, 110
Broad Street (formerly Broadgate) 1, 2, 4, 8
Broadwood, James 18
Broadwood, Johannes 3, 18

181

Brougham, Henry (later Lord) 40, 41, 62, 80-2, 127, 139
Brown, Alexander 4, 8
Brown, Charles Armitage 147, 160
Bruges 69
Brussels 69, 70, 140
Burdett, Sir Francis 24
Burghley, House of 31, 33, 34, 46
Burke, Edmund 25
Burlington House 24
Burslem, Revd William 33
Byron, Lord 4, 24, 25, 26, 33, 43, 49, 50, 53, 64, 67, 78-85 (*passim*), 100, 103, 104, 106, 115, 116, 119, 121, 128, 133, 134, 137, 139, 146, 163, 171
Byron, Lady (Annabella Milbanke) 80, 81, 83
Byron, Mrs (Byron's mother) 4, 50

Caithness 166
Calais 102
Cameron Highlanders, The 67
Campbell, Thomas 121, 136
Canning, George 23, 107
Cargill, James 8
Carr, Sir James 35
Castlereagh, Viscount 23, 35, 39
Catherine Street 27-8, 51, 62, 76
Catholic Emancipation 24, 31
Cenci, The 126, 151
Censor, The 27, 28, 31, 38, 51
Chalk Farm (Tavern), 156-170 (*passim*)
Chalmers, James 4
Champion, The 52-68, 71-83, 89, 90, 92, 94, 97, 103, 107, 112-14, 127, 135, 136
Chaplin, Charles 33
Charlotte, Princess (daughter of the Prince Regent) 48, 128
Chatsworth 63
Childe Harold's Pilgrimage 49, 50, 78, 119
Christie, Jonathan Henry 148-61, 163-7, 169, 170
Christ's Triumphal Entry into Jerusalem 55, 75, 82, 126, 135

Clare, John 98, 114, 122-3, 171
Clarke, Mrs Mary Ann 27
Clermont, Mrs 80
Clewer 5
Clifford, William 36
Cobbett, William 35-7, 47
Cockspur Street 21, 68, 74, 157
Coddington, Samuel 33
Colbourn, Henry 136
Coldbath Fields Gaol 48
Coleridge, Samuel Taylor 25, 43, 63, 98, 113, 138, 144, 145
Colnaghi, Caroline Antoinette—*see* Mrs Caroline Scott
Colnaghi, Dominic 21, 26, 157, 158, 160, 162
Colnaghi, Mrs Elizabeth 21, 26, 36, 37, 119
Colnaghi, Francesca 21, 75, 86, 91, 94, 106
Colnaghi, Martin 21, 158, 160
Colnaghi, Paul 21, 22, 28-9, 37, 68, 92, 95, 117, 125, 157, 158, 160
Colnaghi, Peter 106, 119
Conder, Josiah 95
Constable, Archibald 55, 109
Constable, John 125
Coriolanus 53
Corn Law, The 58, 62
Cornwall, Barry—*see* Bryan Waller Procter
Correction Wynd 16
Courier, The 25, 63
Court of King's Bench 39, 40, 42
Covent Garden Theatre 47, 53, 55-6, 135
Croker, John Wilson 24, 137, 151
Croly, George 130
Cunningham, Allan 130, 143

Dale, David 10
Darling, Dr George 75, 96, 100, 123, 158-67 (*passim*)
Davis, Ann 5
Davis, George 5
Davis, John (royal locksmith) 5, 7
Davis, John (Bow Street runner) 158

Index

Dean, David 51
Dee, the 3
Delattre, Jean Marie 17
de Luppé, Viscount 90-1
De Quincey, Thomas 148, 169
Descent of Liberty, The 62
de Staël, Madame 50, 139
Dewar, William 2
Dieppe 69
Dods, Thomas 13, 15, 17
Dods, William 13
Don, the 3
Drakard, John 30-47 (*passim*)
Drakard's Paper 47, 48, 50-2
Drakard's Stamford News 30-47, 121
Drury Lane Theatre 47, 57-8, 73
du Bois, Edward 35, 45, 51, 68
Duelling 43, 45, 81, 138, 146, 149-67 (*passim*)

East Campbell Street Secession Church 9
East India Company, The 105, 107, 112
Eastlake, (Sir) Charles Lock.108, 113, 114, 121, 171
Eclectic Review, The 95
Edgeworth, Maria 134
Edgware Road 53, 54
Edinburgh 3-5, 9-11, 87, 125, 137, 138, 140, 142, 143, 148, 153, 154, 160
Edinburgh Monthly Magazine, The—see *Blackwood's Magazine*
Edinburgh Review, The 30, 41, 43, 56, 57, 64, 65, 93, 100, 109
Edwards, Captain 70
Elgin, Lord, and the Marbles 73
Ellenborough, Lord 35, 40, 48-9
Elmes, James 114
Emma 77-8
Erdman, Professor David V 144
Essays of Elia, The 127, 134, 136, 138
Eton College 5
Examiner, The 24, 38, 40-1, 47-49, 54, 57, 62, 74-5, 81-2, 84, 139
Exeter, Marquis of 31, 33, 34

Fare Thee Well 80-2, 103, 133
Farquharson, William 1, 2
Finnerty, Peter 35, 39
Fleet Street 23, 24, 47, 51, 170
Flogging, military 32, 35, 36, 39, 41, 42
Folkestone, Lord 42
Foote, Maria 55
Foster, Sir William 107
Foulkes, Evan 33-4, 46
Fulham 17, 151

Galt, John 147, 148
Gandy, Edward 113-14
Geneva 101, 116
George III 5, 7, 17, 39, 123-4
George IV—*see* The Prince Regent
George Inn 34
Giaour, The 50
Gibbs, Sir Vicary 34, 36, 38-40
Gifford, William 30, 95, 170
Gilchrist, Horatio 45
Gilchrist, Octavius Graham 30, 33, 43, 45, 113, 114, 120-1, 145-7
Glasgow 9-13, 102, 137
Glass, Revd Lawrance 16, 29, 50
Glass, Margaret—*see* Margaret Scott
Globe, The 31
Godwin, William 128-9
Gold's London Magazine 114, 136, 140-1
Gordon Highlanders, The 67
Grant, Charles 65
Great Marlborough Street 54, 66
Grenville, Lord 23
Grose, Mr Justice 42
Guardian, The 164
Guthrie, John James 158-9, 163

Haddo House 15
Haileybury College 105
Hamilton, Sir William 140
Hamlet 54
Harvard University 99
Haydon, Benjamin Robert 21, 49-50, 54-6, 64, 66-71, 73-5, 82-100 (*passim*), 103-4, 108, 111-12, 114,

117, 119, 126-7, 135, 137, 139, 154, 162-3, 168, 170
Hazlitt, William 20, 49, 54, 56-7, 61-2, 64, 72, 74, 83-4, 97-8, 100, 109, 114, 117-20, 127, 130, 138, 140-2, 145, 147, 171
Heber, Reginald 76
Henniker, Lord 33, 46
Hessey, James 78, 95, 163, 169
Hill, Thomas 51, 53, 62, 68, 72, 92, 132
Hobart, Lord 13
Hobhouse, John Cam (later Lord Broughton) 25, 104, 137
Hogg, James 76, 110, 153, 171
Holland House 84
Holland, Lord 163
Hood, Thomas 169
Hoppner, Richard Belgrave 103
Horse Guards Parade 13, 27
Horsemonger Lane 48, 49
Hotel D'Angleterre, Brussels 70
House of Mourning, The 95-8, 116
Hume, Joseph 20
Hume, Mrs 20
Hunt, James Henry Leigh 13, 20-1, 23-5, 32, 38-40, 47-50, 57, 61-3, 66, 68, 74-5, 81-3, 85, 104, 109-10, 115, 137-9, 142, 149-50, 171
Hunt, John 24-5, 38-40, 48, 61, 68, 139
Huxter Row 8
Hyde Park Corner 17

Ireland 23-4, 35, 39
Ischia 107, 121

Jamieson, Dr John 10, 142
Jeffrey, Francis (later Lord) 43, 56, 57, 163, 170
Jennyns, Joseph Clayton 97
Jerdan, William 81
Jersey 86
Jones, John Gale 35
Judgment of Solomon, The 54, 68

Kean, Edmund 53-4, 121, 171
Keats, George 99
Keats, John 24, 73, 75, 78, 82, 98-100, 109, 113, 114, 126, 129-30, 137-40, 147, 160, 168, 171
Keats, Tom 99, 139
Kelly, Fanny 58, 73-4
Kemble, Charles 135
Kemble, John 53
Kew Lane 135-6
Kew Meadow Path 136
Kidston, Revd William 9, 10
Kilburn 54
Kinnaird, Douglas 81
Kinnaird, Lord 81, 104, 107
Kinross 131
Kintore, Earl of 13
Kirkup, Seymour 108
Kynoch, John 67-8

Lamb, (Lady) Caroline 80
Lamb, Charles 20, 25, 43, 49, 57-8, 68, 73-4, 112, 116, 127, 129, 134-6, 138, 144-7, 153, 163, 169, 171
Lamb, Mary 49, 73
Lamia 129
Latin America 32
Lawrence, Revd Benjamin 26
Lectures on the Literature of the Age of Elizabeth 119
Leslie, Professor John 148
Libel, Law of 35, 38, 41, 48
Liberty of the Press 38, 39
Lincoln 38-40, 42, 46
Lincoln Rutland and Stamford Mercury, The 31, 32, 43
Literary Gazette, The 81, 151
Liverpool, Earl of 45, 66
Loch Lomond 11
Lockhart, John Gibson 11, 110, 137-40, 142-4, 146-56, 159-170 (*passim*)
Logan, George 67-8, 70-1, 117
Logan, Robert 67-8
Loire, river 88
London Magazine, The 108-51, 153, 159-60, 169, 170

Index

Longman, Hurst, Rees, Orme and Brown 53, 55-6, 59, 68-9, 72, 74-6, 78, 95, 97, 101, 104, 115, 168
Louis XVIII 54, 56, 74
Louvre, the 56, 71, 72
Lovell, Daniel 23, 26-7
Ludgate Hill 135, 140, 156

McCrie, Dr Thomas 142
McCulloch, John Ramsay 153
McCulloch, William 105, 107
Macfarlane, Charles 130
Macfarlane, Peter 107
Mackay, Alexander 13
Mackintosh, (Sir) James 25, 50, 56-7, 62, 64-5, 84, 95, 97, 105-7, 113, 139-40, 143, 163
Mackintosh, Lady 56-7, 84, 97, 106, 113
Maclaren, Charles 154
McMahon, Colonel John 43
Macready, William 135
Maginn, William 110, 138, 142, 147-8, 168
Maida Place 53-4, 56, 69-71, 78
Mardocks 105, 106, 113
Marischal College 8-9, 14, 25, 155, 163
Marylebone High Street 26
Maturin, Charles Robert 128, 132
Melancholy of Taylors, On the 57
Melmoth the Wanderer 132
Melville, Viscount 18, 23
Milan 102, 103
Mill, James 107
Mirandola 135
Mitchell, Thomas 49, 50
Mitford, Mary Russell 148
Moira, Earl of 26
Moncrieff, Robert Scott 10
Montagu, Basil 43
Montagu, Lady Mary Wortley 103
Monthly Mirror, The 19
Moore, Francis 15, 17
Moore, Thomas 43, 49-50, 52-3, 63, 67, 78, 104, 113, 115, 121, 139, 145

Moreau, General 53
Morning Advertiser, The 51
Morning Chronicle, The 25, 65, 74, 82, 160
Morning Herald, The 51, 55, 62
Morning Post, The 24, 25
Morris, Dr Peter—*see* John Gibson Lockhart
Morris, William 157-8, 167
Mortlake 112, 118, 124, 136, 137, 145
Murray, John 77-8, 81, 95, 99-100, 104, 137-8, 143-4, 163
My Friends and Acquaintances 103

Naples 107, 121-2, 130
Napoleon Buonaparte 14, 18-19, 36, 41-2, 50-1, 54, 56, 61, 64-5, 67-8, 71, 74, 99
Nash, Frederick 108, 114, 129
National Library of Scotland 23
Nelson, Lord 19-21
Newcomb, Richard 31-2, 43, 45
Newcomb, Richard (Jnr) 31-2, 43, 45
New Monthly Magazine, The 136
News, The 24
New Times, The 152, 156
Noel, Colonel (later Sir) Gerard N 46, 97
North, Christopher—*see* John Wilson
Notes of a Journey through France and Italy 61

Observer, The 159
Oddy, Joshua Jepson 33-4
Ode to a Nightingale 130
Old Bailey, The 164-5, 167
O'Neill, Eliza 121
Ostend 69
Ottley, William Young 111

Paddington 54, 68
Palais Royal 69, 77
Palmerston, Viscount 19, 65
Paris 21, 25, 28, 56, 59, 61, 68-9, 71, 75, 84, 88-91, 97-101, 108, 114, 116, 118, 129
Parisina 78

Paris Revisited in 1815 74-8
Park Place (now Park Road) 78
Parliamentary Reform 4, 34, 72-3, 111-12
Pastorini, Joseph 15
Patmore, Coventry 135, 168
Patmore, Peter George 103, 130, 135, 137, 140, 143, 146, 150, 152, 156-70 (*passim*)
Paul's Letters to his Kinsfolk 76, 142
Peacock, Thomas Love 107
Peevor, John 13
Peninsular War 27, 50
Pepper, John 33-4
Perceval, Spencer 31, 39, 44-5
Père Lachaise cemetery 91-2, 94, 97
Perry, James 25, 65, 82-3
Perth 10
Peter's Letters to his Kinsfolk 138, 142
Pettigrew, Thomas Joseph 157-8, 161, 167, 170
Phillip, John 169
Piccadilly 80, 82, 111
Pitt, William 14, 17, 26
Place Carrousel 71
Poems Descriptive of Rural Life and Scenery 122
Political Register 35, 47
Pope, Alexander 121, 145
Pope, Professor Willard B 171
Portland, Duke of 23
Portsmouth 19
Prince Regent, The (Prince of Wales and later George IV) 7, 24-5, 29, 39, 42, 48, 54, 61, 81, 82, 128
Princess of Wales, The (later Queen Caroline) 7, 48, 128
Princess Royal, The 7
Procter, Bryan Waller (Barry Cornwall) 114-16, 135, 171

Quarterly Musical Magazine and Review, The 123
Quarterly Review, The 30, 77, 99, 104, 137, 138, 151, 160, 168
Quatre Bras 67, 70

Queen Caroline—*see* The Princess of Wales
Queen Charlotte 7
Queen Street 4, 102

Raphael 72
Recluse, The 66
Redding, Cyrus 136
Rejected Addresses 51, 58
Renier, M 69
Reynolds, John Hamilton 73, 82-4, 113, 130, 157, 161-3, 171
Rice, James 113, 161
Richardson, Joanna 160
Richard the Third 53
Rimini 138-9
Ritchie, Joseph 92, 99-100
Roberts, William 101
Robinson, Henry Crabb 66
Rome 73, 106-8, 114, 121, 147
Rouen 59
Round Table, The 97
Rousseau, Jean Jacques 59, 97
Royal Academy 15, 54
Royal Bank of Scotland 10, 11
Ryan, James 158

St Helens, Lord 33
Saint Malo 86-7
St Martin-in-the-Fields 26, 162-3
St Marylebone Church 26
St Nicholas Church 169
St Nicholas Lane 16
Santa Maria del Carmine 102
Schoolhill 3
Scone 10, 142
Scotsman, The 153-4
Scott, Alexander (John's father) 1-23 (*passim*), 29, 37, 74, 101, 118, 169
Scott, Alexander (Jnr, died in infancy) 9, 169
Scott, Alexander Dick (John's brother) 9, 17-18, 20, 23, 33, 101-2, 118-19, 125, 129, 169
Scott, Caroline (Colnaghi) 21-3, 26, 28, 33, 37, 41, 49, 53, 57, 63-4, 68-71, 79-100 (*passim*), 106, 112,

Index

119, 130–2, 137, 150, 154, 157–71 (*passim*)
Scott, Caroline (John's daughter) 37, 41, 53, 75, 112, 119, 169
Scott, Mrs Catherine (John's Mother) 1, 5, 7, 9–11, 16–17, 19–23, 27–8, 33, 37, 63, 101–2, 107, 118–19, 154, 169–70
Scott, Miss Catherine (John's sister) 3, 11, 70, 75, 101, 108, 154
Scott, Eliza 8, 101
Scott, Hannah Kidston (later Mrs Macfarlane) 8, 64, 101, 107–8
Scott, Helen 8, 63, 75, 101
Scott, Jane 3, 16, 101, 142
Scott, John—*his career is sketched in the Chronological Outline on page 172*
Scott, John Anthony 80, 112, 119, 169
Scott, Margaret (later Mrs Glass) 2, 4–5, 7, 14, 16, 18, 29, 33, 37, 50, 101, 131, 154, 169
Scott, Marion 8, 101
Scott, Mr (of Edinburgh) 9
Scott, Nancy 3, 5, 7, 14, 18, 101
Scott of Ancrum 7
Scott, Paul Alexander 26, 33, 37, 41, 53, 84, 86, 91–6, 116
Scott, Thomas 160
Scott, (Sir) Walter 4, 10, 18, 33, 52, 55, 67, 72, 76–8, 110, 115, 125, 137–60 (*passim*), 168–70
Scotts of Dunninald 7
Secession Church 5, 14, 16, 142
Seine, the 98–9
Severn, Joseph 160
Sheath, Challis 46, 75
Sheen Lane 112
Shelley, Percy Bysshe 82, 107, 116, 126, 151, 171
Sicilian Story, A 115
Siege of Corinth, The 78
Skene, George 4
Sketches of Manners, Scenery Etc in the French Provinces, Switzerland and Italy 167
Sketch from Private Life, A 80–1
Smith, Horace 51–2, 72, 84, 113–14, 124, 132, 137, 150–2, 155–6, 160, 163, 167–8, 170–1
Smith, James 51
Snow, Mrs 7
Soane, George 72
Soane, (Sir) John 72, 74
Somerset House 20, 28
Southey, Robert 52, 115
Spain 27, 32, 50
Spencer, Earl 163
Stamford 30–34, 37, 41, 45–6, 97, 113, 145, 147
Stamford and Boston Gazette, The 31, 43, 45
Statesman, The 23–4, 26–7, 36, 135
Steward, Dugald 93
Stoddart, Dr (later Sir) John 62, 65, 152–3, 156
Strachan, John 3
Strachey, Edward 107
Strada—see Thomas Barnes
Strand, The 28, 31, 52
Stuart, Daniel 25
Sun, The 26, 81
Surrey Gaol 48
Sydenham 45, 51

Table Talk 118, 127
Talfourd, (Sir) Thomas Noon 127, 135–6, 159
Tavistock Street 125
Tax, newspaper 28
Taylor, James 78
Taylor, John 78, 95, 97–8, 159, 163, 169
Terry, Daniel 77
Thackeray, William Makepeace 77
Thanksgiving Ode 84
Theatre Royal, Aberdeen 8
Thomèry 98–9
Throgmorton Street 72, 155
Times, The 7, 25, 52, 62, 65, 74, 152
Trafalgar, Battle of 18
Traill, James 149, 157–70 (*passim*)
Travels and Opinions of Edgeworth Benson 131, 134–5

Venice 4, 71, 103-7, 128, 134
Vesuvius 107
Vevey 116
Victory, HMS 20
Visit to Paris in 1814, A 59, 63-6, 74-7
Voltaire 126

Waggoner, The 122
Wainewright, Thomas Griffiths 117, 124-5, 129, 132, 138, 160, 171
Walter, John 25
Wardlaw, Ralph 10
Wardlaw, William 9-10
Wardle, Colonel Gwyllym Lloyd 27
War Office 13, 15, 16, 17, 19-20, 23-4, 27
Waterloo, Battle of 67-70, 74-5, 78, 119
Watson, Hugh 158-9
Watt, Adam 2
Waugh, Revd Alexander 163
Waverley 55
Weathercock, Janus—see Thomas Griffiths Wainewright

Weedon Lodge 84
Wellington, Duke of 50, 66-8, 74, 88, 119
Wells Street Chapel 163
West Lodge 136
Whitbread, Samuel 26
Whitehall 13, 17, 65
Wilkie, (Sir) David 49, 64, 68, 71, 111, 163, 171
Willett, Wilmer M 26
Wilson, John 110, 137-48, 169
Windsor 5, 7, 52, 123
Winton, John 2
Wordsworth, William 57, 66-7, 75, 79-80, 83-4, 91, 94, 97-8, 113, 115, 121-2, 126-7, 134, 138, 144-5, 163, 170-1

York, Duke of 13, 17, 27, 36
York Street 125, 136, 162
Young, Catherine—*see* Mrs Catherine Scott

OHIO UNIVERSITY LIBRARY

Please return this book as soon as you
have fi   it In order to avoid a
fi   date